Advertising, the Media and Globalisation

D0420436

This book offers a critical, empirically-grounded and contemporary account of how advertisers and agencies are dealing with a volatile mediascape throughout the world, taking a region-by-region approach.

It provides a clear, systematic and synoptic analysis of the dynamic relationship between media, advertisers and agencies in the age of globalisation, and in an era of transition from 'mass' to 'social' media.

Advertising attracts much public criticism for the commercialisation of culture and its apparent impact on social and personal life. This book outlines and assesses the issues involved, with regard to how they are manifested in different national, regional and global contexts. Topics covered include:

- advertising as an object of study
- global trends in the advertising industry
- advertising and the media in motion
- current issues in advertising, media and society
- advertising, globalisation and world regions.

While maintaining a contemporary focus, the book explains developments over recent decades as a background to the globalisation of what it calls the manufacturing/marketing/media complex.

John Sinclair is an Honorary Professorial Fellow in the Australian Centre at the University of Melbourne. He has become internationally acknowledged over the last twenty-five years for his research on the globalisation of media industries. This has been published in the leading journals of the field, as well as various books, notably *Images Incorporated: Advertising as Industry and Ideology* (1987); *New Patterns in Global Television: Peripheral Vision* (1996, edited, with Stuart Cunningham and Liz Jacka); *Latin American Television: A Global View* (1999); and *Contemporary World Television* (2004, edited, with Graeme Turner).

Advertising, the Media and Globalisation

A world in motion

John Sinclair

 Routledge
Taylor & Francis Group

LONDON AND NEW YORK

First published 2012
by Routledge
2 Park Square, Milton Park, Abingdon, Oxon OX14 4RN

Simultaneously published in the USA and Canada
by Routledge
711 Third Avenue, New York, NY 10017

Routledge is an imprint of the Taylor & Francis Group, an informa business

British Library Cataloguing in Publication Data
A catalogue record for this book is available from the British Library

Library of Congress Cataloging in Publication Data
Sinclair, John, 1944-
Advertising, the media and globalisation: a world in motion / John Sinclair.
p. cm.
Includes bibliographical references and index.
1. Advertising – Social aspects. 2. Mass media. 3. Globalization – Social aspects.
I. Title.
HF5821.S577 2012
659.1 – dc23
2011041862

ISBN: 978-0-415-66882-8 (hbk)
ISBN: 978-0-415-66883-5 (pbk)
ISBN: 978-0-203-14364-3 (ebk)

Typeset in Sabon
by Taylor & Francis Books

Contents

List of figures

List of tables

Acknowledgements

This book is the culmination of an Australian Research Council Professorial Fellowship funded over 2005–9 for Discovery Project DP0556419, 'Globalisation and the media in Australia: an integrated analysis of trends and impacts, with special reference to the advertising industry', and I gratefully acknowledge the ARC's financial support over that time.

The Fellowship was hosted by the Australian Centre at the University of Melbourne. I thank the Director, Professor Kate Darian-Smith, and my colleagues in the Centre for welcoming me into a stimulating, congenial and interdisciplinary research environment. The subsequent writing-up phase has been enabled by an appointment as Honorary Professorial Fellow in the Faculty of Arts, with facilities kindly provided by the School of Historical and Philosophical Studies.

During the data collection phase, I am grateful to have benefitted from an exceptional level of research assistance and collaboration provided by Dr Rowan Wilken. For the material specifically on Brazil, thanks are due to my correspondents there, Professors Cassiano Ferreira Simões, Neusa Demartini Gomes and Othon Fernando Jambeiro.

I am very glad to be able to acknowledge my daughters Catalina and Isabelle for timely advice and assistance in their respective areas of professional expertise, and to express my heartfelt appreciation for the constant support from my partner, Dr Janet Hall.

Finally, thanks are due to *Advertising Age* for permission to use material from their Data Center, and to my editors at Routledge, Aileen Storry and Eileen Srebernik, for their help with obtaining permission for the images used here, and more generally in shepherding this work to completion.

Chapter 1

Advertising as an object of study

Advertising is the key link in the mutually-sustained global expansion of consumer goods and service industries and the media of communication which carry their commercial messages. In most countries of the developed and the developing world alike, the largest advertisers, many of them global corporations, have determined the direction and character of media development because of their demand for the means (that is, the 'media') which allow them to reach potential consumers. Media organisations thus stand or fall on their capacity to provide content which will attract such consumers as audiences, as the revenue from advertising provides the major source of income for media owners, and motivates their business strategies.

Understood in this corporate context, it is evident that it is advertising which gives the aptly-named 'commercial' media their characteristic look and sound, and orients their content towards the kind of audiences which advertisers want to reach. Much more than the source of the images and brand names which form the surface of consumer culture, advertising is actually the life-blood of commercial media, and the motive force behind media industry development. Yet, also to be taken into account is the intermediary role of advertising agencies, which act as brokers of media time and space, as well as in their more obvious role of devising and implementing advertising campaigns. This triumvirate of advertisers, media and agencies forms the institutional bedrock of consumer culture, an integrated relationship which may be referred to as the manufacturing/marketing/media complex.

Manufacturing, marketing and media

Not all advertisers are manufacturers, of course, for although it is goods of all kinds, from cars to shampoo, that dominate in advertising content, there are important categories of service advertisers which are also prominent, notably retail and finance. The point is that it is the advertisers, whether of goods or services, who are the source of the revenue which is the prize in the elaborate game now being played out between the 'old' media of television and print, and the 'new' media, notably the internet, and which provides the very conditions of existence for the advertising agencies and the other marketing 'disciplines'.

Marketing can be thought of as a cultural industry that seeks to connect the producers of consumer goods and services with their potential markets, and indeed, to bring those markets into being. For decades, the conventional wisdom of the marketing textbooks is that marketing is defined by a strategic 'mix' of at least 'four Ps': Product, Price, Place and Promotion. Product refers to the product-market strategy in terms of which a product is designed with a particular target market in mind, a process in which the role of yet another P, packaging, is not to be underestimated. Price is a matter of positioning a product relative to the price behaviour of its competitors in a given market – indeed, in some accounts, positioning in a broader sense, and especially in relation to branding, is another P in its own right. Place has to do with distribution, or ensuring that the product is physically accessible to its target market; so only the final 'P', promotion, has to do with advertising as such.

In that light, advertising is just the most visible and public dimension of a much broader but still quite familiar set of practices intent upon harnessing our ways of life to commercial purposes. These include sponsorship, notably of sport and the arts; in-store displays, sales promotions, competitions and giveaways; and direct marketing, such as telemarketing. In the past, media advertising has been referred to in the industry as 'above the line', while these various forms of non-media marketing are seen as 'below the line'. However, particularly given the commercialisation of the internet over recent decades, marketing gurus have since declared that 'there is no line' (Cappo 2003: 101). Not only is media advertising ever more incorporated with sales promotions – for instance, television commercials (TVCs) for giveaway toys in McDonald's – but advertising campaigns are now devised on a 'cross-platform' basis, meaning that such campaigns are scheduled to be mounted across traditional media, the internet and perhaps other more direct 'touchpoints' where they can reach prospective consumers. Marketing practitioners and textbooks now tend to conceive of advertising in the context of what they like to call 'integrated marketing communications'. This may sound like just industry hype, but it does express how advertising is now linked in strategically to the other dimensions of marketing, and to other forms of promotion (Belch 2009).

The advent of the internet has transformed the meaning of advertising media. For even if the line between them is being erased, we still need to distinguish between the 'old' (sometimes called 'traditional' or, somewhat prematurely, 'legacy') advertising media of television, radio, newspapers and magazines, cinema and outdoor; and the 'new' advertising medium of the internet, for a number of reasons. Whereas the old media deliver a sales message to a prospective consumer, that message has to motivate the consumer to respond at a later time and in a different place: for instance, having seen a

TVC, the consumer has to go to a store to buy the product, if the message's 'call to action' is to fulfil its purpose. With the internet, the consumer can respond to an advertising message then and there, such as clicking to add the product to a virtual 'shopping cart' and paying on line with a credit card. The point is not just that the internet thus eliminates delay and distance in such consumption transactions, or even that it combines the functions of both advertising medium and retail store, but that it is an interactive medium which has established itself as a transactional space in its own right. The rapid rise of deal-of-the-day services such as Groupon provides a dramatic example.

The interactive properties of the internet have precipitated a shift in the balance of power between advertisers and consumers, just as they have caused the still-dominant advertising media of television and print to lose growth in advertising revenue in favour of the internet. While it is easy to overstate the differences, audiences for television and print can be thought of as aggregated and 'passive' in the sense that they have very limited channels for response, whereas internet users individually and actively wield the power of the freedom of (inter)action which the internet has given them. From the advertisers' point of view, internet users are more focused targets than media audiences, but it is more difficult to engage them before they click away to something else. The media owners, for their part, argue that the large audiences which they can deliver to advertisers are still better value, or offer better 'ROI' (return on investment) than the internet, because of their sheer size and diversity, particularly for non-specialised products and services. Meanwhile, the advertising agencies have to convince the advertisers that only they have the expertise to guide them to the most strategic placing of campaigns across both old and new media platforms.

What is clear is that the relatively comfortable relationship which has existed between advertisers, agencies and media throughout the golden age of mass media in decades past – in which the media would offer content that could attract audiences so as to sell access to those audiences to advertisers via the agencies – is a 'business model' which has been put under severe pressure by the advent of the internet. Meanwhile, on the internet itself, emergent new business models compete for hegemony. In this environment, not only is there a realignment taking place within the manufacturing/marketing/media complex, but the very meaning of 'advertising' as we have known it is in flux.

The meaning of advertising

When we talk about advertising in everyday life, none of the contexts which have been discussed here applies – we don't bother drawing a line between advertising and other forms of promotion, nor do we distinguish between, say, TVCs and sponsored search results on the internet – it's all just advertising, particularly in the critical public discourse which marketing attracts. Even in academic critique, the meaning of advertising as an object of study is hazy. Yet it is also selective: advertising content, such as the TVC, has attracted much attention from academic critics because of the rich symbolism of its images, and the inferences which can be drawn about its cultural meanings and presumed effects. By contrast, classified advertising in newspapers, except perhaps for the personal columns, is a barren field for cultural analysis, and hence quite neglected. However, in the context of the current struggle between old and new media, the 'migration' of classified advertising from newspapers to the internet is a central issue. So, as with the blind men and the elephant, it is crucial to be clear about what kind of advertising we are talking about in any debate, and to understand the quite different angles from which various academic fields approach advertising as an object of study.

As Liz McFall observes, a 'textually fixated' academic approach to advertising has predominated for decades, largely on the assumption that advertisements are 'prime source material for divining the "spirit" ... of the age'. She argues in favour of the study of 'advertis*ing*' rather than of 'advertise*ments*' (2004: 2–3). While it would be blinkered and boring to try to ignore the actual content of advertising, the emphasis in this book is on advertising as an industry, seen in its relation to advertisers and media, and in the context of globalisation.

The study of advertising excited a great deal of research and theoretical critique in the 1980s, but that was in an era in which Marxism and feminism were extremely influential in setting the agenda for media and communication research, and in those distinct but not unrelated perspectives, advertising was seen as a prime instrument for the reproduction of consumer capitalism and patriarchy. As the next section explains, the emphasis in that era fell more on advertisements than advertising as such, a focus of inquiry which was interesting and useful for a time, but which soon reached its limits. In the 1990s, the study of advertising came to be seen within a larger, more anthropological context, framed within the broad context of consumer culture and the society which supported it. While advertising was thus cast in a more general mould, the 2000s have seen a shift of attention towards a quite specific advertising practice, namely that of branding, particularly in its relation to popular culture and new media. Some of the best contemporary academic work is on branding, rather than advertising as such, and its role in consumer culture. This chapter will trace these shifting paradigms in defining advertising as an object of critical analysis and research over the last few decades.

Advertising as a field of study and research

Marxist critiques

In the 'how-to' marketing textbooks and the trade journals, there is no doubt that advertising is a commercial practice, whereas in the humanities and social sciences, it is seen as a cultural and social phenomenon, albeit with an underlying economic purpose: a 'culture industry' in the critical sense of Adorno and Horkheimer's classic paradox from 1944 (1977). Even within the Marxist tradition to which they belong, in which advertising is seen as an inherent tool of capitalism, there are some more 'economic' and other more 'cultural' critiques, for both were elements in Marx's own analysis.

The question with which Marx began his major work, *Capital*, was how it could be that goods, or 'commodities', which he defined as any objects that satisfied wants, were able to conceal the exploitative real relations between capital and labour under which they were produced. For Marx, labour was the only true source of value, but the 'mystique' of the commodity made it seem that the value was in the object itself. To be under this illusion was what Marx famously called 'commodity fetishism'. Intrinsic to his analysis of the commodity was the distinction between use value and exchange value. Use value was just that – what an object was useful for, its utility – but exchange value was what someone would give for it in exchange: that is, to buy it. For Marx, it was in exchange that the commodity became fetishised, that is, when its illusion overshadowed the truth of the labour that produced it, and particularly because it was being exchanged for money. In practical terms today, we are talking about the difference between what a certain 'good' is good *for*, and the price we are prepared to pay for it. So, Marxists see advertising as having the function of creating the mystique around commodities, thus endowing them with exchange value. This is both an economic and an ideological function.

Marxist critiques of advertising became extremely influential during the 1970s and 1980s, ascribing to advertising an instrumental role in the perpetuation of capitalism, and the power to manipulate the masses, and so control demand. Whereas the Marxist economists Baran and Sweezy took a classic political economy approach in their analysis of the basic economic purposes advertising served for capitalism in its 'monopoly phase' (1968), others put more emphasis on the ideological dimension. Stuart Ewen, for instance, saw advertising as 'an apparatus for the stimulation and creation of mass consumption' which enabled corporations to assume 'an expansionist and manipulative approach to the problem of popular consciousness' through the 'imperialization of the psyche' (1976: 81). In such a view, media audiences were seen as 'cultural dopes' (Garfinkel 1967) who were attracted by the 'free lunch' of entertainment and information, and then 'sold' as a 'commodity' to advertisers (Smythe 1977). Some even argued that this involved a form of 'work' which audiences performed for capitalism, in manufacturing themselves into compliant consumers (Jhally 1987). Thus, there are Marxist perspectives in which the production of audiences is seen to be at least as important as the production of ideology. One authoritative contemporary political economist of communication defines the process of 'commodification' seen to be involved in both these dimensions – consumer goods and audiences – as 'the process of transforming use values into exchange values' (Mosco 1996: 141).

The 'cultural turn'

The definitive account of advertising's function in such transformation of use value into exchange value was Judith Williamson's influential book of 1978, *Decoding Advertisements*. She drew on then current semiological methods, the analysis of how meaning is produced within images, to show how magazine advertisements were structured so as to invoke common cultural meanings familiar to readers, and associate them with a given product. That is, she argues that readers are drawn in to an advertisement and must 'work' to supply the cultural knowledge it requires to be made sense of, and this involves associating some mythic qualities with the product. The kind of cultural Marxist and semiological structuralism which she applied has greatly influenced and persisted in other more recent work, notably that of Robert Goldman, who has coined the notion of 'commodity-sign' to explain how advertisements endow 'commodities' (this time, meaning goods and services) with exchange value: 'Advertising is an institutional process in a political economy of commodity sign-value' (1992: 224).

Like Williamson, Goldman concentrates on advertisements rather than advertising. For even if they use the rhetoric of political economy, these writers' object of study is really signification, or how meanings are produced within advertisements, and they analyse these meanings with little or no reference to the advertisers or agencies which produced them, nor the media in which they are placed. The 1980s saw considerable growth in the number of studies of this kind published, particularly with the impetus given by feminist scholars' critical interest in the changing representation of women in advertisements. Similarly, the identity politics which flourished in that decade and into the 1990s encouraged many studies of how the subordination of ethnic minorities and 'others' was signified in advertisements (O'Barr 1994; Frith 1997). Indeed, such semiological work fairly dominated the field of advertising studies over that era, the 1990s being the decade of the 'cultural turn'. This was defined by a broad movement away from classical Marxist political economy in favour of 'an increasing concern with symbolic systems, systems of meaning and the self-reflexive', which put the study of advertising at 'centre-stage' (Miller 2002: 172–73).

Ethnographic studies

Yet by the mid-1990s the semiological trend had largely exhausted itself, and a more industry-oriented approach was coming to the fore. This had the overall benefit of taking advertising 'as an entire institution not merely the textual end-products of its processes' (Cronin 2004a: 3), which more particularly meant close attention being given to the dynamic relationships within what has been referred to here as the manufacturing/marketing/media complex. In the field of anthropology, the empirical work of the time employed that discipline's characteristic methodology of ethnography, which usually involved the researcher working in an advertising agency as a participant-observer. Thus, Brian Moeran spent a year in an anonymous agency in Tokyo, observing how organisational conflicts within the agency and in its relations with its clients were negotiated in the conduct of certain campaigns in which he participated (1996). Again, Daniel Miller's extensive study of material culture and consumption in Trinidad involved him in sitting in on meetings between agencies and clients, though more as a 'fly-on-the wall' than a participant (1997). A few years later, Steven Kemper's *Buying and Believing* (2001) appears, in which he draws on interviews with advertising and media personnel, and ethnographic studies of consumers' households. Next we have William Mazzarella's *Shovelling Smoke*, 'an ethnographic study of globalizing consumerism', based on his participant observation in particular campaigns in an international agency in the city formerly known as Bombay (2003). Miller's, Kemper's and Mazzarella's studies in particular exemplify a recent shift which will be examined below, namely the setting of the study of advertising within the wider analytic framework of consumption in general.

Instead of the Marxist view of monolithic manipulation wielded by a smoothly functional apparatus of capitalism, all of the ethnographic studies show the highly contingent character of the advertising business, and the delicate relationships which agencies must manage not only with their clients but also between their own divisions, notably the 'creatives' (copywriters and art directors) and the 'suits' (the executives managing the clients' accounts). Interestingly, the studies are all in non-Western settings, but the structural tensions, both internal and external, are common, and found in both 'global' and 'local' agencies.

Meanwhile, back in the West, there were also sociologists whose research directly engaged them with the actual practice, and practitioners, of advertising at this time. Sean Nixon examined the aftermath of the 1980s 'creative revolution' in Britain through interviews with young creative personnel in London. In a period when British advertising was being held up as an exemplar of the nation's 'creative industries', and its corporate leaders were being awarded knighthoods, Nixon's focus was upon the cultural formation and lifestyles of the (mostly) young men involved in the brash 'new lad' style of advertising of that era, the mid- to late 1990s. Apart from the insight it affords upon advertising as a highly-gendered practice, Nixon's study demonstrates the relevance of 'informal cultures and subjective identities of advertising practitioners' (2003: 5) in understanding advertising as a social institution, as the TV series *Mad Men* was later to do so well, but in the form of a compelling dramatic narrative.

Anne Cronin is another British sociologist of this era who approached the study of advertising via interviews with advertising personnel (2004a). She finds them to be preoccupied with the legitimacy of advertising as a business, although as true believers rather than as cynics, and with the need to keep their clients convinced of the value of their work in a competitive environment. More than this, in Cronin's highly theorised account, advertising is seen as both cause and effect of contemporary capitalism, and as having a mythic quality, both in its perceived social influence, and its capacity to stand as 'an index of the social' (2004a: 2). Thus, in her view, advertising is to be understood not so much as an institution, than as a discourse in which mutually-reinforcing beliefs about its power circulate between the agencies themselves; academic critics and the regulators of advertising; and popular culture. A similarly elevated perspective is shown in her suggestion that the Marxist critique of commodification reveals an ontological anxiety about the fragility of the boundary between persons and things (2004a: 125–26).

Consumer culture

For all the focus in these works of the 1990s and 2000s on advertising as such, whether as an institution or a discourse, it should be stressed that they were appearing in a context in which there was a paradigm shift taking place, in that the study of advertising was being eclipsed by the more inclusive analysis of 'consumer culture'. One of the most useful and influential formulations of this shift came from Mike Featherstone, who argued in favour of the concept of consumer culture to characterise contemporary capitalist societies, not as a form of the familiar moral condemnation of 'consumerism', but analytically, with

> a dual focus: firstly on the cultural dimension of the economy, the symbolization and use of material goods as 'communicators' not just utilities; and secondly, on the economy of cultural goods, the market principles of supply, demand, capital accumulation, competition and monopolization, which operate *within* the sphere of lifestyles, cultural goods and commodities.
>
> (1987: 57, italics in original)

In the 1990s, another prominent contribution came from Scott Lash and John Urry, who argued that the economy and culture were becoming ever more integrated: 'the economy is increasingly culturally inflected and … culture is more and more economically inflected' (1994: 64). They particularly see an 'aestheticization' of economic production, meaning that goods, and services, have come to be designed to attract certain kinds of consumers and to fit with their lifestyles: indeed, the concept of lifestyle became very much a buzzword of the 1990s. Prior to the 'cultural turn' of that decade, it was sufficient to have a life, but the discourse of marketing, and its critique, promoted the idea that we each needed a lifestyle, a way of defining ourselves in terms of a distinctive pattern of consumption that we would assemble for ourselves. Lash and Urry capture the self-conscious, knowing relationship they see between individuals and their consumption as 'aesthetic reflexivity', or 'the semiotization of consumption whose increasingly symbolic nature is ever more involved in self-constructions of identity' (1994: 61). Their thesis is that contemporary changes in social structure have liberated individuals from traditional social constraints and categorisation, 'a process in which agency is set free from structure' (1994: 5), giving them the opportunity to define and express their subjectivity as never before, and they do this through their choices in consumption. Note that while Featherstone maintains a 'dual focus' on economy and culture, Lash and Urry tend to push the balance until culture eclipses economy, as they see advertising as a model for all of the culture industries, which are defined by their common function in achieving 'the transfer of value through images' (1994: 138).

Lash and Urry's concept of an 'economy of signs', like Goldman's 'political economy of commodity sign-value' cited above, and the triumph of exchange value over use value in Marxist accounts like that of Baudrillard (1981), are all manifestations of the cultural turn as it became manifested in the critical academic study of advertising, with all of them explicitly or implicitly ascribing to advertising a pivotal role in bringing about consumer culture, or its variant, consumer society. Yet this is to raise a number of theoretical and conceptual issues which we should now go on to consider: the very notion of consumer culture/society, and its ostensible value system of 'consumerism', must be questioned; the meaning of use value and exchange value in Marxist political economy needs be revisited; and the concepts of commodity and commodification require clarification and reassessment. All this is in the interest of furthering our understanding of advertising's much-vaunted capacity to bestow value and cultural meaning upon goods and services.

Concepts and issues in the critique of advertising

One of the most frequent and trenchant criticisms made of Lash and Urry's thesis about the 'culturalisation' of goods and services in the genesis of a consumer society is that this view is mistaken in positing a new and decisive phase in the history of capitalist modernity, and that in any case, to do so is too 'epochal'. Against such a view, Nixon cites McKendrick et al.'s The Birth of Consumer Society which locates the 'consumer revolution' firmly in eighteenth-century England (1982, cited in Nixon 2003: 28–30), while McFall, in her critical investigation of the supposed transition of advertising from a stage of 'information' to one of 'persuasion', demonstrates just how far commercial culture already had become pervasive in nineteenth-century England (2004).

Yet leaving aside what McFall calls the 'obsessive presentism' of theorists such as Lash and Urry (1994: 189), even a literal-minded semantic questioning of the consumer culture/society concept poses the question of how it can be distinguished from other kinds, or phases, of culture or society. In particular, the term implies an opposite: a 'producer' culture or society, either as its antecedent or contemporary antithesis. While there is a rough sense in which we can contrast the characteristic subsistence living of the working masses under early industrialisation with the relative affluence and complex occupational structure of the contemporary West, there clearly is a case for a more nuanced and differentiated way of thinking about such social typologies and their transformations, and for exploring them empirically. If it makes any sense at all to talk about a 'consumer society', its arrival is better thought of as the result of incremental shifts rather than a qualitative, epoch-defining leap.

'Consumerism'

Furthermore, it is not just a matter of developing more sophisticated ways of conceptualising types of society and of paying more attention to actual processes of historical transformation, as there is also the issue of the complex baggage carried, not so much by the consumer culture/society couplet in itself, as by 'consumerism', the total ethos of social values on which it is said to rest. This is a term familiar from both academic and popular critiques of how we live now, and used by both conservative and progressive sides of the spectrum, yet it is a normative term, almost devoid of analytic meaning: 'the concept itself is contested, complex and contradictory' (McLeod 2007: 5). On the conservative side, religious traditionalists contrast the material values of consumerism as a threat to the spiritual ideals according to which they believe we all should live our lives, although business interests see it as the salvation of global capitalism, and see it as their mission to spread it into the developing world. On the other hand, Jackson Lears identifies the American left-liberal critics of consumerism as manifesting 'a preference for production over consumption, a manipulative model of advertising as social control and a masculine bias that led them to typecast the mass of consumers as passive and feminine' (1994: 3). He is referring to influential writers such as John Kenneth Galbraith and Vance Packard in the 1950s and 1960s. Yet the critique of consumerism also has very contemporary advocates in the form of environmentalists, the 'greenies' who see consumerist values to be a major obstacle in their project of achieving a more sustainable way of living for the world (Smart 2010). As if to confuse the issue even more, 'consumerism' was the name given to the social movement formed by advocates for consumer protection and resistance that developed in many 'consumer societies' in the 1970s. Gabriel and Lang sum up these diverse usages of 'consumerism':

(1) A moral doctrine in developed countries.
(2) The ideology of conspicuous consumption.
(3) An economic ideology for global development.
(4) A political ideology.
(5) A social movement promoting and protecting consumer rights.

(2006: 8–9)

For all the frequency with which it is used in denunciatory public discourse, the normative assumptions of the concept are not always spelled out. However, a definition provided by Peter N Stearns in his *Consumerism in World History* may suffice: 'Consumerism describes a society in which many people formulate their goals in life partly through acquiring goods that they clearly do not need for subsistence or for traditional display'. He goes on to implicate 'advertisers seeking to create new needs' as an integral part of such a society (2006: vii). However provisional this definition might be, it does identify two key issues in both the academic and popular versions of the debate about consumption: the idea of artificially-created needs, and the question of display. Critics of consumerism try to establish a line between needs and wants, or 'true' and 'false' needs, but this is necessarily arbitrary. As Baudrillard has put it so convincingly, beyond the most basic physical requirements for sustaining life, in all societies, needs are socially given – as individuals, we are obliged to consume in accordance with our social belonging, and 'no one is free to live on raw roots and fresh water' (1981: 81).

Consumption as display

As for consumption as a form of display, this also is a universal phenomenon familiar to anthropologists, but better known in the critical discourse from Thorstein Veblen's observations of how the newly-rich beneficiaries of late nineteenth-century industrialisation in the US spent their wealth and leisure in 'conspicuous consumption'. That is, for members of this new 'leisure class', consumption was enjoyed not just for its inherent pleasures, but for the way in which it drew attention to their status (1965). However, half a century later, consumption in the US and other industrialised societies had been democratised to the extent that the motivation researcher Pierre Martineau could wryly observe, in 1957, 'within the limits of conformity we can develop individualistic styles in all areas of consumer wants to show our colourful, interesting personalities through our tastes' (quoted in Arvidsson 2006: 57).

For the influential French sociologist, Pierre Bourdieu, 'taste' was about how the dominant social class, not individuals as such, expressed their cultural power. Consumption choices were not necessarily a conspicuous show of wealth and status, but a subtle assertion of superiority cast in aesthetic terms, as 'cultural capital' (1984). In this view, individuals claim membership of the dominant class by their choice of liquor, car or holiday destination, but the point is that in doing so, they affirm the authority and standing of that class.

Although Bourdieu gives us the insight that social class is defined by relations of consumption as well as by relations of production, most contemporary observers are now inclined to see our life in society as characterised by many factors other than class, and including not just the obvious ones of age and gender, but subjective life choices such as subcultural membership or identification with certain lifestyles. Whereas Marxists like Bourdieu saw modern society as uniformly capitalist and based fundamentally on class, postmodern thinkers have been more likely to see a society of fragmented cultural affiliations, in relation to which individuals define their identities by consumption choices. So, while one person defines herself with her high-tech bike, preferred brand of energy drink, and her iPod, for her housemate, it's all about cowboy boots, bourbon, and vintage country & western recordings.

In this scenario, while there is no longer a dominant class asserting its cultural authority over all, neither is it a pluralistic, democratic society of consumption, for there is still what Bourdieu called 'distinction' to be made amongst the meaning of the goods chosen – designer brands in favour of their imitators, for instance – but they stand in multiple systems of relation to each other, rather than a single, dominant hierarchy. Furthermore, to function in these systems, that is, for each of us to be able to choose goods for ourselves and to evaluate other people by their choices, and to understand the nuances and contexts in which those choices are made and expressed, we still require cultural capital – maybe even more rather than less than required by class society. Thus, 'distinction' remains an inherent characteristic of the 'aesthetic reflexivity' endemic to contemporary consumption, but, as anthropologists have long known, there is nothing particularly postmodern about the phenomenon of people asserting their social identities through the display of goods.

Use value and exchange value

More than for their inherent usefulness or competitive social display, there is an anthropological argument that goods are necessary in all societies 'for making visible and stable the categories of culture' (Douglas and Isherwood 1979: 59). As these authors explain: 'Goods are endowed with value by the agreement of fellow consumers. ... Enjoyment of physical consumption is only a part of the service yielded by goods; the other part is the enjoyment of sharing names. ... by far the greater part of utility is yielded ... in sharing names that have been learned and graded. This is culture' (1979: 75–76). Furthermore, the exchange of goods is seen to have a fundamental anthropological function. Arjun Appadurai, following Georg Simmel, argues that 'It is exchange that sets the parameters of utility and scarcity, rather than the other way around, and exchange that is the source of value' (1986: 4). For Appadurai, the meaningful criteria of exchange are governed by 'regimes of value' which enable exchange to take place not only within cultures, but between them, thus making trade possible (1986: 14–15).

This anthropological perspective, that goods do not so much derive their meaning from culture, but on the contrary, provide culture with meaning, perhaps surprisingly finds some resonance with modern Marxists. Baudrillard is notorious amongst them for his rejection of use value in his analysis of consumption, in favour of a semiotic hierarchy of symbolic exchange value, although, like Bourdieu, he largely restricts the meaning of such value to its role in making and keeping class distinctions (1981). That is, for Baudrillard, the cultural significance of goods forms a kind of pecking order which reflects and reinforces the social system. More recently, however, there is the contribution of Adam Arvidsson, who draws on the current strain of 'autonomist' Marxism to argue that the 'productivity of consumers', that is, the cultural capital which they collectively produce and which marketers exploit in brand advertising, is a kind of 'immaterial labour' which forms the context of consumption, 'within which goods can acquire use-value' (2005: 242). Yet by 'use-value' here, he means the social identity and cultural belonging bestowed by the consumption of goods, because for Arvidsson, use value is the good's cultural meaning, not its utility. However, since Baudrillard's sense of 'exchange value' seems to correspond to Arvidsson's 'use-value', it is difficult to see how Marx's classic distinction, if it cannot be made to hold, can have either usefulness or meaning in the contemporary analysis of consumption.

Commodification

As we have seen earlier, in Marxist critical discourse, 'commodification' has become a key concept. However, if goods and services are commodities, and audiences are commodities, and even 'advertising is itself a commodity' (Goldman 1992: 33), it becomes difficult to know what is not a commodity, and just what the concept of commodity can help us understand or explain. That is, it seems to be not so much a heuristic and analytic concept as a rhetorical and critical trope used to denounce all cultural forms in which commerce is seen to encroach upon spheres of life where it ought not to belong. However, the concept of commodity in itself does not tell us how objects come to acquire value. For Marx himself, commodification was a moral concept, for he saw it as a form of corruption, or 'universal venality' (cited in Hirsch 1977: 105n). Usually the term is applied to situations where what was once free now comes with a price attached; where what was once publicly available has become privately held; and where what was once natural and authentic has been contaminated, diluted, dumbed down or otherwise degraded, and then packaged for mass, or perhaps niche-market, consumption as goods and services of some kind. Thus, for example, health and fitness become 'commodified' as bottled water, home gym equipment and sports shoes; or childhood is commodified by Barbie, Lego, Harry Potter and so on.

'The treatment of the commodity in the first hundred or so pages of *Capital* is arguably one of the most difficult, contradictory and ambiguous parts of Marx's corpus' (Appadurai 1986: 7). For those not schooled in Marxist discourse, the concept of commodity itself can be confusing. While Marxists do commonly refer to advertised, branded products as commodities, such usage completely inverts the hierarchical relation between brands and commodities now understood in contemporary 'bourgeois' (non-Marxist) economics. In the current business literature, for instance, commodities are seen as fungible and undifferentiated, merely the raw materials from which products, whether as goods or services, are made for exchange (Pine and Gilmore 1999: 6). Indeed, Marx himself specifically had in mind commodities like corn, iron or silk, which, although there may be variations in quality, are generic: one load of corn is much like any other. By contrast, advertising creates differentiation between products. While some differences can be actual, such as in quality, origin or design, what distinguishes Coca-Cola from Pepsi, for example, is mainly the brand image which advertising gives it. Indeed, when advertisers talk about 'commoditisation', what they mean is their fear that their brand will lose its distinctive image, and the product become readily substitutable for any other of its kind, just a kind of cola drink rather than a Coke.

At this point it is useful to reflect on the social nature of goods, especially the kinds of goods, and services, which we most commonly find advertised in the media. In his analysis of the 'commercialization effect', Fred Hirsch (1977) distinguishes between 'positional goods' and 'material goods'. Positional goods are those which are scarce and difficult to obtain more of, such as 'leisure land' for country retreats or beachfront homes, whereas it is always possible to manufacture more material goods. Because positional goods are expensive, they are socially exclusive, held by members of the wealthy classes, and are a symbolic display of that position, but material goods are comparatively cheap and access to them is, in principle, democratic. The point is underscored in one of Andy Warhol's legendary quips: 'You can be watching TV and see Coca-Cola, and you know that the President drinks Coke, Liz Taylor drinks Coke, and just think, you can drink Coke too. A Coke is a Coke, and no amount of money can get you a better Coke' (1975: 100). While it is not unusual for real estate to be advertised on television, the ads will be for project homes rather than the mansions with 'absolute waterfront' advertised in the quality press.

As was suggested above, advertising plays heavily upon systems of social distinction, but the reality for any given individual is that their membership of the consumer society depends upon their position within the distribution of purchasing power. Nevertheless, the kind of 'commodities' characteristically advertised on television are 'fast moving consumer goods' (FMCG), the sort of everyday purchases we all make at the supermarket – packaged foods, household cleansers, personal care products and the like. As we shall see later in this book, the global manufacturers of such goods are found listed amongst the biggest advertisers from one country to another, and they still favour television as their medium. More importantly in the present context, these are the kinds of products which rely heavily on advertising to establish and maintain their identity as brands.

Figure 1.1 'The fetish of the commodity': Andy Warhol's art commented ironically on the symbolic value of branded goods

Advertising and the branding paradigm

'In fields where there is little real functional difference between the products on offer, the choice the consumer makes will be made largely on intangibles ... on factors such as trust, service, reputation and design' (J Walter Thompson agency memo, cited in Davidson 1992: 24–25). We have seen that advertising's prime purpose is to 'add value' to a commodity, which it does by fostering intangible associations of a product in prospective consumers' minds, while the media, whether mass or niche, provide the means by which those consumers can be reached and formed into a market. Particularly since the era of large-scale corporate takeovers of brands in the 1980s, advertising has become consciously harnessed to the process of branding. Branding itself is not new, having quite ancient origins in the trade mark, the elementary purpose of which was to 'uniquely identify' the maker of a given product, to differentiate that product from its competitors (and imitators), and to provide an assurance of quality and consistency to the buyer (Aaker 1991: 7). Nor is advertising the only means by which branding is achieved, though it is 'the most visible, spectacular and eye-catching' of the several marketing functions involved (Moor 2007). These cover all of the previously mentioned 'four Ps', plus the fifth P of packaging. Product design and packaging are particularly important as vehicles of branding in the FMCG category.

Branding came into its own in the nineteenth-century industrial era, when, rather than buying bulk, generic goods like oats, weighed out by the grocer, shoppers began to identify their preference amongst the packets they now found on the shelves – would it be Quaker, Scott's Porage or Uncle Toby's? At around the same time, householders were coming to appreciate the convenience of branded products, like Ivory, Pear's or Lifebuoy soap in packets, rather than having to make their own lye soap at home. In this way, manufacturers were using the distinctiveness of brands, materialised in packaging and in-store display (Cochoy 2004), to establish a direct relationship with consumers, so that the traditional intermediary role of the retailer was bypassed by the brand itself serving to sell the product, a shift which ultimately was to result in the 'self-service' supermarket (Lury 2004: 19). Over time, the retailers too came to realise that they had to adopt some of the characteristics of a brand if they were to prosper in a shifting and competitive market – Sears, Roebuck in the United States, Selfridge's in Britain, David Jones in Australia, to name a few.

With the rise of the press, then radio and television coming to dominate social communication in the twentieth century, branding found its supreme vehicle in the advertising which impelled the commercial growth of these media. More than uniquely identifying a product or its manufacturer, advertising enabled brands to acquire cultural meanings, such as status distinctions (Harrod's versus Marks & Spencer); associations with certain kinds of people (the Marlboro man); and even something like their own personalities (stylish Lexus versus reliable Toyota). Branding makes the difference between 'what the manufacturer makes' and 'the meanings and values delivered by what the consumer buys' (Lannon 1985, quoted in Davidson 1992: 123).

In the business management literature, the capacity to bestow such value upon a certain good or service, that is, to transform a product into a brand, and sustain it as such, is called brand equity. According to one marketing authority, brand equity is composed of:

- brand loyalty, or the ability to retain satisfied customers;
- familiarity and recognition of a brand name and/or symbols;
- perceived quality of products offered under the brand name;
- associations, including positioning of a brand relative to competitors;
- other proprietary brand assets, such as control of distribution outlets.

(Aaker 1991)

In other words, the greater part of brand equity consists in the relation of a brand with its actual or potential consumers, at the overarching level of culture. As early as the 1950s, the advertising industry has been referring to this quality of a brand – to evoke loyalty, familiarity and positive associations – as 'brand image', which is the kind of character or personality with which a product is endowed as a 'public object' (Gardner and Levy 1955, quoted in Arvidsson 2006: 55). Arvidsson has argued that consumers, rather than being the passive dupes of the marketers, actually participate in the making of a brand, albeit unequally. His insight is that brands capitalise upon 'people's ability to create trust, affect and shared meanings: their ability to create something in common. ... it is the meaning-making activity of consumers that forms the basis of brand value' (2005: 236–37). However, this does not amount to the all-out victory of the sovereign consumer: there is a hegemonic struggle going on in which marketers constantly seek to engage and mobilise the 'meaning-making activity' of consumers with their branding.

Common meanings created collectively by people (whether a nation, or a subculture) is one of the main things we mean when we talk about 'culture', so in other words, Arvidsson's view is that although it is people who create cultural meanings, what brand marketers do is to pick up on these meanings and exploit them by associating them with particular products and services. This is a capitalism which is more reflexive in the sense that it recognises the rise of an independent popular culture, but seeks to bring it under control to serve commercial interests, just as consumers, in this view, are more reflexive in understanding their own responses in relation to advertised goods.

In order to understand the branding function of advertising more fully, we need to consider here, first, the issue of how economic value can be transformed into cultural value, and vice versa; and second, what it is about popular culture which branding exploits, and how it uses the media to do so. We shall see that although there are brands which have been established as icons on the national, and even the global level, branding also works hand-in-hand with market segmentation in the practice of brand management, so that some brands are quite narrowly targeted towards particular demographic groups. Perhaps the area leading this trend, and with the greatest implications for the use of new media, is in marketing brands towards youth, such as Crumpler and Red Bull.

Brands as corporate property

The large-scale corporate takeover of brands which began in the 1980s has endured to become a characteristic of globalisation, with sometimes long-standing brands being acquired in a process of continued global corporate expansion and consolidation of brand portfolios: just to name one, Procter & Gamble's acquisition of Gillette in 2005. Branding has become a major means by which all global corporations maximise the advantages that accrue to them via globalisation, particularly the opening up of huge new markets and licensing opportunities, and the rationalisation of distribution systems (Arvidsson 2006; Holt 2002). In this perspective, we see that the brand is not so much a mere image in the form of a logo or symbol and set of cultural associations, but a form of intellectual property, and as such, 'an important immaterial asset in contemporary capitalism' (Arvidsson 2005: 238).

What is being traded in the corporate transactions is brand equity – that is, brand image is given a financial value so that it can change hands. Since there are high costs and often also long years involved in building up brand equity, corporations that want to take over an existing brand via acquisition or merger have to compensate the seller, not just for the investment embedded in the brand, but for the meaning it commands as a public object. The elusive, intangible quality of a brand image is thus given a concrete value, or specific, calculated quantity. Since the 1980s formal accounting methods of putting a figure on both the present and future value of brands have become standardised to facilitate such takeovers and mergers, which in effect are methodologies for transforming quality into quantity (Lury 2004). Once again, the trademark can be seen as the ancestor and paradigm of the legal protection with which brands are now surrounded, but patents, copyright and design rights may also apply. All these rights prevent competitors from imitating or otherwise encroaching upon the brand's equity, thus protecting the company's investment in developing or acquiring the brand. As well, in the era of corporate globalisation, intellectual property law has become something of a weapon to wield in maintaining market power and eliminating local competitors, especially in new markets (Moor 2007).

Branding and popular culture

The question of how cultural value becomes bestowed upon products through branding can be usefully approached by looking at the meaning which certain branded goods have within national popular cultures. In an era in which national governments have allowed discourses of national belonging to become more grounded in popular culture and its commercialisation by the media, commercial television, in its dual historical role of nation-building and the forming of national markets for advertisers, has led many contemporary nations, both developed and developing, to become 'imagined communities of consumption' (Foster 1991: 250). In their role as consumers rather than as citizens, large sectors of the national population choose to express their national belonging by making purchases of certain brands which are represented to them as embedded in an everyday, popular national culture that they identify with as their own. For example, Oreo cookies in the US; McVities digestives in Britain; and Tim Tam biscuits in Australia. '[I]t is in consumerism that we most express our sense of social belonging. ... Culture is the society we build with our brands' (Davidson 1992: 124). Thus, in addition to whatever utility branded goods may have, and however much they may mark our social distinction as individuals, they also can express our belonging to a nation.

'Brands are products that are famous', quips Martin Davidson (1992: 25). Indeed, just as mediated popular culture sustains a world of celebrities, so it does also for the world of goods. However, if brands are the celebrities, then commodities are the masses, and as Marx could not have anticipated, it is actually brands, not commodities which are fetishised. Modern-day Marxists would have to agree that branding contributes to the mystique that conceals the value of the labour which made the product: it is essential to what they mean by commodification. In that light, it is branding, not commodification which transforms use values into exchange values, or to put it another way, branding is a process through which commodification takes place.

The analogy of brands with celebrities can be taken further, however, in that just as celebrities each have their particular characteristics which define them in relation to each other and form a kind of pop culture moral universe – Angelina Jolie as saintly mother, as against the irresponsible Britney Spears, for example – so do brands acquire identities in relation to each other in popular culture. As with celebrities, these can be but are not necessarily in opposition to each other – McDonald's versus KFC, for instance – nor even in a hierarchical relationship, like Mercedes and Volkswagen. Rather, and once again, like celebrities, brands present us with a huge field of identities, each defined by its difference from the others, yet meaningful only in relation to them. Like the stars at night, we know how to recognise each one by its position relative to the others, though unlike the stars, that position can change over time. The relational aspect is fundamental. We acquire the capacity to recognise, differentiate and associate not so much from advertising, as from everyday popular culture, but of course, those two spheres draw upon each other. Advertisers seek to associate celebrities with their brands, and these associations can pass into popular culture, though perhaps in unintended ways. For example, Michael Jackson's hair catching on fire during the filming of a Pepsi Cola commercial in 1984 became part of the popular mythology about the late celebrity's plastic surgery (Taraborrelli 2004).

This is what Arvidsson means when he argues that consumer perceptions are 'beyond the direct control of capital' (2005: 242). Far from imposing brand images upon unwitting targets, brand managers have to protect their brands from falling victim to ridicule or disrepute. In the US, for example, a T-shirt available over the internet asking 'Got dope?' is a parody of the long-running 'Got milk?' campaign. Young consumers are particularly prone to participate in parodies and spoofs of branded advertising, and new social media such as YouTube allows the rapid diffusion of such material on a global scale. At the same time, advertisers and their agencies are fascinated by the internet's ability not only to target young consumers, but to exploit their social networking behaviour. Even before the advent of Web 2.0, the social media phase of internet development which has enabled interactive services like Facebook, specialist agencies were engaged in 'cool hunting' – market research into youth culture trends – and 'bro'ing': the mobilising of word-of-mouth recommendations of a brand (Klein 2000: 72–75).

With Web 2.0, all this has gone on line, so what used to be called 'peer pressure' is now mediated through posts on social media sites, instant messaging, blogs, email and other forms of online communication. Where once the brands marketed towards youth were 'shaped by the noises coming from the street' (Mort 2000: 277), the internet has allowed marketers to do their cool hunting on line, and opened up the possibility of 'buzz' or 'viral' marketing, by 'stealth': that is, strategically planting advertising or other marketing material on the internet where it would be picked up and passed on by users, thus creating 'buzz' around the brand. An early but internationally-known example is the 'Subservient Chicken' from Burger King, which since 2004, has been obeying commands typed in by users (Howard 2004; Deuze 2010).

As well as giving marketers access to cool and sceptical young consumers via social networking, Web 2.0 has been characterised by the phenomenon of 'user-generated content', and this too has been exploited by some major brands. Advertisers such as PepsiCo's Frito-Lay snack food brand Doritos have in recent years run competitions for users to submit TVCs to be shown during the US's premium television advertising event, the Super Bowl. Online judging is part of the selection process (York and Mullman 2009). Similar competitions have since been run by Doritos in Australia and the UK. On the other hand, Domino's Pizza had the embarrassment of two employees posting a video of themselves playfully contaminating pizza ingredients on YouTube, showing that some user-generated content can create quite the wrong kind of buzz (York 2009). Thus, both social networking and user-generated content have become 'touchpoints' at which brands can engage with the popular culture of youth, but it is a struggle for brand managers to ensure that it occurs on their own terms. Rather than the mass of 'cultural dopes' that consumers were taken to be in the past, manipulated by and in thrall to the cultural authority of media and advertisers, the coming of the internet has shifted the balance so that consumers, particularly young ones, are now seen to use brands in their own way, 'to construct social relations, shared emotions, personal identity or forms of community' (Arvidsson 2006: 18). The popular culture forms thus created have set new limits upon the credibility and standing which advertisers can claim for their brands.

Advertising, the media and globalisation

In this final section, we will take account of how the study of advertising and the media can be understood in relation to globalisation. The concept of 'globalisation' has become a cliché of our times, but that is because of the need for an inclusive term able to cover the huge economic, political and sociocultural changes which we are experiencing on a world scale. Nevertheless, we also need to be specific about the contexts to which discussions of globalisation refer. In the humanities and social sciences, globalisation has meant a massive enlargement of the scope of our studies, principally from a national to an international, or more accurately, transnational framework. In an era in which capital and labour are on the move from one nation to another, and media and markets are distributed across borders, our understanding of economy, polity, society and culture can no longer meaningfully be bounded by the borders of the nation-state.

As will be outlined in the next chapter, and understood in the context of globalisation, the advertising industry is best seen as a service industry which supports the foreign investment of global advertisers and stimulates global media development. Yet it will also be shown that the advertising agency business itself is highly globalised in its organisation, as well as being a force for globalisation in national media and consumer markets.

To take the last point first, many, perhaps most, of the brandnames that we know via advertising and other modes of marketing in our national markets are in fact owned by global corporations. Interestingly, Lury points out that most of the major global brands are fifty to a hundred years old, that is, older than most of their consumers (Lury 2004: 101). From that perspective, we see that, at least in the main consumer capitalist societies, people experience brands just as they do their national language: as we have just seen, brandnames and their cultural meanings are an integral aspect of the everyday world in which each of us must learn how to function. Major brands like Coca-Cola can truly say 'Always Coca-Cola' after having been part of many national cultures for generations, just as McDonald's, with its happy meals and birthday parties, has secured a place in the childhood memories of those who do not remember a time when there was no McDonald's in their country.

Importantly, however, brands have extended themselves over space as well as time. Thus, just as the older brands were not always household names throughout the world, even now, they are not literally 'global', but certainly a massive presence in the developed nations, and the globalised zones of the developing world. They belong to companies which grew from local to national scale, mainly in the US and Western European countries, and then became what were called the 'multinational' or 'transnational' corporations which came to prominence in the 1960s and 1970s. Furthermore, in the FMCG field in particular, a limited number of corporations are concealed behind a whole host of brands. Mention has already been made of how Procter & Gamble, perennially the world's biggest advertiser, acquired the Gillette brands Duracell and Braun, thus adding to its huge stable of brands which currently ranges, just to mention the field of cosmetics and fragrances, from Old Spice and Max Factor to Hugo Boss (Procter & Gamble 2009).

On the other hand, while some global brands have had an extended period of development, contemporary marketing and media institutions have allowed many others to achieve global reach in a matter of decades (Frith and Mueller 2003: 1). The most striking phenomenon in recent times has been the sudden rise of communication and information technology corporations, so that we now find Google, Microsoft, Apple and Nokia amongst the top brands in annual surveys, followed by others that also have achieved global presence within a fairly short time, but have more to do with contemporary leisure activities and lifestyles, such as Ikea and Starbuck's (Millward Brown 2010).

Regarding the globalisation of the advertising and marketing communication industries then, this occurred as the US- and European-based consumer goods and services corporations spread themselves into foreign markets in the 1960s and 1970s, for advertising agencies from their home countries also set up offices abroad, both to serve existing clients, and to capture new ones. Thus, many advertising agencies themselves became 'transnational corporations' over this period, with a presence in both the developed and the developing world, and the power to establish how advertising was to be conducted. In more recent decades, as will be explained in the following chapter, these advertising agencies have gone on to form themselves into truly global organisations.

Talk about the globalisation of the media usually can be pinned down to one or both of two contemporary tendencies: the capacity of media corporations, such as publishers, television and film studios to distribute their products across national borders, and, as implied in the previous discussion, the transnational, interactive character of the internet: Subservient Chicken can be accessed as easily by friends in Melbourne as Minneapolis or Manchester. Again, it was the 'transnationalisation' of the manufacturers of brandname consumer goods in the 1960s and 1970s, and their advertising agencies, which created demand for advertising space and time. This put pressure on national governments to liberalise their media in the 1980s, at the same time as new technologies, notably international satellite television, broke down the borders of the national media systems which had prevailed until then. This in turn allowed several media corporations to internationalise themselves, such as Time

Warner, Sony and News Corporation, although, as will be discussed in following chapters, global media corporations do not necessarily carry global advertising. In the internet era, new modes of media globalisation and advertising have seen the rise to global dominance of Google.

The expansion of what has been called here the manufacturing/marketing/ media complex in the 1960s and 1970s generated a critical literature, and indeed, became part of a major world controversy over 'cultural imperialism' that was played out in academia, public discourse and even the United Nations. Advertising was seen as responsible for 'the export of consumerism' and a force threatening the diversity of national cultures with homogenisation (Schiller 1979: 24). By the 1980s, writers were in a position to document and analyse the actual process of advertising's internationalisation and its impact on what was then called the 'Third World' of developing nations (Sinclair 1987), and to provide a comprehensive critical assessment of subsequent developments in that decade (Mattelart 1991). By the early 1990s, with the end of the Cold War which formerly had given context and purpose to the cultural imperialism debate, coupled with the rapid growth of the internet, the era of globalisation had arrived.

This chapter has outlined the transformations in the intellectual frameworks within which the critical study of advertising has been set as it has developed in the humanities and social sciences over the last few decades. A number of significant shifts become apparent: from the study of advertisements, or the content of advertising, to the study of advertising as an industry and social institution; from Marxist to more anthropological approaches in theory and in method; from a focus on advertising itself to the broader context of consumer culture; from the analysis of advertising practices in general to the process of branding in particular; and from seeing advertising in relation to any specific national society in favour of a perspective on advertising as a globalised phenomenon. We now turn to look in some detail at how this has occurred.

Chapter 2

Global trends in the advertising industry

While some argue that globalisation began with colonialism, in the case of global advertisers, agencies and media it is, of course, a much more recent phenomenon, though not quite so recent as might be thought. The last two decades of the twentieth century may have been the era when 'globalisation' became a common discourse, a way of thinking and talking about the world, but the emergence of what we have called the manufacturing/marketing/media complex on an international basis developed over the whole of the twentieth century. Indeed, the US advertising pioneer J Walter Thompson opened up a London office as early as 1899 (Mattelart 1991: 3), but then as now, it was the advertisers who were the real prime movers. This chapter will outline the stages by which advertising came to be a global industry, looking at the globalisation of the advertiser clients, media and agencies, but with an emphasis on the recent past, and the changes under way in the present.

Globalisation of advertiser clients

If we look at international league tables of the world's very biggest advertisers, such as *Advertising Age*'s Global Marketers report each year, it is evident that fast moving consumer goods (FMCG) and automobile conglomerates predominate. Reference to official and unofficial corporate histories of these companies shows that, typically, they have their origins in the late nineteenth or early twentieth century, often beginning from quite modest local enterprises in the United States or Western Europe (though later in the case of the Japanese companies), then building themselves, usually through mergers and takeovers, into major national corporations in their country of origin, and subsequently branching out into the rest of the world. For example, of the 2010 list of the top ten global marketers ('Global Marketers 2010' 2010), Coca-Cola is the paradigm case (McQueen 2001), although the world's largest advertiser is also its oldest: Procter & Gamble dates from 1837 (Dyer *et al.* 2004). The Anglo-Dutch Unilever and Swiss-based Nestlé both were formed from smaller companies which had begun in different countries in the nineteenth century, but had already begun to establish overseas markets before the First World War (Jones

2005). L'Oréal and Johnson & Johnson also date from this era. In automotive, Ford and General Motors both began overseas ventures soon after their inception in the first decade of the twentieth century, although much more international growth took place in the period between the World Wars (Farber 2002).

Yet even for these prime movers, it is the decades after the Second World War which mark the high tide of international expansion. Just as we think of the present, or at least, about the last two decades, as the era of globalisation, the 1960s and the 1970s were the age of the 'transnational' or 'multinational' corporation. The reconstruction of war-ravaged Europe in the 1950s had created foreign investment opportunities for US-based companies in particular, but the 1960s and 1970s saw several European corporations also join in the quite intense process of setting up subsidiaries and joint ventures, and licensing and franchising their brands, in foreign markets both in the developed and developing world. While some of this investment was in 'export platform' initiatives, that is, manufacturing goods in cheap labour countries for sale in the corporation's home market, of more significance was the setting up of manufacturing in and for the foreign markets themselves. Some of these markets actively sought such investment on the rationale of 'import substitution': that is, attracting manufacturing to their own soil, rather than importing finished goods. Thus, this phase saw new consumer goods and automotive industries established by the transnationals in Australia, South Africa, Latin America and Asia (Vernon 1971). One of the first books to critically analyse, and to name, this new 'globalization process' [sic] cites several indicators of the exceptional rate of growth: for instance, that the percentage of sales of all US companies manufacturing abroad which were derived from the foreign markets almost doubled between 1961 and 1970 (Barnet and Müller 1975: 260).

At this stage, the corporations were transnational or multinational in the sense that management was centralised in the head office in the US or Europe, and all the overseas offices were directly under that control. As globalisation progressed, however, and entered a period of large-scale mergers and takeovers in the 1980s, management became more complex. For example, Philip Morris, US makers of the global cigarette brand, Marlboro, sought to diversify into the food industry, and took over General Foods in 1985, thus acquiring the Maxwell House, Jell-O and Oscar Mayer brands (Castro 1985). There was a further takeover of Kraft Foods in 1988, and then of Nabisco in 2000 (Kraft Foods Inc. 2002). The parent company which ultimately overlooks the management of the scores of brands made by these and other companies in the conglomerate is now known as Altria Group, but the member companies are still managed separately, even on a country-by-country basis (Brat 2009). This process of conglomeration is not just an 'American' phenomenon: similar stories can be told for the scores of brand divisions marshalled under such European-based counterparts as Unilever and Nestlé. Nor is the group organisational model exemplified by Altria unique to the FMCG category, as it distinguishes the automotive field as well: notably, the Volkswagen Group now incorporates Audi, SEAT, Škoda and Bentley, amongst other distinguished European marques (Volkswagen Group 2009).

This mode of corporate expansion, that is, the continued acquisition of companies in a related, or even the same, field, and at the same level of production, is called horizontal integration. This is a characteristic of what are known as oligopolistic markets, that is, where the market is dominated by a handful of suppliers, as is the case in FMCG and automotive. Furthermore, since companies in oligopolistic markets tend to compete more in terms of advertising than price, which stabilises the market in their favour and keeps out prospective competitors, advertising is said to be a barrier to entry. That is, would-be new entrants have to launch themselves with levels of advertising expenditure comparable to the incumbents (Baran and Sweezy 1968; Comanor and Wilson 1974). Thus, the conglomeration process tends to encourage high expenditure on advertising, both domestically and globally.

As far as globalisation is concerned, the point is more that as the core companies become more complexly interpenetrated with other companies through takeovers and mergers, and more decentralized in their operations, the component companies are no longer necessarily controlled by a head office located in the country of origin – in fact, the country of origin becomes less relevant to their functioning. This globalisation of ownership and control is manifested in many ways, including the recruitment of key executive personnel from the foreign operations: for example, Australians have served as global CEOs (Chief Executive Officers) of the iconic US corporations Coca-Cola, Ford and McDonald's in recent times. While it might be an exaggeration to characterise this whole development as 'disorganized capitalism' (Lash and Urry 1994), clearly there is a great organisational as well as spatial distance between the highest level of management and the actual conduct of the companies in the many national and world-regional markets in which they operate. Accordingly, there is a 'process of interpenetration of firms and markets' (Mattelart 1991: 36) such that these corporations are now more truly said to be global than transnational or multinational.

As we have noted, it was the 1960s and 1970s that marked the crucial phase in this transition to the globalisation of today: the era when the world's cities became illuminated with the logos of globalising corporations on the electric signs across their skylines. Less obviously, the massive overseas expansion of US and European-based manufacturers in that era was accompanied by a corresponding expansion in service industries, such as banking, insurance, consultancies and advertising. As we shall see in more detail later in the case of advertising, the service companies were motivated not only by the need to follow their major home market clients into foreign markets so as to retain their business, but were also looking to open up new markets for themselves, most obviously in the case of banking. The number of overseas offices of US banks tripled in the late 1960s, for instance (Barnet and Müller 1975: 259).

Finally, there was one other kind of business which was actively being internationalised in this same era: television. Many governments around the world welcomed the new medium on the grounds of its potential for national cultural development and education, but given its even greater commercial potential, and its appearance at just this point in world history, coinciding as it did with the age of corporate expansion, television was soon harnessed to consumer capitalist modernity as its supreme vehicle for advertising.

Globalisation of advertising media

While print and radio were well established as advertising media in many countries before the Second World War, it is really only with the advent of television that it became plausible for corporations to contemplate mounting advertising campaigns on a global basis. Even then, television had to go through an initial 'nation-building' stage in each country in which it was adopted, and by no means were all of those countries open to commercial advertising. In general, European countries implemented directly or indirectly state-controlled, public service regimes for television, ranging from the BBC model in Britain, which had no advertising, to countries such as Spain, where the state system was subsidised by the acceptance of advertising. Most of Asia and Africa instituted direct state control, with restricted or no advertising. The major countries of Latin America, however, implemented television on the commercial model propagated by the US, and with transmission and reception equipment, technical assistance and programme content supplied by the established US networks. There were early attempts to sell advertisements in programmes to be shown in chains of countries in the region, but these were not successful, and were soon abandoned (Sinclair 1999).

For not only was television a nation-bound medium in its organisation and regulation, but also in its physical and technical implementation – each country developed its own national broadcasting structure. The advent of television via international satellite in the 1980s changed that profoundly, though it did not necessarily result in global advertising campaigns, nor even in common programming. When pan-European satellite services became available in the 1980s, global advertisers and their agencies soon found that it brought more problems than advantages, at least until the 1990s when it became technically possible to pick and choose in which particular territories under the satellite footprint they would run their ads (Chalaby 2008). The experience of STAR TV in Asia is another example of how the global, or at least regional, technical capacity of a communication medium to cover immense territory is frustrated in its commercial potential by the realities of linguistic, cultural, regulatory and political differences between nations. STAR began as a pan-Asian service, but very soon found it could not attract audiences, and hence advertisers, on that basis. Yet subsequently, with the cunning management and diplomacy of

Rupert Murdoch, STAR found success once it tailored its offerings to the specific national markets under its footprint (Thomas 2006).

International satellite television was the first of two major innovations in recent times to make possible the much-vaunted globalisation of the media – the other being the internet, which we will come to presently. However, the European and Asian experiences just described suggest that, from the point of view of the traditional commercial function of attracting audiences to be sold to advertisers, the globalisation of the media has been over-rated. Writers at the end of the 1990s such as Robert McChesney declared that a US-based '*global* commercial media market has emerged full force' (1999: 78 italics in original), but the first decade of the new century has seen an emerging critique of the assumption that just because certain media interests are present every-where, that they therefore must be dominant (Flew 2007). Certainly, there is considerable substance to McChesney's argument that the spread of neoliberal policies throughout the world in the last decades of the twentieth century has facilitated a process of media globalisation. Equally, though, it can be argued that the advent of satellite technology actually hastened the liberalisation of television markets in Europe and Asia, as governments could see how difficult it had become to continue to control television signals coming in to their national territory. In any case, it is quite another question as to whether the extension of television and other media across borders therefore facilitates the running of advertising campaigns on a global basis, an issue to which we shall return.

Global media conglomerates

In some respects, television and other global media industries have similar characteristics to the FMCG, automotive and other manufacturing industries of their advertiser clients, including a tendency to oligopolistic structures. Indeed, there are major media corporations which have based themselves on manufacturing. Sony is an interesting case, as it exemplifies a particular kind of global corporation, a media company which enters the media field from a basis in industrial manufacturing, in its case, looking for 'synergy', or cross-stimulation, in the horizontal integration of its media 'hardware' with 'software' divisions. Also, it was Sony which brought home the reality of glo-balisation in the US, when it acquired Columbia TriStar film and television interests and CBS Records in that country in 1989. This showed dramatically that globalisation was more than just something that US-based companies did to the rest of the world, but that the US itself was subject to the forces of globalisation. In the US, horizontal integration between manufacturing and media has had a long history, notably in the case of General Electric, which branched into radio in its early days by setting up RCA, and still today has a major involvement in media via its 49 per cent ownership of NBC Universal. In other instances, media corporations have had a base in financial or commercial services, though this is more of a European phenomenon: an example is Silvio Berlusconi's Mediaset in Italy, which is integrated with financial and other media companies (Herman and McChesney 1997).

News Corporation can be regarded as an archetypical model of how the confluence of neoliberalism and technological developments became business opportunities which could be exploited. While News has its origins and still dominates the press in Australia, it has become a high-profile media conglomerate with a truly global character, albeit strongly identified with the person of its Chair, Rupert Murdoch. It has a history of risk and debt-prone but strategic international acquisitions, first of press interests in the UK and US; then network television in the US and international film production and distribution based in the US (Twentieth Century Fox); followed by the extension of its satellite television interests from the UK and Europe to all of Asia and Latin America (Herman and McChesney 1997: 70ff).

A crucial aspect of News Corporation's structure is that it is vertically as well as horizontally integrated; that is, not only can it recycle print content from *The Times* and *The Wall Street Journal* in *The Australian*, for example, but because different stages in the same chain of output are strategically connected, notably production and distribution, News can supply its television channels with films it produces itself in the Fox studios. Similarly, News can cross-promote its various businesses from one outlet to another: newspaper entertainment pages can favourably review the corporations' films and television programmes, for example. Even further, News is in a position to coordinate the pursuit, and defence, of its broader economic and political interests on an international basis.

However, at the stratospheric level at which global corporations make mergers, achieve their integration and synergies, and establish their economies of scale and scope, Murdoch has modestly protested that News Corporation is a relative 'minnow'. Indeed, News ranked fifth amongst the corporations which made up the first of the two tiers into which Herman and McChesney classified the global media corporations in the mid-1990s, as measured by volume of sales (1997). Heading that list was Time Warner. Ten years later, in the annual ranking of 'the world's top media owners' compiled by the global media-buying agency ZenithOptimedia, based on income from advertising, News was second, but a distant one: Time Warner was still first, with nearly double News' revenues (2007).

In 1996, Time Warner had merged with Turner Broadcasting, thus acquiring Cable News Network (CNN), the world's leading cable news service, and so enabling synergies with Time Warner's own channels such as HBO through its cable service provision activities. In 2000, Time Warner seemed to have reached the high watermark of media conglomeration, when it became merged with the internet company America On Line (AOL). This was hailed in the business press at the time as the triumphant, strategic fusion of 'old' and 'new' media, AOL being a major provider of internet services both in the US and internationally. However, the venture suffered in the stock market's disillusionment with new technology companies and the consequent 'dotcom crash' at the end of that same year. Furthermore, the company's 'walled garden' subscription (rather than advertising) model failed to attract subscribers, and neither did the expected synergies between old media content and new media distribution eventuate (Ellis 2002).

As to News Corporation's new media initiatives, Murdoch was actually criticised, and even publicly criticised himself, for being relatively late in his embrace of the internet. However, News' acquisition of the then leading youth-oriented social networking site, MySpace, and the subsequent creation of an internet division, Fox Interactive Media (FIM) in 2005, was a definitive move into the digital media of the Web 2.0 era. The timing took advantage of both the availability of greater bandwidth to share images, music and video, and the rise of the user-generated content phenomenon, where users were seen to be 'the same audiences that are most attracted to Fox's news, sports and entertainment offerings' (Murdoch, quoted in Schulze 2005). Thus, News was also exploiting its vertical integration of ('old' media) content and ('new' media) distribution, seeking to attract and hold young internet users who could be exposed to advertising while they enjoyed free access to News' sites. At the same time, the integration of print and television content with internet access meant that News could offer advertisers 'cross-platform' deals for buying advertising space and time across the different media. However, this old/new media venture also failed to meet expectations, and News eventually sold MySpace at a heavy loss in 2011 (Saba 2011).

Significantly, these cases demonstrate that in practice, the distinction between old and new media does not hold, at least as far as their corporate ownership is concerned, and neither are moves into new media necessarily profitable. It is true, for example, that newspapers have suffered massive losses of revenue to the internet, and that television revenues have levelled out in the same process, but because the major media-owning companies are becoming integrated across both old and new media, they can potentially balance the losses of the former with the gains of the latter. Such gains remain elusive, however. What seems crucial is not the size and extent of their corporate holdings as such, but the mode of strategic integration, horizontal and vertical, with which they are able to 'monetise' their traditional media assets through harnessing them to the internet as a marketing medium. There is much more to be said about this in Chapter 3.

Globalisation of the advertising industry

Some of the oldest names in the US advertising industry began to establish offices in foreign countries as early as the 1920s, serving the clients whose accounts they held at home – J Walter Thompson for General Motors, N W Ayer for Ford, for example. A further wave of expansion occurred after the Second World War, particularly into Europe, Latin America and Asia. Armand Mattelart has described this as the 'imperial' phase of advertising's internationalisation (1979). The 1960s and 1970s, as we have seen, were decades of great expansion abroad by the transnational manufacturing corporations of the era, coinciding with the spread of television to many countries. However, rather than open their own branch offices, in this phase the agencies were more inclined to go into a partnership or acquire a minority stake in a local agency. The advantages of this mode of entry were, on one hand, to lower the strong US profile of the industry in an era when national governments were becoming ever more sensitive to the inroads of 'cultural imperialism', and on the other, to give the incoming agency access to the local knowledge of the market which was held by the resident agency. The latter advantage became ever more important as investment flowed into culturally alien areas like the Middle East.

As in the imperial phase, agency expansion was motivated by the need to follow their clients from the home market into whatever foreign markets they chose to do business with, but by this time, the agencies had acquired their own motivation and dynamic, and thus had their own interests to pursue: they were not entirely in a subservient, functional relationship with their clients. Relative to the competitive US domestic market, foreign markets offered new opportunities, such as the local clients who could be introduced to more sophisticated styles of advertising, although the major factor was that the US agencies had experience with the new medium of television. This was not only in making and placing television commercials (TVCs), as they still do today, but in actually producing programs for sponsors. This was commonly done until the 1960s, when television production became more independent of advertisers.

Thus, the US agencies were entering the new markets with the comparative advantages of 'American know-how', to recycle a phrase of the time, and their experience with television. While both inside and outside the advertising industry in many countries, there were those who opposed the US incursion, others again derived benefit from it. In Australia, for example, where television had been adopted in 1956, the influx of US agencies that began in 1959 provoked, on one hand, the formation of a pressure group in resistance, but on the other, a series of partnerships (Walker 1967). However, then as now, the greatest advantage in such relationships for the local partners is the access which it gives them to the big transnational or global clients which the foreign agency brings with them. Ultimately, then, the major motivating benefit for both the foreign and the local agencies with which they partnered was derived from the fact that the advertiser clients were internationalising, and needed their services. At the time, this was known as a 'common account' arrangement: if an agency held a client's account in the US and it was willing to open up offices wherever that client had subsidiaries abroad, it would be given that client's business in those markets also (Sauvant 1976). While this arrangement protected the agency's relationship with the client in the US domestic market, the agencies had everything to gain from overseas expansion, as just explained. Between the second half of the 1960s and the early 1970s, the 'billings' (the total amount which an agency charges the client) of the top ten US agencies grew 12.6 per cent internationally, but only 1 per cent domestically ('Madison Avenue goes multinational' 1970).

The third phase is that of globalisation proper, in two senses: first, in that a discourse about globalisation emerged to facilitate and legitimise the process; and second, in that the international advertising industry came to be characterised by much more than just US agencies serving US clients on a transnational basis. The origin of the relevant aspect of globalisation ideology is usually attributed to a Harvard management guru, Theodore Levitt, who proclaimed 'the emergence of global markets for standardized consumer products on a previously unimagined scale' which had overcome 'accustomed differences in national or regional preference' and now required 'the standardization of products, manufacturing, and the institutions of trade and commerce' (1983: 92–93). The leading British advertising agency of the 1980s, Saatchi & Saatchi, helped to build itself into a global corporation by taking up Levitt's doctrine (Mattelart 1991). Saatchi & Saatchi foresaw 'the world of a few mega-agencies handling the megaclients' (cited in Magnet 1986: 39), and threw themselves into bringing this prophesy about. Their efforts entailed a significant role in a major restructuring of the advertising agency business at a global level during the 1980s, and leading the elusive and still controversial quest for how to create 'global brands', the standardisation of products and their advertising throughout the world.

In this section of the chapter, we will systematically examine the key trends in the advertising agency business which were set in train in the 1980s and which continue to be formative today: first, the incorporation of international agencies into holding companies at a global level; second, the integration of other marketing services into these same groups; third, the separation or 'unbundling' of advertising's two traditional functions of creating advertising campaigns and placing them strategically in the media; and finally, the continued influence of common accounts, now in the form of 'global alignment', in structuring the contemporary advertising industry.

Concentration of the mega-groups

For all its seminal influence upon the concept and conduct of advertising as it spread across the globe, Madison Avenue within one decade found itself incorporated into a totally new world order. Impelled by competition for globalising clients, the 1980s saw the peak of a longer-term trend to concentration in an intense period of mergers and acquisitions, as well as the establishment of a new set of ground rules for the structuring of the industry. By the end of the decade, the advertising industry had assumed a truly global character,

Figure 2.1 Mad Men, requiem for the glory days of Madison Avenue

rather than that of an internationalised US institution, with a complex structure extended globally at two levels, and a new capital basis.

The model for the new corporate structure did already exist in the US, but it was when British companies adopted it and bought up US agencies using capital raised on the stock market that the rules of the game were rewritten and the global industry's centre of gravity shifted fundamentally. Prior to this period, advertising agencies were owned by their principals, and usually carried their names, rather like law, accountancy or architecture firms, whose professional status the advertising agencies could only envy and mimic. This is why some of the older names still retained have bewildering acronyms: BBDO, for example, comes from a time in the 1920s when Messrs Barton, Durstine and Osborn merged with Mr Batten's company to become one of the first agencies on Madison Avenue. Others sound like the partnerships they once were: Young & Rubicam comes from the same era (Tungate 2007). It was agencies such as these which, as has just been explained, built themselves into transnational corporations in their own right as, using their own capital, they pursued their major clients into foreign markets in the 1970s, thus creating the 'TNAA': the transnational advertising agency (Anderson 1984).

What happened under the new model was that these TNAAs were brought together under the umbrella of a small number of holding companies at a higher, global level of management. To appreciate the reason for this very major development, we need to take into account the issue of 'client conflicts'. This relates to one of a number of 'tribal rules' which have governed the manufacturing/marketing/media complex for decades; basically that an agency must not hold the accounts of competing products or services. Other such consequential rules are that agencies must not own media interests, nor should advertisers own agencies (Tunstall 1977: 56). These rules are mutually enforced – if an advertiser discovers that their agency has taken on a competing account, that client will take their business to another agency. Their concern is not so much the philosophical problem of whether an agency can serve two masters, but fears that the industrial secrets of their strategies and campaigns will be leaked to their competitors. It will be evident that client conflict becomes problematic in the world of fewer agencies chasing fewer clients, especially where those clients have ever more brands to advertise.

McCann Erickson is a US agency with 'imperial' credentials which opened up offices in Europe and Latin America between the World Wars in the service of the Standard Oil Company, or Esso, for whom they devised such international campaigns as 'Put a tiger in your tank'. In 1960, its domestic and international operations were separated from each other, but grouped along with a 'second-string' division to handle competing accounts, as well as a number of non-advertising marketing companies, all under a holding company, the Interpublic Group (Tungate 2007: 174). With the acquisition of a number of agencies in London, culminating in 1978 in a merger with Lintas, once the 'in-house' agency of Unilever, Interpublic was able to present itself to global clients as a 'double network' able to insulate competing accounts in quite separate international agencies, which were nonetheless all under the same corporate ownership and ultimate management. As we have seen, a similar two-tiered corporate structure is common in consumer goods manufacturing. Significantly, the architect in the Interpublic case, then president Marion Harper, was said to have been inspired by General Motors, which had its Buick, Cadillac, Chevrolet, Oldsmobile and Pontiac makes all competing with each other (Mattelart 1991: 7). The holding company, then, may be thought of as the parent company which handles all finance and corporate matters, while the member TNAAs are like brands, and in fact are often referred to as such in the trade press.

Without question, it was the US-based Interpublic which established the holding group model of organisation and its corporate solution to the client conflict problem, and this made it the world's largest advertising entity by the early 1980s. However, by 1986, the UK-based Saatchi & Saatchi had taken over that position. As well as adopting the Interpublic model, Saatchi & Saatchi raised huge amounts of capital from the London Stock Exchange. Traditionally, advertising agencies had used their own private funds for take-overs and mergers: they were not listed as 'public' companies whose shares could be bought and sold on the stock exchange, nor were investors inclined to see advertising as a sound business. With their move into the financialisation of the advertising industry, the Saatchi brothers, Maurice and Charles, were able to make a series of takeovers of companies bigger than themselves, both in the UK and the US, culminating in the biggest takeover in advertising history, that of the US TNAA Ted Bates in 1986 (Magnet 1986). However, the stock market crash of 1987 and a shareholder revolt led to the Saatchi brothers being ousted from the agency which still bears their name, but is now part of the French-based Publicis group, while they themselves later re-emerged with another international agency, M&C Saatchi (Tungate 2007). Their relative decline should not detract from their historical significance in transforming the advertising industry in the 1980s, with their promotion of the holding group model, their ideology of global advertising for world brands, and their rapacious approach to raising capital for expansion.

A more durable and consequential challenge to traditional US supremacy over the world advertising industry came from Saatchi's former finance director, (Sir, since 2000) Martin Sorrell, who in 1985 acquired a publicly-listed company, Wire & Plastic Products, now better known simply as WPP, and made it into a holding company which gathered beneath it some of the most distinguished US agencies of the imperial era. In 1987, Sorrell successfully launched a hostile takeover of J Walter Thompson, and then in 1989, acquired Ogilvy & Mather, WPP thus overtaking the Saatchis as the world's biggest advertising network (Mattelart 1991). In the 2000s, WPP bought Young & Rubicam, a major TNAA of previous decades, and yet another, Grey Global, in 2005 (Tungate 2007). The idea that advertising is a US-dominated industry dies hard, however: for instance, in order to give an example of US hegemony in international communication, a current popular textbook states that the world's top three agencies of 2005 were based in the US (Thussu 2007: 28). Indeed they were, but they were all owned by the British-based WPP, which as we have just seen, is funded by capital of indeterminate national origin on the

British Stock Exchange. Even by the end of the 1980s, it was evident that 'Americanisation' had become superseded by a more complex 'world modernity' and globalisation of capital, of which the Saatchis and WPP were the harbingers (Mattelart 1991: 37).

Yet, it is nevertheless the case that the biggest holding group of the 2000s has been the US-based Omnicom. Like its UK counterparts, Omnicom also took shape in the 1980s, though precipitated by a takeover attempt by Saatchi & Saatchi on one of its component TNAAs, Doyle Dane Bernbach (DDB). Admired for its creative work in Madison Avenue's halcyon years, particularly its famous understated print ads for Volkswagen, DDB went into a merger with BBDO and Needham Harper, all taking shares in the new holding company. The trade press called it the 'Big Bang' (Tungate 2007). Still, by the end of the decade, WPP had overtaken Omnicom as the world's biggest holding group, as measured by total revenue ('World's 50 Largest Agency Companies' 2011).

By no means has the globalisation of advertising since the 1980s been confined to the UK–US axis, however. The French Publicis Group, with origins in European advertising dating from 1926, and inheritor of various US agencies of decades past, today includes the latter-day Saatchi & Saatchi, as mentioned, as well as Leo Burnett, a TNAA which originated in Chicago in the 1930s, and 49 per cent of Bartle Bogle Hegarty, the UK agency known amongst other things for its creative work with Levi's over many years (Pincas and Loiseau 2006). Publicis was the world's third-largest group in 2009. Other significant French connections are Paris-based Havas, in seventh place, which was originally a major press agency with roots in the nineteenth century, and these days, owner of Euro RSCG Worldwide, which is headquartered in New York, and also of Arnold Worldwide, in Boston ('World's 50 Largest Agency Companies' 2011). Returning the compliment is 'the first agency born international', the Paris-based TBWA, now owned by Omnicom (Tungate 2007: 132).

Looking further afield, there is the strong presence of Japanese companies in *Advertising Age*'s top agencies of 2011: three of the top 15 are Japanese. The largest is Dentsu, which, in the 1970s and early 1980s, prior to the era of the holding groups, was consistently the world's biggest advertising company. Dentsu is still predominantly an advertising agency in its own right, as distinct from a holding company, but it does have its US agencies grouped under Dentsu America, as well as a minority stake in DYR, a joint venture with WPP's Young & Rubicam, which dates from 1981, and 2 per cent of Publicis. The other Japanese groups are Hakuhodo and Asatsu-DK, though WPP has a holding in the latter ('World's 50 Largest Agency Companies' 2011). As will be discussed in Chapter 5, these agencies do the bulk of their business in the Japanese market and the Asian region: often 'global' agencies have their markets mainly in a certain world region, and in that sense are not literally global but certainly transnational.

To sum up at this point, Table 2.1 lists the principal global holding companies in order of size, and the main TNAA brands which belong to them.

Table 2.1 Global holding companies and their corresponding TNAA networks, including media-buying agency divisions, shown in italics

WPP (UK):	JWT, Ogilvy & Mather, Young & Rubicam, Grey; *Group M*
Omnicom (US):	BBDO, DDB, TBWA; *OMD*
Interpublic (US):	McCann Erickson, DraftFCB, Lowe; *Universal McCann*
Publicis (France):	Saatchi & Saatchi, Leo Burnett; *Starcom, ZenithOptimedia*
Dentsu (Japan):	Dentsu, DYR (+ 2 per cent Publicis)
Aegis (UK):	*Media agencies only: Aegis Media, Carat, Isobar, Mitchell*
Havas (France):	Euro RSCG, Arnold Worldwide; *MPG*

Source: 'World's 50 Largest Agency Companies' 2011.

Also shown are the media-buying divisions: the concept of the media-buying agency is explained separately in the section below on unbundling. A final observation is that all of these companies are publicly-listed – particularly since the 1980s, the scale of global expansion and consolidation has been too great to be funded out of the companies' own profits.

Integration of other marketing services

That's just the networks in the business of advertising: the holding companies have emerged as vertically and horizontally integrated conglomerates of companies across the whole field of 'integrated marketing communications', reflecting the degree to which the advertising revenue which sustained the traditional media is now being redirected into new media and non-advertising modes of promotion. Accordingly, in addition to its stable of international advertising agencies, providing 'full-service', creative or media-buying services, a contemporary holding company typically incorporates, first off, a digital agency to deal with internet advertising, followed by companies in cognate marketing 'disciplines' such as public relations and market research, as well as specialist service companies, such as pharmaceutical or ethnic-specific marketing.

The structure of these mega-groups illustrates even more clearly than the manufacturing or media corporations how the principles of integration are made to work. Horizontal integration is basic to the management of client conflicts, and as we have seen, this was one of the main factors which led to the formation of the holding groups in the first place. For example, Colgate and Unilever are competing global clients, but WPP is structured to cater for them both, with Young & Rubicam handling Colgate, while Ogilvy & Mather takes care of competing brands for Unilever. If the clients need public relations services, they can be referred to different companies in that field too, notably Burson-Marsteller or Hill & Knowlton, also available on a global basis.

Meanwhile, vertically-integrated companies in the group can provide a range of services to support advertising: media-buying, of course, but also market research from Millward Brown or TNS, and non-advertising services in branding and design, direct marketing and promotions, and specialist areas such as healthcare and multicultural marketing. Significantly, in recent years WPP has generated less than half, around 45 per cent, of its world revenue from advertising and media, indicating how important 'below the line' marketing has become: compare this figure, for instance, to the 28 per cent derived from branding, healthcare and other specialist communications, or 10 per cent for public relations. Omnicom's figure for advertising and media was even lower than WPP's, 43 per cent in 2008, though Interpublic and Publicis were both higher, at 54 and 64 per cent respectively (Agency Report 2009).

The advent of a commercialised, user-friendly internet in the 1990s saw the formation of dedicated internet advertising entities within the holding groups, either as separate companies, or as divisions of the agency networks. The feverish years of the dotcom boom in the latter part of the decade, with its millenarian 'new economy' rhetoric, overnight software fortunes, and the threatening rise of Google meant that the groups dared not be a part of it. The inevitable collapse, in April 2000, effectively brought this dawning period of the digital age to its end, but a more measured approach has since emerged. The groups tend to favour having a digital branch of one or more of their advertising networks, such as Omnicom's DDB which has DDB Tribal; Publicis, however, has a separate corporate division, Digitas, a major acquisition it made in 2007 ('World's Top 50 Agency Companies' 2009).

As will be examined in Chapter 3, the internet and other new media have opened up a highly technical side to the placing of advertisements and the targeting of audiences, effectively a third area of expertise, after the traditional advertising services of designing advertising and placing it in the media.

Unbundling of creative and media-buying

When people outside the advertising world ever think of what advertising agencies do, they just suppose that they make and place advertisements. That is quite right, but such a common-sense understanding needs considerable elaboration. When advertising 'agents' first appeared, largely towards the end of the nineteenth century, they were basically brokers who sold newspaper space to advertisers, and received a percentage of the sale as commission from the newspaper. Only in the twentieth century, as print media became more developed and diverse, and with the advent of radio, did advertising agencies become identified with the additional service of designing and actually producing advertisements for their advertiser clients (or later again, coordinating production by various freelance specialists). For decades thereafter, these two basic functions of placing and making advertisements would be handled by the one 'full-service' agency, along with ancillary services such as market research.

Even in the decades of international expansion, as outlined earlier, the newly-formed TNAAs were full-service, the organisational mode most comfortably adapted to the golden age of television.

However, along with the rise of the holding companies, the 1980s began to see the 'unbundling' of advertising's basic functions with the business of strategically purchasing media space and time being hived off from the 'creative' business of devising and executing advertising campaigns, in quite separate agencies, though usually vertically integrated under the one holding group, as Table 2.1 shows. Already in the 1960s, a French company, Carat Espace, had launched itself throughout Europe, on the business model of being able to negotiate much lower prices from the media when buying very large amounts of space or time on behalf of big advertiser clients – in effect, acting as wholesalers (Mattelart 1991; Tungate 2007). Such agencies, incidentally, are in a position to onsell space and time to smaller agencies, as well as cater to advertisers. Acquired by a British company in 1989, Carat has since been reorganised as the Aegis Group, which with its media-buying and market research divisions, has been the world's sixth-biggest advertising agency group since 2007 ('World's 50 Largest Agency Companies' 2011).

An advertising holding group without any creative division is the exception rather than the rule, however. Publicis also started out as a French media-buying company, in 1970, but built itself up into the world's third-biggest group in 2009 with the acquisition of US and UK full-service TNAAs. It was when it incorporated the original Saatchi & Saatchi agency that it also acquired Zenith, a media-buying agency the Saatchis had started in 1988. The Publicis Group has long since reorganised this as ZenithOptimedia, which is now set alongside its other media-buying operation, Starcom MediaVest. WPP has a corresponding set of media-buying agencies, mainly MediaCom and Mindshare, under the banner Group M. Similarly, the US-based agencies have their media-buying operations, Omnicom with OMD Worldwide and PHD, and Interpublic with Universal McCann (UM), Initiative and others. Havas has MPG. Neither Dentsu nor Asatsu-DK, the Japanese agencies in the world's top ten, has separate media-buying divisions ('World's 50 Largest Agency Companies' 2011).

The fact that the holding groups have multiple media-buying companies under their umbrellas, just as they do creative networks, suggests that client conflict can be just as much an issue to be managed in media-buying as in creative campaigns. This is because media-buying is not only a matter of getting media space and time for the best price, but involves the crucial matter of media planning. Like a creative campaign, media planning involves strategies which a client does not want to risk being leaked to competitors. Media planning is about the selection of the media best able to reach the target market, the schedules to be followed, and whatever mix of 'platforms' is to be used. In addition to the conventional old and new media options – press, television, outdoor, cinema, internet, etc. – these platforms will often include non-media channels, such as direct mail, in-store promotions or some form of experience marketing, or perhaps the shameless 'through-the-line' practice of product placement.

Indeed, if we look for the reasons why media-buying was unbundled from the creative side of advertising, one explanation is that advertisers had become sceptical about the ability of traditional media to reach their target audiences. What had glistened for them about the golden age of television in particular was that it reached huge relatively captive national audiences that could be measured as a known quantity and paid for accordingly. With the advent of the video recorder and the remote control, the technologies which for the first time enabled time-shifting and 'zapping' of TVCs, advertisers became disillusioned with the effectiveness of television as an advertising medium, and began to show more interest in below-the-line approaches.

Apart from the advertisers being uncertain about what they were paying for, there were other factors in play in the 1970s and 1980s which were fundamentally transforming the basis on which advertising agencies derived their income. The traditional commission system had long been at the heart of the manufacturing/marketing/media complex: as explained above, advertising agencies established themselves on a business model of selling media space and time to advertisers and being paid a commission by the media. This has given them a pivotal intermediary role, but ambiguously so: are they 'agents' of the media, or their clients, the advertisers? Historically, in France, where the move to media-buying specialist agencies began, a 15 per cent commission system was the norm: in other words, the agency would pay the media 85 per cent of what the client paid them. The US and UK also operated on a similar system, although in Australia, the commission was more like 10 per cent, but with a fee-for-service charged directly to the client. Note that under the 15 per cent regime, clients were not paying separately for the creative work they were getting, as the commission covered that as well as providing the agencies with a generous margin of profit. Advertisers were right to suspect that the arrangements over commissions between agencies and media worked to their detriment (Cappo 2003; Sinclair 1987).

However, in 1976, even before the wave of deregulation which swept through the West in the 1980s, the Office of Fair Trading in the UK declared the commission system to be an illegally restrictive trade practice, as it was being used to keep new entrants out of the business. This led to an increase in the number of what were called 'media independents' in the UK, in line with the European trend (Mattelart 1991). In the US, there already were media-buying agencies, but on a very small scale. With the European example on one hand and pressure from advertisers looking for more transparency and better performance on the other, the major full-service agencies in the US recognised that 'the good old days' of 15 per cent commissions were over, and hived off media-buying into separate companies. Since then, a range of remuneration models has developed, but basically creative work now has to be paid for with some form of fee-for-service, while the media-buying agencies, as already explained, make their money from wholesaling media time and space to clients and smaller agencies (Cappo 2003: 37).

There is reason to believe that even in the absence of a commission, media-buying is more profitable than carrying out creative work: with media-buying there is room to buy cheaply by negotiating huge discounts from the media, and to sell at whatever price the client will pay, whereas the fee-for-service for creative work is more transparent – what you see is what you get. Furthermore, within the holding group structure, a group can funnel the total media-buying requirements of its several creative agencies through its rather fewer media-buying agencies to obtain considerable buying power with the media. This capacity is perceived as attractive to large clients wanting to minimise their marketing costs, but does not augur well for the traditional media, television in particular. For example, by the beginning of the 2000s, as consolidated agencies faced off against consolidated media companies, more than 70 per cent of television advertising sales in the US was under the control of only nine major media buyers (Cappo 2003: 34). On the other hand, because advertising agencies are no longer able to derive commissions from the media as they did in the 1960s and 1970s, they have less of a vested interest in recommending media campaigns to their clients. This situation in turn has given impetus to the trend away from conventional advertising forms such as the TVC, and towards social networking media and more direct and measurable non-media forms of promotion. As well, it exerts pressure for more intensive commercialisation of entertainment and information in the media, and fudges the line which formerly existed between media content and the advertising it carried, as will be examined in Chapter 3.

Global alignment

At this point we can now see how Saatchi & Saatchi's self-fulfilling prophesy of a world of mega-agencies handling mega-clients has been brought into being by means of the global group or holding company. Table 2.2 provides data extracted from *Advertising Age*'s Agency Report 2009, and not repeated since, which while not strictly comparable, nevertheless demonstrates the degree to which the then four largest holding groups were depending on their largest clients, the global advertisers.

Some of these relationships have been of very long standing, which is unusual in an industry more often characterised by constant uncertainty and chopping and changing in agency–client relationships. WPP claims to have an average length of relationships with their top ten clients of 50 years, and Publicis of 45 years, remembering in both cases they are counting the time with their component agencies prior to the formation of the group.

As we have seen, long-standing agency–client relationships were formed in the imperial phase of agency expansion abroad when the common account

Table 2.2 Percentage of revenue derived by mega-groups from largest clients

WPP	2007 largest clients: British American Tobacco, Ford, GlaxoSmithKline, IBM, Johnson & Johnson, Kraft, Microsoft, Nestlé, Procter & Gamble, Unilever. Percentage of revenue derived from these ten largest clients: 19%. Percentage of revenue derived from largest client, Ford: 6%. Claims to service 345 of *Fortune* Global 500 companies.
Omnicom	2007–2008 largest clients included Daimler, Nissan, BMW, Mercedes and VW. Percentage of revenue derived from ten largest clients: 16.7%. Percentage of revenue derived from 100 largest clients: 47.4%. Percentage of revenue derived from largest client, Daimler: 4%.
Interpublic	2006–2008 largest clients included General Motors, Johnson & Johnson, Microsoft, Unilever, Verizon and US Government. Percentage of revenue derived from ten largest clients: 26%. Percentage of revenue derived from 100 largest clients: 55%. Percentage of revenue derived from largest client, General Motors: 5%.
Publicis	2008 largest clients included Procter & Gamble, Coca-Cola, Toyota and Nestlé. Percentage of revenue derived from 20 largest clients: 43%. Percentage of revenue derived from largest client, P & G: 8%.

Source: Agency Report 2009.

concept was advantageous to both parties, although there were instances in which agencies had to maintain unprofitable offices in certain locations just to keep the client's business at home, or to fend off a competitor ('Madison Avenue goes multinational' 1970). Existing agency–client relationships were important also in the transnational era, when US or UK agencies could gain entry to new markets by forming a joint venture or partnership with an existing local agency on the strength of having one or two big clients from their home market to sweeten the deal.

However, once again it was the 1980s, with the global brands discourse introduced by the Saatchis, which was the crucible of change. As early as 1984 in Australia, for instance, clients of the stature of General Motors and Colgate-Palmolive were 'being realigned to suit international arrangements' (Shoebridge 1984: 21). In other words, these and other big clients, such as British Airways, were reassigning their accounts to the one agency network on a worldwide basis so as to position themselves for running global campaigns, and also to cut costs, looking for the 'economies of scale' which the Saatchis had promised. Previously, so long as the clients were advertising on a regional or national market-by-market basis, the accounts could be assigned to different agencies accordingly. This client-generated movement towards agency 'consolidation' or 'global alignment' accelerated in the 1990s, and played havoc with embedded local–global agency arrangements (Leslie 1995). In the case of Australia, once again, even by 1991 there was no wholly Australian-owned full-service or creative agency within the top 20 agencies, and as the decade proceeded, several of the next-largest remaining Australian agencies became integrated into global groups. As one Australian agency owner explained, on merging with Ogilvy & Mather, 'Half the business [advertising clients] is international and half is local, and we were only available for half the business' (quoted in Sinclair 2006), meaning that in order to gain access to global clients, they have to join a global group with which such clients are globally aligned.

Thus, global alignment has been a crucial mechanism in bringing about the world of mega-agencies serving mega-clients, as the Saatchis foretold. However, the actual scenario today is rather more complicated than the globalisation discourse would suggest. Rather than one client having only one agency on a worldwide basis, conglomeration amongst clients has been such that it is the brand rather than the client as such which is represented by an agency network. Indeed, it can be argued that this aspect of globalisation has been one factor which has heightened the significance and the value of brands. Some global advertiser clients today parcel out their various brands to a number of agencies, and these agencies might belong to more than one holding group. This is evident in Table 2.2, in the case of both Procter & Gamble and Unilever, which are diversified FMCG corporations with hundreds of brands in several divisions, and in various parts of the world. Again, *Advertising Age*'s annual Global Marketers 'dots' report provides elaborately-detailed data on 'Multinational Agency Network Assignments', which shows how, for example, Coca-Cola has a 'lead' agency network or 'agency of record' in the form of McCann-Erickson in most world markets, but there are more than a dozen other agencies on its 'roster', across several of the holding groups, which also have accounts for Coca-Cola brands in one or more countries (2009). The reality is that what we call globalisation is in fact moderated by 'local', national and world-regional factors, and that industry practice is even more intricate and the structures more diverse and fluid than this account has been able to describe up to this point.

Emergent global structures

What we have seen so far is how the world advertising industry has formed itself into a small number of complexly-integrated holding groups which incorporate creative advertising agency networks along with media-buying specialist agencies (known more briefly, if confusingly, as 'media agencies') and businesses in a series of other marketing 'disciplines', including internet or digital advertising, as well as public relations, market research, direct mail and similar 'marketing services'. These structures are a manifestation of how 'integrated marketing communications' has eclipsed the mediacentric advertising we have known in the past. It was noted previously how the two biggest groups are earning less than half of their income from advertising as such, symptomatic of a trend away from conventional media advertising and towards a wide range of 'below the line' forms of promotion. In this final section of the chapter we will examine some notable cases of new-generation agencies and networks which embody this trend and which show how the advertising industry is searching to adapt to the new scenario.

New marketing hot-shops

For all the conglomeration which has gone on at the most abstract level of global management, it is in the nature of advertising that, on the ground, there is still room for small agencies, especially creative 'boutiques' or 'hot-shops'. For creative work, the barrier to entry is low – without any capital, two or three copywriters and/or art directors with industry awards and a good reputation with clients can set themselves up as an agency. However, the successful ones are subsequently picked up by the holding groups, and incorporated into their structure. This is one way in which the holding groups can buy in the creative talent of the moment without necessarily incurring the risks and costs of developing it themselves. This process has been a fairly constant feature of the industry in the UK, from even before the 'creative revolution' of the 1980s. Collett Dickinson Pearce (CDP) is the best case in point. Not only did they produce advertising campaigns memorable to Britons (such as 'Happiness is a cigar called Hamlet'), but also fostered the careers of film-makers Ridley Scott, (Sir) Alan Parker and (Lord) David Puttnam. However, the agency did not remain independent, as Dentsu acquired a 40 per cent stake in 1990 (Tungate 2007). By 2009, it had become Dentsu London.

Crispin Porter & Bogusky is another example, but from the US, and very much of the internet era. In contrast to the print and television campaigns for brands such as Benson & Hedges from CDP, Crispin Porter & Bogusky became renowned for the interactive games, online user discussion groups and viral content it devised for a campaign – against smoking. Burger King's Subservient Chicken, mentioned in Chapter 1, is the best known of the more recent work from this agency. Creative Director Alex Bogusky is explicit in his embrace of interactive marketing: 'The future of advertising doesn't exist. The party is coming to an end for everybody' (cited in Deuze 2010: 462). Originating in Miami, but now with other offices in the US and UK, Crispin Porter & Bogusky has been progressively absorbed by MDC Partners. MDC is the tenth-largest of the global integrated marketing communications holding groups, publicly traded and based unobtrusively in Toronto, and composed of several other specialist marketing and advertising companies under its umbrella ('World's 50 Largest Agency Companies' 2011).

Some of Australia's best-known creative hot-shops of the classic media advertising decades of the 1970s and 1980s have also been integrated into the major holding groups. The Campaign Palace was absorbed into George Patterson, and hence Y&R and ultimately WPP in 2005, while Mojo, known internationally for its 'shrimp on the barbie' TVC for the Australian Tourism Commission, ended up as Mojo Publicis ('Agency Report Card' 2009). In an interesting variation, David Droga, an Australian-born senior creative executive with Publicis, left them to open up a new-generation agency in New York in 2006, Droga5, doing viral work for clients such as the youth fashion label Ecko, although rumoured at the time to be in joint venture with his former employer. Within two years, Droga5 established its first overseas office – in Australia ('And then there were three' 2007; Sophocleous 2006).

Not only are there creative hot-shops, but other notable initiatives have been in the media planning and strategy, and marketing services areas. In London in 2000, three former members of PHD, an Omnicom media agency, founded Naked Communications. The name was to declare their intention to offer 'raw ideas', reaching consumers with innovative strategies stripped of media preferences. Naked said they were not so much 'media neutral' as 'communications agnostic' (Tungate 2007: 260). By 2007, Naked had offices in eight countries, including two in Australia, and was working with global clients of the calibre of Coca-Cola and Unilever (MacLennan 2008). Yet although WPP had shown interest in acquiring Naked, it was the Australian-based, publicly-listed marketing services group Photon which successfully bought it early in 2008. Number 20 on *Advertising Age*'s 'World's 50 Largest Agency Companies' in 2011, Photon Group's holdings cover 22 companies, including two leading creative agencies, across several marketing services divisions in Australia. Internationally, it has companies in 13 countries, mainly Naked offices, as well as some online agencies in the US (Photon Group 2011). As with MDC's tenure over Crispin Porter & Bogusky, Photon's acquisition of Naked would indicate that while not all the hot-shops fall to the biggest of the holding groups, there are second string companies, outside the traditionally dominant centres though inside the Anglosphere, also driving the global trend to concentration.

Micro-networks

Just as this minor league of holding groups is emerging on the world scene, we also need to take account of a number of largely creative agencies which have internationalised themselves in recent decades, very much on the model of the imperial advertising networks of the past. These are known as 'micro' or 'mini' networks, because of their comparatively modest scale, with only a small but strategically-placed number of international offices acting as hubs for certain regions. Once more we can take as a guide *Advertising Age*'s 'World's 50 Largest Agency Companies', as ranked by worldwide revenue, and identify three such micro-networks (2011). Number 26 is Wieden & Kennedy, which began in Portland, Oregon in the US, its first client being Nike, whose marketing strategies have been the object of quite intensive critique from cultural studies and anti-globalisation perspectives (Goldman and Papson 1998; Klein 2000; Lury 2004). Wieden & Kennedy is privately owned, and full-service, though with an emphasis on its creative work. Founded in 1982, it opened up an office in Amsterdam the following year to service the Nike account, and subsequently has established offices in Tokyo, Shanghai and New Delhi as hubs for those key national markets in Asia, and São Paulo in Latin America ('World's 50 Largest Agency Companies' 2011).

At number 31 is M&C Saatchi, the agency which the Saatchi brothers founded after being sacked from the original agency which, however confusingly, still bears their name, and which is now one of the networks under Publicis Groupe. M&C Saatchi claims to be 'international from birth', as offices sprang up like dragon's teeth in London, Sydney, New York, Hong Kong and Singapore in 1995. The agency promotes the 'brutal simplicity' of the creative work which is their strong suit, but it is worth noting that there are branding and strategic consultancies, a digital agency and specialist companies under their corporate umbrella, not all of which bear the M&C Saatchi name, in which respect the company looks more like a second-tier holding company than a micro-network (M&C Saatchi 2011). Similarly, they tend to have multiple offices in selected national markets rather more than the other micro-networks being examined here, and their clients tend to be large and prestigious national advertisers, rather than global ones, looking for conventional media advertising. As a matter of interest, Maurice Saatchi is still actively involved with the agency, but Charles left in 2006 ('World's 50 Largest Agency Companies' 2011).

Founded by three former members of Omnicom's TBWA in London in 1982, Bartle Bogle Hegarty (BBH) is at number 43 in *Advertising Age*'s list. A leading light in Britain's creative revolution of the 1980s, and closely associated with Levi's as a client (Tungate 2007), BBH now has international offices serving the largest national markets in Asia and regional hub offices in New York, Singapore and São Paulo. However, in order to raise the capital for the overseas expansion, BBH sold a 49 per cent share of itself to Leo Burnett in 1997. Publicis thus acquired this share when it incorporated Leo Burnett into its group, so BBH cannot be regarded as an independent mini-network ('World's 50 Largest Agency Companies' 2011).

As these cases show, there is no pure, 'ideal-type' model of the micro-network, each of these companies having some variation – Wieden & Kennedy is full-service and not publicly-listed; M&C Saatchi is structured more like a mini-holding group with a range of marketing services; and Publicis owns a substantial minority share of BBH. Nevertheless, the trimmed-down, creatively-focused, regional hub approach exemplified by these companies does represent one significant trend in how marketing communications has developed over the last two decades in the direction of flexible specialisation.

Made-to-measure

Finally, a recent corporate experiment illustrates how the manufacturing/marketing/media complex is casting around for new business models, and that size and market power is no guarantee of success. This is the case of Enfatico, an agency created by WPP specifically to serve, at least in the first instance, just one client: Dell Computers. Dell had built up its strong market position on the basis of direct sales over the internet or phone, rather than through conventional retail stores. With a decision to expand into retail selling in 2007, Dell announced that WPP would be setting up a dedicated agency to handle its business: 'We believe this is the first time a global client and agency have come together to redefine the "agency" on such a scale' (cited in 'WPP takes Dell's \$4.5bn global biz' 2007).

After a period in which WPP attracted the scorn of the world advertising trade for its indecision in naming the new entity (Project Da Vinci, then Synarchy, and eventually Enfatico), its new CEO declared it to be 'a next-generation agency with a diverse mix of marketing services and talent – all uniquely orchestrated to drive value for Dell and future clients' (cited in 'New Dell-WPP shop' 2008). That is, Enfatico was to offer Dell bespoke marketing services, integrating expertise from WPP's various companies, but clearly WPP expected that this new model of client service would attract further global advertisers. However, less than a year later, during which time it had attracted only one other client, WPP abandoned the concept of a stand-alone company, and folded Enfatico into its Y&R Brands division, a portfolio of companies in several marketing communications specialities (Parekh and Bush 2009). This experiment in providing custom-tailored marketing for just one or two clients is not likely to be repeated for some time.

'The internationalization of advertising mirrors but also facilitates the internationalization of capital' (Leslie 1995: 404). In this chapter, we have seen how, over the twentieth century, advertising agencies formed international networks, primarily in response to the various stages of the internationalisation of the clients they served, but also to press their own comparative advantage in new markets abroad. In the decades in which this process coincided with the establishment of television systems throughout the world, many countries settled into a regime in which the commonly-available and dominant means of social communication was given over in part or whole to commercial advertisers, actively abetted by their agencies, and advertising as an institution became embedded as part and parcel of national culture. Yet in the 1980s, with the advent of new communication technologies, seismic shifts in the structure and conduct of the advertising industry, and the triumph of neoliberal ideology, the stage was set for a more intricate and global set of relations to develop within the manufacturing/marketing/media complex.

A similar architecture of conglomeration across the component advertiser, agency and media sectors has produced a world in which there is an apparent proliferation of choice amongst brands, agency services and media options at ground level, but above which is built an elaborate structure of corporate concentration. However, over the last decade or so, new communication technologies have brought about a fundamental shift in the relations between the manufacturing/marketing/media complex and 'the people formerly known as the audience' (Rosen, cited in Turner 2010: 80), bringing to light the delicate balance and tensions in the structure. That is the stuff of the next chapter.

Chapter 3

Advertising and the media in motion

That moment we all know from the opening credits of *The Simpsons*, when the family crowds together on the couch in front of their television, is an ironic and already nostalgic image of the golden age of mass media now coming to its end. The media have been 'mass' to the extent that for generations they have provided a more or less common culture of information and entertainment to a national, heterogeneous audience, an audience that certain kinds of advertisers still gladly pay to reach. Indeed, advertising revenue has underwritten that common culture, and advertisements have been a significant part of it. Television in particular has been the dominant advertising medium, and the television commercial, or TVC, has made its own distinctive contribution to mass culture. For example, the Hovis 'Bike Ride' ad in the UK, Wendy's 'Where's the beef?' in the US, and Telstra's 'Not happy, Jan!' in Australia each found a place in their respective national popular cultures. First it had been the newspaper which formed the nation as an 'imagined community' (Anderson 1983), and then broadcasting, but especially television, which developed a very public and accessible culture in each nation to which it was introduced; not always but characteristically, and ultimately, on a commercial basis. In this way, the major means of social communication in most modern societies had come to rely financially on funding from the manufacturers and retailers of consumer goods and services, in the form of advertising.

However, there is now a crisis in the comfortable and enduring media ecology in which the revenue from large national advertisers is channelled through advertising agencies to motivate and reward press barons and broadcasting corporations in their supplying of information and entertainment attractive to mass audiences. The crisis has undoubtedly been provoked by new technologies, both in hardware and software, but we shall see that it is far too simple to think of it as a confrontation of 'old' and 'new' media technologies. The crisis is both economic and cultural: economic in the sense that the classic 'business model' of the manufacturing/marketing/media complex is under challenge, as new and old players alike cast around to find alternative ways of 'monetising' their assets; and cultural in that the public sphere and relatively common culture formerly sustained by national mass media is breaking up as media audiences undergo 'fragmentation'. To the extent that advertising can be taken as a reflection of society, what we see in the reflection is this crisis.

However, we should not exaggerate the alleged imminent 'death' of mass media. Certainly, there has been a general slowdown in the rate of newspaper circulation and revenue growth, just as national free broadcast television networks have been losing audiences to pay-TV and other alternatives, but the state of play varies from one country to another. Indeed, in the developing world, especially in the much-vaunted new national markets of Asia and Latin America, mass television remains in robust health, as we shall see in Chapter 5. Within the developed world, there are interesting variations: for example, only in Britain has the pre-eminence of television been overtaken by the internet as the preferred advertising medium, because so much of the television audience is commanded by the public, advertising-free network, the BBC (Creamer 2009). In Australia, newspaper advertising revenue still increases, because newspaper owners also own the most popular internet portals and can offer 'multi-platform' placements to advertisers (Varley 2010). This example also serves to illustrate that 'new' media do not replace 'old' media in a zero-sum game, but merge and adapt.

Nevertheless, against this background, the advent of the internet and other new media have most certainly put into play a much more fluid set of relations than has existed for decades within the manufacturing/marketing/media complex. This chapter begins by reviewing the common business models which have defined those relations at different stages, and outlines the impact which new media are having upon them. The unique and unprecedented character of the internet as an advertising medium is then considered, and the different stages and modes of its commercialisation are outlined. Amongst the new global media corporations to which the internet has given rise, Google is given special attention here, for its dominance of search as an immensely popular and profitable new form of advertising, and the challenge which that presents both to advertising agencies and traditional media corporations. In particular, 'Google has conditioned the world to expect free stuff' (Wright 2008), which has undermined newspapers' attempts to build a paywall around their content, and even threatens the subscription model for television. The chapter explains how the battle between free, advertiser-supported content, and paywall-protected intellectual property has emerged as perhaps the most significant issue in the contemporary global mediascape.

The capacity of the internet to be accessed by mobile phones and other devices; its ability to give access in turn to other media, notably television; and its unique facility to allow users' responses and input, and engage in online social interaction; are major technological features underlying a fundamental shift in the character of what we still call, from radio days, 'audiences'. These developments are outlined in this chapter, having regard to the issue of whether and how power relations between consumers and producers might be undergoing a rebalance in the transition from mass to niche audiences. Finally, as conventional media advertising messages become easier to avoid, advertisers are looking to commercialise information and entertainment content itself. The chapter ends with a review of the main ways in which this is being done.

Advertising and the media – a relationship in flux

Classic models of advertising–media relation

The first advertising agencies emerged with the advent of newspapers and a mass audience able to read them. By the end of the nineteenth century, a popular commercial press had developed under the likes of Lord Northcliffe in the UK, Scripps and Hearst in the US, and the Syme family in Australia. The sale of advertising space allowed newspapers to be sold well below cost, thus increasing their circulation and profitability, particularly where news catered to popular demand. As mentioned in Chapter 2, advertising 'agents' as such first arose as brokers of newspaper space, selling it to advertisers for a commission from the newspapers, but they later came to provide advertisers with copywriting and eventually the range of creative and other marketing services we are familiar with today. The advent of radio broadcasting in the first half of the twentieth century met with quite different institutional arrangements in the UK, where it was established under the auspices of the state, and the US, where it was allowed to develop on a commercial basis, though not without resistance from public interest groups. Australia sought to take the best of both worlds with a 'dual' regime. In the decades between the World Wars, radio flourished as an advertising medium in both the US and Australia on a 'sponsorship' system. This involved the sale of airtime to advertisers, with the agencies not merely acting as brokers, but as producers of programmes. For example, for 20 years from 1935, the original BBDO agency in the US produced *Cavalcade of America* for the DuPont chemical company. Under this system, the sponsors effectively owned the time, and could rule in and rule out what could be said, who could be represented, and so on (no 'Negros', for example) – this was not only a self-serving but very conservative ideological influence on radio content (Barnouw 1979). In Australia, George Patterson, the largest agency, set up the Colgate-Palmolive Radio Unit, while J Walter Thompson produced programmes for Lever Bros (now Unilever) (Walker 1973).

However, the flaws in the sponsorship system were exposed in the US in 1959 – this was already the television era – when it was discovered that a popular quiz show sponsored by Geritol vitamin supplements was rigged. This scandal produced a fundamental shift in how the business of broadcasting was conducted. Rather than advertisers buying airtime by the hour and having their agency produce the programme, the broadcasting networks took charge of supplying the programming themselves or commissioning it from independent producers, and selling commercial 'spots' of time to advertisers. Advertisers could still pay to have themselves named as 'sponsors' of a given programme, but programming costs were such that they would have to share the available spots with other advertisers (Barnouw 1979; Myers 2009). This now traditional assemblage of relations between advertisers, agencies and media consequently put much more emphasis on audience measurement in the form of ratings, since advertisers wanted to be assured of the size and composition of the audience they were reaching with their spots, measured as cost per thousand, or CPM. As for the agencies, while they had been dispossessed from their former role in supplying programming, much more scope was opened up under the new 'spots and dots' regime for the media buying and planning side of the business, while their creative energies would be absorbed for decades to come with 15, 30 and 60-second commercials. The British experience, with commercial television being institutionalised under ITV, subjected to relatively strict regulation, and obliged to compete with the BBC, has been quite different, but it has resulted in much the same familiar features of television as a 'consumer delivery enterprise' (Bunce 1976).

Thus, the principle upon which commercial television has operated throughout its golden age, since the demise of the sponsorship system, involves a quarantining of advertisements from the programming content in which they appear, and a structural separation of advertisers, agencies and media. This system has also entailed an implied bargain with the audience: that they will accept the advertisements which are bringing them the information and entertainment they want at no apparent cost. However, as noted in Chapter 1, from a certain Marxist theoretical point of view, this social contract ideal is a fraud: the programming is a 'free lunch' to attract audiences that can then be 'sold' as a 'commodity' to advertisers (Smythe 1977); indeed, for audiences to watch advertisements is actually to 'work' for capitalism when they are supposed to be at leisure (Jhally 1987). We shall see that these arguments from the mass media age have taken a new twist in the era of social media. The immediate point is that the dominant advertising medium for more than a generation in the UK, US and Australia, for all its 'commercial' character, has maintained a stable convention of the separation of advertising from programming content, and it has derived its revenue from advertisers rather than audiences.

Yet the advent of subscription television, or 'pay-TV', forced a fundamental distinction from the prevalent 'free-to-air' (FTA) model of broadcasting, in that, under the subscription model, viewers must pay a service provider to gain access to a 'bouquet' of channels. The service provider, in turn, pays the channel, the content provider. The initial marketing pitch for pay-TV was that subscribers could opt out of the implicit contract of FTA broadcast television, that is, they could pay not to have to watch advertisements. Yet in practice, there are many pay channels which carry advertising, while some others do not. Usually subscribers are offered a 'basic' selection of those channels that do have advertising, but they may in fact, by paying more, obtain access to 'premium' channels, such as movie channels, which do provide content without any advertising. In spite of this barrier, by far the bulk of revenue earned in the pay-TV industry comes from subscriptions, so much so that some now consider investment in pay-TV to be one line of defence media corporations can make against decline in advertising revenues from broadcast television (Barnett 2010). As we shall see, the pay-TV business model is similar to the 'paywall' model now being implemented by certain of the print media.

In addition to these business models which have grown out of broadcasting history – sponsorship, delivering audiences, and subscription – the advent of the internet has presented one more, in the form of search advertising. Search is a fundamental function which everyone needs to use the internet, for which we go to the services on offer from the main 'search engines', Google, Yahoo! and Bing. The search engine's basic business model rests on its ability to offer and sell advertising, but not on any platform other than its own. Instead of attracting an audience with the offer of information or entertainment content, as with traditional media, search engines attract users to the service itself. In both cases, the audiences or users collected are then 'sold' to advertisers, but in distinct ways. In particular, traditional media depend on large advertisers, who place their advertising via an advertising agency. Yet on one hand, search advertising has in principle diminished the need for any intermediary, such as an advertising agency, at the same time as it has enabled the rapid rise to power of Google, by far the most successful search engine in the field.

While the advertising agencies have developed their specialised internet or digital divisions which advise advertisers on internet strategies, buy internet advertising on their behalf, and provide other services, advertisers, whether large or small, can go straight to Google, thus 'disintermediating' the agencies. Google's AdWords system sells the advertising space which appears next to the results which it provides you with when you search for a keyword (advertisers must bid for their position in the list next to any given keyword), with 'pay-per-click' being the unit of measurement charged to the advertiser, if you show interest by clicking through to their website. This system is attractive to advertisers because it puts the buying of advertising on to a performance basis, increases the calculability of return on investment (ROI), and gives their advertising global reach (Spurgeon 2008).

Yet while Google does attract large advertisers like AT&T and Amazon, US data from 2010 showed that the ten biggest advertisers only accounted for 5 per cent of Google's revenue at that time (Learmonth 2010), which would validate Spurgeon's 'long tail' analysis, that 'the tail of the demand curve can be cumulatively more valuable to advertisers than the head' (Spurgeon 2008) – and more valuable to Google. Similarly, the long tail has been one of the most striking effects of social media on the global advertising scene. While most global corporations have become actively involved with one form or another of social media ('Brand giants go social' 2011), most of Facebook's advertisers, to take the most significant example, are small and medium-sized businesses, and they too use the self-serve ad systems on the site rather than go through a media-buying advertising agency (Lee 2011). It is evident that the vast majority of advertisers who support the internet form a vastly different range than the usual list of large 'national' (and global) brand advertisers who dominate traditional media advertising. This is a significant trend which not only has implications for the sidelining of the agencies, but also suggests that advertising is now more diffuse than in the era of mass media.

The transition from 'old' to 'new' media

To mention Google and search advertising is to invoke the current crisis, often characterised simply as a confrontation of the 'old' media by the 'new'. Yet even before the internet erupted into the mediascape in the 1990s, a seismic shift was under way in the substructural relationship between advertisers, their agencies and the media. Already with the advent of the remote control and the video cassette recorder (VCR), audiences for television could customise their own viewing and were free to 'zap' or fast-forward over ads. Advertisers could no longer be assured that viewers were actually watching the TVCs that their agencies were making and placing for them in 30-second spots, the paradigmatic advertising form of the mass media era. Notwithstanding the electronic audience measurement innovation of the people-meter, advertisers were becoming disaffected with television's actual capacity to deliver audiences to them, and the lack of guarantee for their ROI.

Today, even pay-TV, which we have just seen in the light of being the relatively 'new' challenger to the 'old' FTA model of television, is itself faced with competition from newer technologies of access to information and entertainment. In the emerging 'on-demand environment' (Sinclair, L. 2008), broadcast networks are defending their turf with 'catch-up' television, making new digital channels available, and offering films and series over new convergent internet/TV services such as Hulu in the US and YouView in the UK (Whitehead 2010), all of which viewers can record on their new digital video recorders (DVRs).

Just as the traditional television business in its best years was known as having 'a licence to print money', the persistent economic strength of the print media throughout most of the twentieth century was attributable to the 'rivers of gold' which flowed to newspapers in the form of classified advertising revenue. Clearly this is a mundane form of advertising fundamentally different to the publicly visible TVCs for global and national brands characteristic of television, or even the stylish display advertising seen in newspapers and magazines, but the revenue has been crucial to the newspaper industry. However, while newspapers proved themselves able to hold their ground for decades against the inroads made by television into the total advertising revenue available, the advent of the internet has presented a form of competition which is much harder to deal with. Online search quickly established itself as a superior advertising medium for lucrative classified categories such as employment, real estate and automotive. In the US, the free classified ad site Craigslist emerged as a 'newspaper killer' (Hau 2006) in the decade of the 2000s, when venerable titles such as the *Los Angeles Times* were struggling against bankruptcy (Berman *et al.* 2008). The situation was exacerbated over 2008–9 by a marked shrinkage in advertising expenditure caused by the global financial crisis (GFC). This affected both the daily newspaper groups in Australia, News Corporation and Fairfax Media (Tabakoff 2008; Tabakoff 2009), while in the UK, internet advertising grew so quickly that it is now expected to command a third of total advertising expenditure by 2014 ('Online adspend set for further growth in UK' 2010).

However, it is not as if the 'old' medium of print is being ousted by the 'new' one of the internet. As noted in the previous chapters, newspaper companies have responded by creating their own online divisions, or acquiring successful sites, thus seeking to straddle both print and online, and offer advertisers packages for 'cross-platform' exposure. The picture is even more complex on a global scale. A comprehensive study by the World Association of Newspapers shows that although circulation and advertising revenues from print are in decline in the US and Europe, there is consistent growth in Africa, Asia and Latin America, suggesting that the crisis is an affliction of the developed economies. (As we shall see in Chapter 5, broadcast television also continues to flourish in the developing world.) Even more tellingly, the study predicts that 'At no time in the foreseeable future will digital advertising revenues replace those lost to print' ('World press trends' 2009), meaning that even if newspapers are now deriving income from their online as well as print divisions, these revenues combined will not allow them to compensate for the scale of print revenue which they are losing. Hence we can see the profundity of the crisis, and the spur for print media in their search for new business models.

Ultimately, it is not a question of whether a medium is old or new, but whether it is able to give sellers access to buyers in a market: that can mean large corporations still mass-marketing global brands on broadcast television, or tech-savvy individuals selling their old cars on an internet site. Nor is it about the technologies as such, but how the technologies can be embedded commercially and socially via business models that the target audiences find attractive in an environment of ever more choice and social differentiation.

The internet as an advertising medium

Advertisers and their agencies were sluggish in recognising the potential of the internet as an advertising medium during its first decade, the 1990s – quite understandably, as the internet of that era was only a primitive ancestor of what began to be called 'Web 2.0', the social media age, from the mid-2000s.

At first, there was an inclination to see the internet as analogous to traditional media: even by the end of the 1990s, most online advertising was banner advertising, 'much like a billboard on the Info Highway' (Himelstein *et al.* 1997). This was when advertisers began to pay Microsoft's Hotmail for the number of impressions subscribers would see while their free email was loading, with effectiveness being measured by 'click-throughs', the number of subscribers who responded by clicking through to the advertiser's site (Amjadali 1999). From a zero base, internet advertising attracted a small but rapidly-increasing number of advertisers from the mid-1990s, though another essential feature of the burgeoning commercialisation of the internet was a boom in internet web presence: suddenly, businesses found the need to be on the web. The struggle over advertising revenue was yet to come, as newspaper groups and television networks established their sites, really as a promotional extension of themselves and showcase for their content assets. They could hardly ignore the new medium: these were the feverish years of the dotcom boom, with its millenarian 'new economy' rhetoric and overnight software fortunes. Similarly, advertising agencies, although still deeply entrenched in the old media paradigm, began to open up their 'interactive' or 'digital' divisions. The inevitable collapse of the dotcom boom, in April 2000, effectively brought this initial, experimental period to its end.

In the next five years, up until July, 2005, when News Corporation bought MySpace and so signalled corporate recognition of the arrival of the social media era, traditional print and television corporations took a more strategic approach to the internet, looking to find new ways to capitalise upon their content assets by adapting to the new medium, and taking stock of the challenges posed by the new internet businesses. In the advertising industry, some commentators were declaring 'The end of advertising as we know it' (Zyman 2002), while others were still asking 'Is the internet an advertising medium?' (Cappo 2003), even as the remaining barriers fell to it becoming so. Household access to the internet was increasing dramatically in the developed countries, giving advertisers access to consumers who did not have to be assembled in space and time, the way a newspaper or television audience did.

Above all, the internet was distinguishing itself as an interactive medium, through which users were able to respond immediately to the call of advertising. At the very least, this characteristic gave advertisers a measure of their advertising's effectiveness, at best, it might even mean a sale on the spot. That is not to invoke the cliché that the internet audience is 'active' while that of traditional media is 'passive'. Rather, it is more that traditional media require that advertising make sufficient impact for consumers to remember it next time they are in the store or thinking to buy that kind of product, as against the immediate response made possible by the internet. If anything, this property of immediacy, along with its specific targeting of prospects, makes advertising on the internet more like direct mail than media advertising, and even then, without the lag which is still involved in direct mail. It already seems quaint to recall that, in this phase of the internet, it was email rather than the World Wide Web which was the more characteristic vehicle of advertising, seen rather like an electronic version of direct mail (Cappo 2003).

While there continued to be a great deal of experimentation in how the internet could be exploited commercially, a number of distinctive business models were emerging. Microsoft's MSN and America Online Inc represented two alternative models of internet business development that had survived from the first decade, both of which were descendants of traditional media models. On one hand, MSN was offering its communication services free to users so long as they registered, while AOL operated on a 'walled garden' model, in which users only gained access to its services so long as they paid a subscription (Spurgeon 2008). In other words, the MSN model was analogous to a traditional 'old' media model, like FTA television, which attracts an audience on the basis of apparently free content offerings, and then sells access to that audience to advertisers, in the form of advertising time, or space in this case, while the AOL model sought to attract users willing to pay for the services on offer, as with pay-TV, so that subscriptions were the source of revenue. In the US and UK, these two rivals operate as portals in their own right, but elsewhere, have gone into association with traditional media, such as in Australia, where MSN teamed with the media conglomerate PBL, while AOL joined with the Seven Network.

While there no longer can be any doubt that the internet is an advertising medium, advertisers and their agencies seem to have been slow to realise that it is so much more than that. However, businesses like Amazon.com and eBay were not. Like MSN and AOL, both of these companies were also survivors of the dotcom crash, but through having established themselves, not as content vehicles for advertisers nor to attract subscriptions, but as models of 'e-commerce', to use the now seemingly quaint buzzword of the era: that is, they were forms of business made possible by the internet itself. Amazon launched itself in 1995 as an online retailer, initially of books, subsequently CDs, DVDs and a range of other goods. Although it did not become profitable until 2003, Amazon still represents a benchmark model of direct selling over the internet, B2C, business to consumer (Rivlin 2005). In contrast to 'bricks and mortar' retailers, Amazon commercialises the internet's interactive properties by allowing customers to search its database as an online catalogue, and at the same time, via 'recommendation engines', collects information from them about their tastes which can be used later to entice them into further purchases. Amazon now sells space to other 'third party' retailers to advertise on their site, and charges on a click-through basis, but this is just one aspect of various minor ways in which they have experimented with auxiliary commercialisation of their core business model.

By contrast, eBay is in fact totally built on advertising, but of a very specific type. Advertisers may be companies, but more characteristically they are individuals selling goods on a P2P model: that is, person-to-person. What eBay does is to act as an auction broker, charging the seller for their insertion, as in traditional classified advertising, and also a 'final value' fee (Bunnell and Leuke 2000). The most recent wave of internet businesses are the 'deal-a-day' merchants, led by Groupon, which have exploited the fact that the internet is as much a transactional space in itself as a medium for content. They have successfully adapted the traditional marketing ploy of the discount coupon to the online world, and attracted their own kind of advertising in the process.

Thus, while the internet has been readily assimilated into corporate capitalism over the last two decades, this has occurred in unpredictable ways. We have considered how old media have adapted themselves to the interactive, digital age, but should note here that this has not been as smooth a transition as in the past. When television was a new medium, newspaper corporations and commercial radio networks transformed themselves into television broadcasters, where it was a relatively short step to take from the old to the new, and the business model was already in place. Quite famously, the commercialisation of the internet has been less of a corporate than an entrepreneurial phenomenon, characterised by the 'opportunistic experimentation' (Bunnell and Leuke 2000) of individuals, who, either alone or in close partnerships, but backed with venture capital, have founded companies that have gone on to become the dominant ones of the internet era, and have brought them immense personal wealth. This 'revenge of the nerds' narrative is part of the mythology of the digital age (Turner 2010), and some of the entrepreneurs have become household names. Characteristically, they are the founders who now head up publicly-listed global corporations: Bill Gates at Microsoft; Jeff Bezos at Amazon; Larry Page at Google; and until 2011, Steve Jobs at Apple. The story of Mark Zuckerberg at Facebook, and Sean Parker from Napster, has even been the inspiration of the award-winning Hollywood biopic, *The Social Network*.

These corporations, which are active across the whole range of what are still sometimes called the 'hardware' and 'software' dimensions of the internet, are unlike those of the industrial manufacturing and commercial services sectors which previously characterised corporate capitalism. The economic value of applied innovation and knowledge as defining the contemporary age and marking it off from the past are familiar to us from theoretical perspectives on it as a 'post-industrial society', 'information economy' and the like. However, these new corporations are by no means 'post-capitalist': on the contrary, behind the playful and innocent corporate names now stand powerful conglomerates which have been built up through the same kind of strategic takeovers and mergers as we saw with the global advertiser clients and their agencies in Chapter 2. Indeed, as brands, Google, Apple and Microsoft are now ahead of consumer industry brands like Coca-Cola and McDonald's in rankings such as Millward Brown's annual Most Valuable Global Brands (2010).

The rise to such pre-eminence of the global internet-based corporations and the diverse range of business models through which they have achieved it demonstrates how the internet is so much more than a new medium for advertising, and also can be taken as a measure of the exceptional extent of socio-cultural and economic change which the internet has wrought. Yet it should be noted that although the new media companies are built on ways of commercialising the internet which do not involve advertising as we have known it, it is evident that they tend to be more in totally new fields such as software provision and internet services, as distinct from the kind of information and entertainment content – news, television series, films – which are the backbone of old media, and the traditional vehicles for advertising. We shall return to consider their situation presently, but first, we need to better understand the role of what is arguably the most transformative of the new global media corporations, Google.

The rise of search advertising and Google

Even if the internet is so much more than a new medium for advertising, it is nevertheless the case that the world's most valuable brand, Google, has attained that position precisely because of its dominance of advertising on the internet. However, it is not the kind of creative advertising familiar to us from TVCs and splashed throughout the pages of newspapers and magazines, and which social critics like to take as the expression of the Zeitgeist. Rather, Google is the market leader by far in search advertising, characterised earlier in this chapter as a distinctive new model of advertising, and one which capitalises on search behaviour as an intrinsic and elemental form of interaction on the internet, as well as the unique capacity of the internet to hyperlink from one site to another.

Any internet user will be familiar with search advertising, in the form of the 'sponsored links' you find listed along with your search results on Google, and with the internet's versions of display advertising. Internet display ads may be static, but very often include some movement within the frame ('rich media'), while others are more dynamic again, and often quite intrusive: they float or expand across the page, or pop up while the page you want is loading, and take full advantage of the range of audiovisual effects which the internet offers. They have become as much a part of our everyday communication landscape, though at least as irritating, as TVCs on television. Yet search advertising, however dull it may look by comparison to the colour and movement of display, is where the money is. For example, in the UK, over 60 per cent of the £3.5 billion ($US5.6) spent on all forms of internet advertising in 2009 was on search, with display at 20 per cent and classifieds at 19 per cent (IAB UK 2010). Proportionally it was rather less in the US: 47 per cent for search as against 33 per cent for display and 10 per cent for classifieds, of a total expenditure of $US10.7 billion (IAB US 2010). Just to give some broader perspective to these ratios: as of

2009, expenditure on internet advertising as a whole in the UK, with 24 per cent of the total, had overtaken television (IAB UK 2010), but as previously mentioned, this is exceptional. In the US, internet expenditure was about two-thirds that of television (IAB US 2010), while in Australia, internet advertising's 15% of total expenditure still lagged behind television's 25 per cent (Sinclair 2010). Although Google is interested in expanding its display advertising activities, search remains its core business, or as a Google executive puts it: 'Search is still the most monetizable moment on the web' (Rosenberg, quoted in Lee 2010a).

Yet Google is bent upon opening up ever new means for commercialising the internet, to put it mildly. This has been most apparent in such characteristic Web 2.0 properties as MySpace and YouTube. As Spurgeon argues, Google has been particularly prescient in seeing how it could profit from the internet's interactive character by providing services to facilitate connections between advertisers and consumers (2008: 14). For example, at the very point at which MySpace became the most visited site in the US, in August 2006, its then owner, Fox Interactive Media (a division of News Corporation), announced an exclusive deal that had been made with Google to provide text-based search and keyword advertising functions to MySpace and all Fox's other web properties. This gave News Corporation a high quality search function, in effect, by outsourcing advertising sales and management to Google, while Google gave itself a boost by gaining access to what was then the leading global social networking site for its search advertising, and the opportunity to develop the display side of its business as well (Schulze 2006).

It was also in 2006 that Google acquired YouTube, and it continues to work on ways to monetise the video sharing site with advertising and so turn a profit, but without alienating its users. By August 2007 Google announced that it had implemented a system of inserting ad messages which would run on an overlay as a user watched a video clip. If the user opted to click on the overlay, a video ad would play, then allow the user to return to the clip (Helft 2007), the immediate ancestor of the current TrueView system. Research has shown that 'pre-roll' advertisements are unacceptable to viewers. In a related development, Google added applications that aid in gathering data about the ad-related consumption habits of YouTube users. In March 2008, YouTube launched a feature which shows video creators when and where viewers are watching their videos. Called YouTube Insight, it tracks a video's popularity over time as well as geographically (broken down by state inside the US, elsewhere by country). It has rightly been suggested that 'marketers rather than casual users will be clamouring for these tools' (Clifford 2008), particularly with the advent of mobile, location-based advertising.

Indeed, Google has also been making strategic moves into gaining control over other internet measurement tools. One of the most significant of these has been the acquisition of DoubleClick, completed in March 2008 (Teinowitz and Klaassen 2008). Google's interest in DoubleClick lies in the fact that its core business is delivering marketing messages to websites and monitoring how many clicks each site receives. This acquisition, together with that of Teracent in 2009, a company which targets ad messages to a user's location, strengthens Google's position to expand in display ad targeting and mobile advertising (Efrati 2010c). Google's interest in location-based advertising became wholly evident in September 2011 when it began to 'geo-target' its deal-a-day service, Offers, and acquired a restaurant review company, Zagat, in the US (Patel 2011).

Just as Google dominates the search advertising market, Microsoft dominates the internet browser market, but in the last few years has been making strenuous efforts to challenge Google in search advertising. Both Yahoo!, formerly the world's second largest internet advertising company, and Microsoft have shadowed Google's strategies, such as with Yahoo!'s acquisition of Right Media (Beal 2007), and Microsoft's purchase of aQuantive, both in response to Google's acquisition of DoubleClick ('Editorial' 2007). Microsoft actually then sought to enter the search market with a takeover of Yahoo!, in 2008, but this failed. Instead, Microsoft entered a cooperative agreement with Yahoo! in 2009, allowing Microsoft's Bing search engine to overtake Yahoo! in the US the following year with a 14 per cent share of search volume, but still well behind Google with 65 per cent (Nielsen Wire 2010). Facebook's eclipse of MySpace in recent years also presents something of a challenge for Google, as will be outlined below.

Sleeping with the 'frenemy'

From the advertising agencies' point of view, the search companies' activities on the internet are blurring the boundaries between advertising agency and advertising medium, and potentially usurping the agencies' media-buying function, or, as suggested earlier, 'disintermediating' them. This blurring has tended to take place in the area of gaining control over the best proprietary software tools for advertising placement, measurement and management, and in this respect, it's not just about Google. Rather, it was Publicis Groupe, the Paris-based global marketing communications holding group, which initiated a rush of acquisitions in this crucial strategic area with its takeover of a US online marketing specialist company, Digitas, in December 2006, with the aim of extending Digitas' expertise worldwide (Pfanner 2006). Publicis Groupe includes the major media-buying agency networks Starcom Mediavest and ZenithOptimedia, and such creative networks as Leo Burnett and Saatchi & Saatchi. It should be noted that Publicis' purchase was made before Google had made its acquisition of Doubleclick, Yahoo! had bought digital advertising exchange unit Right Media, and Microsoft had purchased online marketing specialist aQuantive, as just mentioned.

There were other significant moves by the global groups into online advertising service companies around this time, notably in May 2007 when the WPP

Group bought 24/7 Real Media, a search optimisation and online ad delivery network. As noted in Chapter 2, WPP is the world's largest global agency group, UK-based, with international media-buying agencies like Mindshare and creative networks like Young & Rubicam under its umbrella, and serving clients of the stature of Ford, Unilever and HSBC. In fact it was WPP's CEO, Sir Martin Sorrell, who had dubbed Google a 'frenemy' just a few months before, and the 24/7 Real Media purchase was therefore interpreted at the time more as a pre-emptive strike against Google, than as an attempt to match Publicis' move with Digitas. Even more revealingly, Sorrell declared that, based on the new acquisition, WPP was entering 'a third major line of business' beyond the traditional media-buying and creative functions, that is, in what he called the 'online technology space' (quoted in Story 2007).

The paradox which gives rise to the 'frenemy' or 'sleeping with the enemy' metaphors is that while taking on Google on its own turf, WPP media-buying agencies remain major customers of Google. Indeed, one source suggests WPP is actually Google's biggest single customer, but even with spending $US 150 million a year, that only amounts to 1.5 per cent of Google's media sales (Mandese 2007). That is, at least as far as its involvement in internet advertising is concerned, WPP needs Google much more than Google needs WPP. For its part, Google continues to make inroads upon traditional advertising agency territory with its servicing of advertisements to newspaper chains and television networks, and more recently, in tailoring online campaigns for clients such as Ford in the US ('Google gets "creative"' 2009). However, a crucial aspect of the clash of interests between the agencies and Google is their struggle to occupy the new specialised areas of business which the internet has opened up in the technicalities of online advertising: the generation, placement, distribution, measurement and general management of online advertisements, as well as research and analysis and trading in ad inventory, all now populating a new digital space between the agencies and the internet.

'Information wants to be free ... '

At this point it is useful to pause and reflect on the apparent contradiction between the public nature of information and entertainment as we consume it, and the private, commercial basis on which it is produced and distributed. In his landmark article, 'Contribution to a Political Economy of Mass-Communication', Nicholas Garnham identified 'cultural and informational goods', that is, media content, as 'classic public goods'. He meant that such goods are out there in public, and are not used up in their consumption – for example, popular culture content like *Seinfeld* is in principle always available for future generations of viewers – so access to them has to be controlled if they are to be commercialised. In Garnham's Marxist language, this is in order to attach exchange value to them (Garnham 1979: 140). He specifies how the cultural industries have dealt with this problem in a number of familiar ways:

- Copyright: making a scarce commodity of the content, or otherwise controlling its supply, as with films and recorded music. Piracy is the risk with this method, Garnham noted, little knowing how much internet downloading and filesharing would come to confront these industries.
- Controlling access through a box-office mechanism or otherwise restricting channels of distribution. Garnham had in mind the cinema and newspapers, but pay-TV is a better example of what is basically the subscription or paid-access model outlined earlier in this chapter. As Garnham notes, the problem with this method is that new technologies come along which offer more efficient economies of scale and so open up access, and make it more difficult then to charge for it. His example is television's threat to the cinema: more contemporary are the internet's challenge to television, and to newspaper content.
- 'Built-in obsolescence through the manipulation of time', such as the newspaper's creation of 'news' itself, and the daily news cycle.
- Creating audiences which can be 'sold' to advertisers: the classic commercial broadcasting 'free lunch' model as previously discussed.

(Garnham 1979: 141–42)

Arguably, it is this same contradiction which is captured in the often-quoted aphorism of counterculture futurist Stewart Brand: 'Information wants to be free. Information also wants to be expensive. That tension will not go away' (Brand 1987). However, Brand was drawing attention to another characteristic of media content as a kind of good, implicit in Garnham's account, which is that the cost of information trends towards zero. All the cost of a film, for example, is in the production costs of making just one, original copy. As more and more further copies are made, the actual costs of materials and manufacturing become negligible. With piracy, of course, even the first copy is as good as free. So, the 'freedom' of information in this discussion can have quite different meanings: the right to have access to it as a public good (that is, it *should* be free); the tendency for it to become cheap or without real cost due to economies of scale; or the fact that once information is 'out there', distributed into the public domain, the owners of the information (who want it to be expensive), have to find ways to restrict its circulation so as to ensure themselves a financial return.

Most recently, the issue of information as being free, in the sense of available at no cost, has been taken up by Chris Anderson, well-known as chief editor of *Wired* magazine, and author of *The Long Tail* (2006). We shall examine below how Rupert Murdoch has been in a controversial pursuit to restrict access to the online content of News Corporation's newspapers by means of a 'paywall', in his averred belief that paid-for content is the future of the internet. Against this, Anderson argues that it is the nature of the internet, and the intense commercial competition which it fosters, that allows companies to achieve economies of scale such that they can provide users with content at no cost. His prime example is Google, which in giving users free search, maps, email and so on, 'turned advertising into a software application' (Anderson 2008: 4). He means that Google operates on a model analogous to the commercial broadcasting model, in that, attracted by its free services (notably Google Search) and content (video, maps, images) it assembles an audience which advertisers will pay to reach (though this audience is online, not in space and time like a normal television audience). He is careful to make the point that media markets of this kind, online or not, involve not just a transaction between buyer and seller, but with a third party, who, as he puts it, 'pays to participate in a market created by the free exchange between the first two parties' (2010: 24). This third party, of course, is the advertiser. There are costs involved, but these are hidden, and crucially, though Anderson plays down this aspect, they are met by consumers, who ultimately pay the cost of the advertising of a product, for that cost is built into the price they pay if they buy it.

In addition to the fundamental notion 'that advertising will pay for everything', Anderson distinguishes a number of business models which offer free software, content or services as a way of commercialising the internet (2010: 20–29):

- Cross-subsidies: offering one free product as a 'loss leader' which entices the consumer to pay for another, such as Nintendo offering software for one of its games free only to consumers who agree to buy another.
- 'Freemium': analogous to the subscription model of television, except that entry is free, while higher tiers or 'premium' content or service levels are only available for payment, such as Yahoo!'s photo-sharing site Flickr, as against Flickr Pro which costs $US25 per annum.
- 'Labour exchange': giving free access to websites or services in exchange for users surrendering something of value about themselves, such as Google's 411 service, which was helping Google to refine a next-generation speech-to-text search engine for smartphones. More generally, this is how commercial websites 'assemble' audiences for sale to advertisers, like in the FTA television model, in offering something apparently for nothing. However, in requiring users to register, become members, open an account, or set up their page on a social media site, they give up valuable information about themselves in the process. Not only does this information give greater benefit to advertisers, in enabling them to target likely prospects, but it can be sold to third parties (Spurgeon 2008: 88–92). Such 'registration' practices raise serious questions of consumer privacy and protection, to be considered further in Chapter 4.
- Zero marginal cost: for content with little real costs, such as bands giving away music on line to market their concerts or merchandise, or to make money from licensing. Magnatune is an example of how this can be done on a 'post-advertising' business model (Wang 2009).

- Gift economy: this is *not* a commercial model. On the contrary, Anderson has in mind here truly free, voluntarily-provided content, such as open source software or collective initiatives such as Wikipedia. Yet, ironically, non-commercial motives and activities have been instrumental in the formation of the internet as 'a market infrastructure': for instance, in the free software movement having paved the way for commercial social media ventures like YouTube (Kelty 2008: 307).

While Google in particular has shown itself to be a master of internet strategy, and used its success in selling advertising on its free search service as a basis for building a global corporation active across an ever-increasing range of software and hardware fields, and in a relatively short period of time, long-standing traditional media corporations with a huge capital investment still in television stations, newspaper plants and the like have been more challenged in finding models for grafting their operations onto the internet. In other words, they are looking for ways of making information 'expensive', in spite of its alleged tendencies towards being free: that is, of controlling access to the content assets which they produce and own as news, television series and so on. This may or may not involve advertising: we shall see that a key issue for these corporations is whether to somehow adapt the traditional free lunch model to the internet era; to protect their content with a paywall on a walled garden or subscription model; or to forge some hybrid model in between.

The quest for new business models

After an 'internet brainstorming session' with senior global personnel in February 2005, and warning US newspaper editors in April how much they were losing advertising revenue to internet sites, News Corporation Chairman and CEO Rupert Murdoch announced in July that News was buying a US-listed company, Intermix, owner of the then leading youth-oriented social networking, photo, music and video sharing site, MySpace (Schulze 2005). MySpace had begun in 2003, and grown to 18 million users by the time of the sale on a '100% viral' basis ('Interview with Richard Rosenblatt' 2006). Other Intermix sites were included in the sale, and absorbed into a newly created internet division, Fox Interactive Media (FIM). While Murdoch was criticised, and indeed criticised himself, for being late in this embrace of the internet, relative to his US competitors, the MySpace acquisition was strategically timed as a definitive foray into the then new era of social media, or Web 2.0. As well as taking advantage of the internet's capacity to digitise and facilitate the exchange of graphics, music and video, MySpace was seeking to capitalise on the content of News Corporation's existing media properties, seeing MySpace's users as 'the same audiences that are most attracted to Fox's news, sports and entertainment offerings' (Schulze 2005).

Another dimension of the strategy was to develop a different model to that of the MSN and Yahoo! kind of portal by making MySpace 'sticky', meaning that users would want to spend a lot of time on the site, downloading, messaging, calling and searching, and thus maximising their exposure to advertising, as well as to being offered the content from News Corporation. As one of Murdoch's lieutenants put it, 'we've bought audience, youth and communities that play to the sweet spots of News Corp's strengths' (Levinson quoted in Helmore 2006). The inherently local–global character of the internet meant that national sites since became seamlessly 'glocalised' into MySpace.com, to give it even greater attraction to increasingly globally-connected young users. However, while MySpace held its leading position in the US for the first few years, by early 2009 it had been overtaken by its main competitor, Facebook (Google Trends 2010), and was falling short of News' revenue expectations, prompting a re-launch in 2010 (Canning 2010), and ultimately, its disposal in 2011 (Saba 2011). News' experience with MySpace shows that corporations are not omnipotent, as their strategies, especially in bridging from old to new media, can and do end in failure.

Facebook's growth, especially amongst users outside the US, had been very rapid since its founding in 2003, and it has enjoyed brisk increases in display advertising revenue. However, it is still a long way behind Microsoft (which actually sells some of Facebook's advertising inventory), Yahoo! and even Google in display sales (Vascellaro 2010). Google's strength remains in search, and it enjoys much greater international reach amongst advertisers than does Facebook, so its annual revenue may be as high as 12 times that of Facebook, even if Facebook does have 650 million global users (Lee 2011). As an article in a News Corporation newspaper admitted, 'While social networking sites such as MySpace and Facebook have exploded in popularity in recent years, they have struggled to generate the kind of revenue and earnings prospects that can sustain them as businesses over the long haul' (Angwin and Steel 2009).

So, it should not be assumed that because the social networking sites enjoy high visibility and novelty, not to mention immense popularity, that they are therefore profitable for the companies which own them. Furthermore, their effectiveness as advertising media remains an open question. The same appears to be true for YouTube. Not everything Google touches turns to gold. Like other new media initiatives, YouTube was started up in 2005 by young entrepreneurial partners backed by venture capital (Graham 2005). Its rapid success with users prompted Google to buy it in October 2006, but leave it to operate as an independent unit. The purchase was considered at the time to be a competitive strike against MySpace (La Monica 2006). Interestingly, Google already had its own social networking site, Orkut, commenced in 2004, but with no advertising or real business plan (Sullivan 2004). Although Orkut has subsequently found very large numbers of users in Brazil, India and elsewhere outside of the English-speaking world, Google continues to look for ways to improve its position in social networking in its primary markets, including the addition of social networking features to YouTube (Efrati 2010a), and enhancements of its basic service, notably Google+, introduced in 2011 (Williams 2011).

In that regard, YouTube should be seen as in competition with the social networking sites for advertising revenue, and like them, but unlike its parent company's profitable domination of advertising on its search engine, You-Tube's global pre-eminence in online video does not translate into profits for Google (Learmonth 2009). In addition to problems that online video shares with social networking sites – how to present advertising in ways which do not alienate users, and how to ameliorate concerns over users' privacy in being targeted by advertising – YouTube carries vast amounts of copyright material, not only user-generated content, and has had to negotiate deals with content owners. These include such major international film, television and music corporations as Sony BMG Entertainment and the Warner and Universal Music Groups, as well as the US broadcasting networks. The arrangements which YouTube has been obliged to make with the copyright owners char-acteristically involve the sharing of advertising revenue, so YouTube faces an inherent cost in having to pay to make copyright material available to meet users' expectations (La Monica 2006; Smith and Vascellaro 2009). Another limitation faced by YouTube and the other social media sites in becoming profitable is that advertisers can bypass the site owners and make use of the platforms themselves, rather than spending to buy advertising space on them. Ford did this in launching its Fiesta in 2009, by seeding a viral video (Learmonth 2009). On the other hand, big advertisers like Ford and Coca-Cola are learning that they need to monitor social media chatter about them to protect their brands (Needleman 2009).

Perhaps the most surprising success of the social media era has been the micro-blogging site, Twitter. As would be well known, Twitter freely enables registered users to post short, 140-character messages called 'tweets' via its website, which other users can opt to follow. From its launch in 2006 until 2010, Twitter did not put ads on the website, nor include them in users' tweets. Nevertheless, various companies in the online technology space, including Google, were already finding ways around this, delivering advertis-ing based on users' keywords, when Twitter announced its 'Promoted Tweets' facility in April 2010 (Hansell 2009; Klaassen 2009; Vascellaro 2009). At the time Twitter was estimated to be worth $US1 billion, and to have 45 million regular users worldwide, mostly outside of the US. Early clients of the new commercial access included Starbucks, Sony and Red Bull. Advertisers' spon-sored tweets appeared at the top of certain search pages, like Google's spon-sored links, tailored to users' keyword history, and discreet clickable icons were given on the home page. By the end of 2010, Twitter was selling adver-tising to appear in individual users' Twitter streams or 'timelines' (Lee 2010b). In addition to commercialising itself in these ways, Twitter by this stage had reached arrangements with Google and Microsoft's Bing to allow them to offer Twitter content in their search results (Arthur 2010; Efrati 2010b). Like Facebook, Twitter is a private company and does not have to disclose its financial performance, so we can only guess at how far these measures have enabled it to translate its manifest popularity into profitability.

While social media have gravitated towards an online version of the classic advertising-supported model characteristic of FTA commercial broadcasting, a corresponding development has been a bid by newspapers to control access to their content by subscription. Like the MySpace venture, this initiative has come from Rupert Murdoch, Chairman of News Corporation, elaborated in a series of moves since September 2007, when News bought Dow Jones and Co, owner of *The Wall Street Journal*. At the time, Murdoch enthused that this was 'one of our most important strategic acquisitions of the last 20 years', in that it was made to converge the *WSJ*'s paid online content model with the global distribution capabilities which News had built up through its newspapers and television networks (Tabakoff 2007). Murdoch soon after specified that the *WSJ* content would be available on what has been described above as the 'freemium' model; that is, with some content being offered free, but premium content being accessible only to subscribers, who, incidentally, would also receive advertising along with it (Steel 2008).

In the following year, News management threw down the gauntlet to the search engine companies, arguing that Google and others that were providing services which aggregated news from newspapers and presented it on their sites in headline and digest form were discouraging users from clicking through to the newspapers' own sites. This meant that the newspapers were not recouping the costs nor getting the commercial benefit of their own content, since the search engines were reducing the appeal of newspaper sites to users, and hence, to advertisers. Google and Yahoo! were 'content kleptomaniacs', Murdoch told the World Media Summit in October 2009. 'Vampires' and 'tapeworms' were other epithets cast about by News executives in the course of this very public challenge to the practice of aggregating free content (Dawber 2009), which says much about the tone of the debate, but did little to legitimise their argument. Of course, there are many different kinds of content which companies aggregate on the internet, and present to attract users and advertisers, but the newspapers' case in particular is that news is content which it costs them to acquire, and they thus claim the right to monetise it. This puts them in conflict with the search engines' business model, which is predicated on being able to offer their services free. Google and Yahoo! argued in defence that they were acting in accordance with existing agreements with the newspapers which allow them to use the content in headline and condensed form (Dawber 2009).

At this stage, News Corporation had already announced its intention to begin charging for its online content as of 2010, and was seeking to mobilise other news organisations in the same cause, notably the *New York Times,*

Hearst and Tribune companies, its rivals in the US. The initial aim was to have a single online registration and pay system which would be used in common by all partners, including News' titles in the UK (Brand Republic Staff 2009). The advent of the Apple iPad, launched internationally in the first few months of 2010, gave the plan further impetus and dimension in the form of Project Alesia, a 'digital newsstand' which was to give iPad and other digital device users a single online address at which they could pay a monthly subscription to access news from any of the partner organisations. However, by October, the plan had to be shelved, because News' rivals could not agree on key issues such as control of subscriber data and how to split the revenue (Worden 2010).

Although the partner organisations have gone on to develop their own pay systems, including News' own tablet newspaper, *The Daily* (Learmonth 2011a), the failure of this collective initiative has been a considerable setback for News Corporation and the large news companies, as an industry, in their attempts to claw back the content and revenue which has gravitated to the internet. As Murdoch himself says, 'Content is not just king. It is the emperor of all things electronic. We are on the cusp of a digital dynasty ... ' (Quoted in Elliott 2010). Yet we have seen that while newspapers have been astute in establishing themselves as an online presence, the modes of access to their content now afforded by the internet, in line with Garnham's and Anderson's analysis outlined earlier, undermine their former control over that access, and hence their capacity to monetise it with advertising. Consistent with Murdoch's rhetoric, one commentator observes, 'We are in the middle of the greatest re-drawing of the boundaries of media empires ... in our time' (Cato 2010). How the media empires, old and new alike, negotiate the terrain of paid versus free is decisive for where those boundaries will be settled: truly, lines in the sand.

Moving targets

The iPad is emblematic of a new phase in the relations of media, advertisers, consumers and the technologies which link them, in that conventional internet access from fixed computers is being greatly augmented by a range of mobile hardware – other tablet devices, wireless laptops and the new generation of smartphones. The iPad in particular not only was welcomed by Murdoch as the saviour of the newspaper industry (Burns 2010), but also magazine publishers have seen it as a way of making up lost ground in digital advertising, enabling them to offer advertisers 'the new-media bells and whistles'; though once again, a mutually satisfactory business model still remains to be worked out (Ovide and Vranica 2010). A trend is already evident in the US for consumers to be spending more time with their mobile devices than home with their TVs and desktops (Elkin 2010). Mobile advertising would appear to be the coming thing.

Yet in spite of the fact that the number of mobile telephones, or cellphones, in the world had outstripped that of internet connections for over a decade, as late as 2009, advertising on mobile phones was still being referred to as 'nascent' (Chang 2009). The exploitation of mobile telephony as an advertising medium had been dogged to that point by the complicated ecosystem of the industry: convoluted and at times tense relationships between the mobile operators (the telcos who provide the mobile services and handle the billing), the advertisers, the content providers and even the handset manufacturers (Wilken and Sinclair 2009). The operators had been favouring a walled garden model to maintain control of access to their subscribers, to whom they could 'push' advertising, usually by text message, albeit restricted by the requirement for subscribers' consent – another significant barrier in itself. Against this, other interests favoured a 'pull' model which would be able to attract subscribers 'off-deck', that is, away from their operators' portals, to an external site which offered entertainment or some other incentive (Haig 2002). Once again in this case, we see respectively the choice between controlled and free access to content, as well as lesser and greater interactivity.

The advent of proprietary operating systems and web browsers, along with other advances in mobile telephone technology, led to the launch of a new generation of mobile phones from 2007, notably Apple's iPhone and Google's Android, which not only gave users access to the internet when on the move, the 'mobile net', but enabled third parties, such as advertisers and other commercial interests, to offer 'apps' (applications, or software) on the various platforms. This is analogous to sponsors providing their own programmes in the early days of television, as described earlier. Furthermore, the new smartphones, like the iPad and other tablet devices that were soon to follow, were vastly enhancing the scope for mobile display advertising in a field still dominated by relatively primitive SMS text messaging. Thus, in order to acquire the technical expertise required to master this new mobile zone in the online technology space, Google bought Ad Mob, a mobile display-advertising specialist company, in November 2009 (Chang 2009), while for its part, Apple then bought a mobile ad network, Quattro Wireless, and launched its iAd mobile advertising service (Patel 2010a).

However, the new technology has altered the assemblage of relations in the manufacturing/marketing/media complex. Some of iAd's first advertisers were reported to be unimpressed with the service, while its capacity to work with advertising agencies was also an issue. Display advertising requires much more creative input than SMS, but Apple's firm control over the agencies supplying that input was delaying the timely appearance of the ads. Advertisers were complaining about this, and the lack of feedback. 'Apple underestimated how tough the new business would be and is still learning the best tactics for dealing with ad agencies. At the same time, ad agencies are struggling to keep pace with the new ad technologies' (Kane and Steel 2010).

Google's activities in mobile advertising not only involve the new field of display, but also build on its established strength with search. Already in 2010, Google announced it was expecting to bring in $US1 billion from mobile search and display around the world, in step with the global growth in smartphone penetration (Patel 2010b). Mobility adds another dimension to search advertising, conceived in the trade literature as 'location-based services' (LBS) or 'mobile local search' (MLS). This is 'the Holy Grail that advertisers have been talking about for ages', in that they can send advertising messages to individuals based on their location, such as their proximity to bars, restaurants and other businesses. The privacy implications are obvious even to its advocates – these are necessarily 'opt-in' services (Truman 2006). Even so, LBS/MLS are forms of advertising attractive to legions of small businesses which want to be sought out, and so will go to Google search instead of the local newspaper as they once would have. Google is also capitalising on its supremacy in mobile search to add a further layer of technology with its Wallet and Offers opt-in services, both involving mobile payment systems (Cheng 2011). More recently, with its purchase of Motorola Mobility, a phone manufacturer and patent holder, Google has made a significant shift from software to hardware, thus consolidating its position in search advertising at the same time as it challenges Apple's market leadership with the iPhone (Fildes and Frean 2011).

Television as you like it

Along with the emergence of the mobile front for advertising, new platforms for television distribution, including mobile, but mainly still in the home, are competing to attract viewers with more choice and control over their viewing, albeit at the cost of even further fragmentation of the traditional television audience. Television has been going through considerable changes for decades: first, the advent of pay-TV challenging FTA's supremacy, and then the internationalisation of distribution via satellites opening up national markets and engendering the multichannel environment, have put television into a 'post-broadcast' era (Sinclair 1999: 162–63; Turner and Tay 2009). The ongoing convergence of television and digital technologies has multiplied even more the choices of how we access television content, resulting in a competitive environment and profound challenges to the corporate owners of television content and its forms of distribution. The quest for assembling audiences that can be sold to advertisers, as in the golden age of mass media, is still a driving factor, but other forms of capitalising upon television content now also are being instituted.

The long-prophesised era of what is generically referred to as internet protocol television (IPTV) started to materialise towards the end of the 2000s with several ventures, beginning in the US in particular. Netflix is a public company which originated as a DVD rental by mail operation, and has since shifted to online streaming of film and some television content. Due to international copyright restrictions, it is available in the US and Canada only. It offers a series of 'membership' (subscription) plans, and is accessible via a range of devices which subscribers may already have in their homes – not only computers, internet-enabled televisions and TiVo DVRs, but Blu-ray players and even some game consoles. The absence of suitable devices in enough homes had hitherto been a barrier to the growth of IPTV. In 2010 Amazon also entered the field, but on a video on demand (VoD), that is, pay-per-view basis (Schechner and Fowler 2010; Verna 2010).

Then there is Hulu, owned by a consortium of media corporations, notably the networks NBC Universal (General Electric), Fox Entertainment (News Corporation), and ABC Inc (Walt Disney Company), all owners of extensive media content which they are seeking to protect even as they capitalise upon it. Initially available only in the US, Hulu launched there in 2008 with access over some existing devices. It operates on a freemium/hybrid business model. Certain content is free, but with advertising: 'we just ask that you sit through some commercials in exchange', says Hulu. More desirable content, and access over a wider range of devices, including Apple mobile products, can be had for a nominal subscription ($US10 in 2010) to a premium tier, Hulu Plus. However, this is not enough to buy subscribers out of the obligation to sit through commercials: Hulu Plus also carries advertising (Hulu 2010).

The hybrid business model reflects the ambiguous position of the media companies behind Hulu as they face the rising demand for IPTV. On one hand, they want to assert their presence in the new digital delivery market, but on the other, don't dare to give away too much of their content for free. Furthermore, to the considerable extent that they also have interests in broadcast networks and pay-TV, they are fearful of 'cannibalising' these other operations. The scene has been complicated by the entry of Google TV, which carries Google's search business model into the digital television field. Google TV is not so much a television service itself, as a platform or portal which enables viewers to search for whatever television content they want to watch from the internet, and for content providers to develop applications for it, as with the smartphones. Google TV uses Google's browser, Chrome, for navigation, and the same Android technology as in its smartphone, enabling compatible applications. Although initially requiring special devices to access it, Google TV is aimed at serving advertisements to viewers along with search results, as with 'original' Google (Efrati 2010d). When it launched in 2010, Google TV had agreements with Netflix and Amazon, but not Hulu, while the national broadcast networks actually blocked their programming from being accessed via Google TV. In addition to concerns about cannibalisation, the networks cited problems with pirate sites turning up in keyword searches via Google TV, and more generally, just losing control of their content as it becomes 'lost' amongst the heterogeneous content options of the internet (Schechner and Efrati 2010). Thus, not only has Google become a threat to the large advertising agencies, but also to the leading media corporations.

Apple is also a contender in the IPTV market: in fact, it had first launched its Apple TV set-top device in 2007, but at $US299, that had not taken off. Recognising price as a problem, a new device was launched in 2010 at $US99, with downloads of some shows, including from certain major networks, available at 99 cents. This is a pay-per-view model, obviously based on Apple's success with its music downloads via iTunes. Not all content providers believe they can flourish in Apple's walled garden however, arguing that at 99 cents, their shows are devalued. Yet for its part, Apple needs access to this and other content so as to keep selling iPads, iPhones and iPod Touch consumer hardware, its core business (Fowler and Schechner 2010).

In the UK, it has been the broadcast networks themselves, public and private, that have initiated YouView, in consortium with broadband providers, as of 2011. Viewers have to buy a set-top box, as with the previously existing Freeview scheme for digital access, but there is no subscription charge to enjoy basic services such as catch-up TV. However, it is also a platform for pay-per-view and third-party programme providers, services for which users pay (YouView 2010). In Australia, there is a FTA, advertising-supported Freeview scheme for accessing digital television; a range of pay-per-view options, including via iTunes and Microsoft's Xbox 360; and some streaming subscription channels in development (Frith 2010).

In the golden age of mass media, networks and equipment manufacturers were presumed to exist in a harmony of interests. These days, they compete over the available pool of advertising revenue and/or are testing the limits of what viewers are willing to pay for, in an environment in which those viewers, like newspaper readers, have been accustomed to getting their content apparently at no cost. In terms of business models, the time-honoured commercial television model of attracting mass audiences for sale to advertisers still persists, as does the pay-TV alternative, but they exhibit various combinations in practice, along with the attempts to integrate the marketing of new consumer electronic devices as an essential part of the equation. The resultant proliferation of choice is both cause and effect of audience fragmentation, and raises questions about the sustainability of so many new services (Steinberg 2009). Nevertheless, the niche audiences being created in the process can be more readily identified and targeted for advertising via the range of interactive, 'addressable' devices in ever more homes, regardless of whether they are there on a FTA or subscription basis. In this respect, television is converging with the internet's capacity to extract information about users for commercial exploitation (Andrejevic 2009).

From the supply side to the demand side

So far we have considered issues raised by the advent of the internet as an advertising medium, and the realignment of corporate interests around it and other new media on offer. If we turn our attention from the corporations and the various permutations of business models upon which media are now offered, and look instead at the abundance of choices consumers have to access information and entertainment, and to communicate and express themselves socially, we gain a quite different perspective. As demonstrated by the range of choices in television access just discussed, viewers are now freed in time and space from the control of broadcast network scheduling and 'appointment television'. The old stereotype of the 'couch potato', unable to reach out and change the channel, is more off the mark than ever. Network television certainly has not gone away, but viewers actively select what they want to watch, and the time and place for it, such as with 'catch-up' or video on demand services, and also have pay-TV and other options over the internet, like You-Tube. Video rental stores still get by, thanks to the popularity of boxed sets of television series. Similarly, newspapers also survive, but compete for readers' attention with internet news sites and blogs.

It is not only the profusion and flexibility of choice which sets the internet era apart from mass media's golden age, but the interactivity which it enables and encourages. Options for interaction between senders and receivers of traditional media are relatively restricted – letters to the editor, talkback radio, the studio audience – and the number of people who can interact at any one time is also limited. Furthermore, the pathway for mediated interaction is principally from receiver back to the sender, not so much laterally, between receivers. The cornucopia of choice and the interactive ease and immediacy of the internet, by contrast, has transformed social communication in a way which rebalances the power relations between senders and receivers, and heightens interaction amongst receivers themselves – indeed, the internet has rendered obsolete conventional paradigms such as sender/receiver, or producer/consumer: hence the term, 'social media'. However, the significance of this transformation and rebalancing is much contested.

On one hand, advertisers find that they have to take into account how their target consumers will react to advertising messages and marketing tactics in general. In the mass media age, brand owners didn't have to fear the scorn and contempt that prospective consumers can now heap upon their brand, for example, by means of a parody posted on YouTube, such as with Microsoft's 'I'm a Mac' campaign launch in the US, to take a mild example (Bulik 2006). This new accountability that advertisers now find themselves having towards their consumers, and the capacity of consumers to react on the internet, whether in negative or positive ways, has led many observers to celebrate what they see as the 'empowerment' of consumers in the form of the 'produser'. First envisaged, well before the internet age, as a 'prosumer' (Toffler 1980), the produser in the contemporary 'digital orthodoxy' discourse (Turner 2010: 57) is the user or consumer who, individually or collectively, is able to participate in content creation (Bruns 2008). This can also be conceived of as a process of 'value co-creation' (Prahalad and Ramaswamy, cited in Zwick, Bonsu et al. 2008).

For, on the other hand, advertisers have recognised the power of user-generated content, and sought to harness it to their own purposes. A notable example, already mentioned in Chapter 1, is the competition which the PepsiCo company, Frito-Lay, has conducted each year since 2007 to attract user-generated TVCs, for its Doritos cornchip brand, to be shown during the broadcast of the Super Bowl. This national football final is a major event in the US television and advertising industry calendar, with advertising time being sold at premium prices. The 2009 winner was particularly well-received by television viewers and on the internet, in spite of being 'sophomoric' in its humour. The producers were two young brothers who wanted to be film directors (York and Mullman 2009).

Such mobilization by the manufacturing/marketing/media complex of the aspirations, creative talents and energies of media users has drawn much criticism in a wider debate about corporate co-option of the affect and 'work' invested in media consumption by both old and new media audiences in general, not just the active produsers themselves. As Terranova has bluntly observed, 'knowledgeable consumption of culture is translated into productive activities that are pleasurably embraced and at the same time often shamelessly exploited' (2000). As also alluded to in Chapter 1, other ways in which corporations seek to capitalise on internet users and social media in particular are crowdsourcing, which is looking for idea generation or feedback from audiences for prospective new products, for example; and buzz marketing. Though first practised on a word-of-mouth, interpersonal communication basis, the internet has greatly facilitated this practice of stimulating discussion or 'buzz' about a product in such a way as to spread it through social networks on a 'viral' basis.

It is not only the creativity and social networking activities of users that can be exploited by advertisers, but also the information about themselves that they offer up both knowingly and unknowingly in the course of their everyday internet use. Whereas in television's golden age the ratings system yielded only a broad demographic breakdown of the mass audience, the internet age is distinguished by unobtrusive electronic means of following users' online tracks – 'behavioural targeting' – as the basis for cultivating niche markets. Just as we pay the true price of 'free' television in terms of the time we spend watching TVCs, and the hidden costs of advertising passed on to us when we consume goods and services, the true price of using internet services such as Google or Facebook is in how we, in using them, necessarily give over information about ourselves which they are able to monetise. In both cases, the illusion of something for nothing overshadows the implicit transaction.

As Andrejevic observes, 'marketers know much more about consumers than consumers know about how this information is being used' (2009: 38). For instance, with their information on users' browsing history, Google and the other search engines can offer advertisers 'interest-based' advertising, that is, ads which are matched to a user's track record ('Google launches targeted ad scheme' 2009). Again, both Facebook and MySpace let advertisers target ads in accordance with information that users have included in their profile. Although the search engine and social media site owners claim such information can't be traced back to any individual user, occasional public gaffes about their data management do nothing to alleviate concerns about privacy and surveillance, and their opaque practices of data collection, storage and ownership (Wright 2008). We can return to consider this issue further in the next chapter.

Desperate advertisers

In the face of the marked shift of advertising revenue towards the internet, and against a background of documented advertiser dissatisfaction with television as an advertising medium (Newman 2008), the traditional wall between advertising and editorial content (that is, information and entertainment) has been crumbling. This has not just begun to happen, as it can be traced back at least to the advent of the remote control and VCR, and the threat they made to the hegemony of the classic 30-second TVC as the preferred advertising format. Even before then, viewers had become accustomed to commercial promotions being presented as content, usually in studio-based genres such as variety shows. Nor is the breach confined to television: magazines in particular have been fairly unapologetic in offering advertisers 'advertorial' environments in which to buy advertising space for many years. Local newspapers also can be shameless about, for example, publishing a favourable restaurant review in the same issue as the restaurant begins to advertise. Even in metropolitan dailies, we are accustomed to finding advertising supplements on specialist topics with all the editorial content based upon the products and services of the brands advertised in it. This is not to mention the number of items presented as news which have been placed by public relations networks, cinema advance publicity being a common example. With television in particular, it is possible to trace a continuum of commercialised content from the relatively mild, though usually unsubtle, practice of product placement, through the multi-platform, multi-sponsor model of reality shows, to the phenomenon of 'branded content', in which programming has been produced at the behest of a particular sponsor.

In the 2009 series of *Desperate Housewives*, Bree arrives home with a new Lexus 4WD/SUV. We know it's a Lexus, because when the other housewives gather around in her driveway, she says so, and takes a few minutes to point out some product features to them. However, the product is actually written into the plot: Annette is jealous and guilty, because of financial difficulty, she has just made husband Tom sell his Mustang. This is product placement, 'product integration' to be specific, in a top rating, internationally distributed series, for a global product. The show was seen even in countries where product placement is illegal, notably the UK at that time. Interestingly however, by the end of 2009, the British Government had acceded to pleas from commercial television to allow it, albeit under restricted conditions, the industry having argued, amongst other things, that they had suffered a dip in advertising revenue associated with the GFC. They hoped to catch up to the estimated 5 or 6 per cent of television advertising income garnered by product placement in the US (Adetunji 2009). Yet even since then, there still is product 'displacement' on British television, with branded products which would be allowed elsewhere on screen pixelated out of existence (Hall 2010).

One of the most successful examples of internationally-formatted reality programming over the past decade or so has been *Big Brother*. In Australia, *Big Brother* was a media phenomenon, not just for reasons similar to those elsewhere in the world, but because of the intensive product placement from many corporations worked into the show itself; its other platforms, namely the website and telephone voteline; and its merchandising. The 2002 series in particular had 15 sponsors, such as Colgate, Nestlé and Foster's. According to the executive producer, the conduct of the show was actually built around the sponsorship deals (Abbott, quoted in Lawson 2002: 8). In addition to sponsorship, the network generated income from mobile phone voting, as well as revenue from cultivating viewers as 'online communities' who registered to enter content areas on offer, effectively opting in to become addressable targets for advertisers (Sinclair 2006). Other reality shows have followed suit in maximising returns from multiple platforms, such as *Lost* in the US (Fernandez 2006), while more generally, multiple sponsorship has become a mainstay of genres such as cooking, makeover and travel shows.

Branded content can be distinguished from product placement or multiple sponsorship insofar as it is programming that has been paid for by one particular sponsor, and is offered as entertainment content. The definitive case is *The Hire* series of short films made for free internet distribution, which were directed by leading international directors, featured some well-known celebrities, and were produced by the Fallon advertising agency (part of Publicis Groupe) for the client, BMW, in 2001–2 (Halliday and Graser 2005; Pavlik 2008). Short-form branded 'infotainment' content like this is well-suited for internet distribution, but can even be found on international cable television, such as the Rolex Spirit of Yachting series on BBC World, CNBC Sports and ESPN Star Sports Asia. Major advertisers who have become engaged in long-form branded content for television include the world's biggest FMCG corporation and advertiser, Procter & Gamble, and Wal-Mart, the world's biggest retailer. Arguing that there are insufficient 'family-friendly' entertainment vehicles for advertising on US network television, both companies were part of a consortium which produced the series, *The Gilmore Girls* in 1999, and more recently, have been partners in the production of a telefilm, *Secrets of the Mountain*, which included product integration as well as TVCs for the two sponsors in the commercial breaks (Vranica and Byron 2010). This model, of sponsors buying airtime and providing the network with their own

Figure 3.1 Dynamic in-game advertising technology can integrate branded products into the game itself as it is played, on a targeted and variable basis

programming, closes the circle with a 'back to the future' version of how commercial broadcasting was first conducted in the early days of radio, as we have seen. Clearly, the traditional ideal of keeping advertising and editorial separate has become more seriously compromised than ever.

Finally, one other medium which is proving amenable to these various forms of commercialisation deserves note, and that is the video game. This is a niche rather than a mass medium, but a significant one, and a useful example of how advertisers are targeting segmented demographic groups, in this case, mainly 18–34 year-old males. Games can be sponsored, as branded content, but more striking, with both online and even packaged video games, is the use of dynamic in-game advertising (DIGA) technology (Hay 2006). This can integrate branded products into the game itself as it is played – the characters' clothes, their food and drink, or the signage around them, for instance – on a targeted and variable basis (Anderson 2010). Advertising agency groups and media owners alike have been establishing 'entertainment' divisions which work across the whole range of such 'below-the-line' content commercialisation (Corlette 2010).

The search for space and time

This chapter has shown how advertisers, in their quest to secure the attention and interest of prospective customers for their goods and services, have taken up the new opportunities afforded by the internet and other new media, and in doing so, have destabilised the formerly quite settled relations within the manufacturing/marketing/media complex. The advertising agencies no longer control access to the advertising media to the extent they once did, since advertisers, large (and especially) small, can go directly to the search engines on the internet. One line of defence has been for the agencies to build up their control over specialist companies in auxiliary technical services such as ad placement and delivery. For traditional media, the challenge has been in how the internet has undermined their control over access to their information and entertainment content, and indeed, fostered the expectation that such access should be free. A number of business models have been erected in response, but none of these exhibits the stability of the past. In the process, the customary line between advertising and editorial content has been smudged, although this tactic runs the risk of devaluing the content assets it seeks to protect.

On the new media side, it is not as if there are secure and uncontested beneficiaries of the ascendance of the internet. Even corporations of the scale and success of Google, Microsoft and Apple must compete in a fluid and complex world in motion, albeit a world very much of their own making. Although they each have come to dominate their respective new media territories, the boundaries are not fixed, particularly as the extension of mobile internet access opens up 'a post-PC platform war' between them and the other big players (Learmonth 2011b). As for the consumers of media in society at large, the new media have enabled much greater access to information and entertainment content, and more interactive, expressive and mobile modes of social communication than ever conceivable in the age of mass media, but at the cost of ever greater exposure to the commercialisation of private life and the fragmentation of a public sphere of citizenship and popular culture.

Chapter 4

Current trends in advertising, media and society

Before the widespread take up of the internet, and social media in particular, a chapter on current trends in advertising, media and society would have concentrated on the ideological messages in advertisements – notably TVCs, glossy magazine ads and billboards – and their presumed social impact. As outlined in Chapter 1, such advertising was seen as a 'sign of the times', and semiotic analysis, that is, treating advertising as a system of signs, was believed to be the means by which the functioning of the society behind that system could be revealed (Cronin 2004b: 354). Such analysis rested on what branding academic Douglas Holt calls a 'cultural authority' theoretical model in which 'Omnipotent corporations use sophisticated marketing techniques to seduce consumers to participate in a system of commodified meanings embedded in brands' (2002: 71).

Studies of this kind can still be found in the global era (Goldman and Papson 2011), but critics of advertising are now less likely to see it as a coded force for ideological conformity, shoring up and reproducing a class-based social structure, but rather, as 'a medium for the reflexive construction of identity', to quote Adam Arvidsson, one of the leading contemporary theorists (2003: 5). At least in the developed world, the trend in advertising towards marketing and branding, as distinct from simple selling, together with the emergence of more streetwise and self-expressive consumers with access to social media, has produced 'a distinctively postmodern mode of sociality in which consumers claim to be doing their own thing while doing it with thousands of like-minded others' (Holt 2002: 83).

While the transition to this postmodern 'commercial culture' should not be seen as 'epochal', in the sense of it being universal and total (Nixon 2003: 16), the concept of a postmodern era of consumption is useful to characterise the principal features of how advertising and consumers relate to each other in the internet age. There are at least two processes now occurring, though in a manner that Scott Lash and John Urry could not have anticipated in their landmark but controversial *Economies of Signs and Space*, cited in Chapter 1. First, now enabled by the interactive capabilities and multiple, lateral choices offered by the internet, there is what they call 'an accelerating individualisation process ... in which agency is set free from structure' (1994: 5): that is, individuals are less bound in to society. Second, they posit an 'aestheticization of material objects' (1994: 4): form becomes at least as important as function, in conjunction with a reflexive or self-aware way of being in which individuals select and combine consumer goods and services so as to express their individual identities to each other. In this respect, taken in the wider context of branding, advertising assumes the purpose of adding value to goods and services by endowing them with cultural meanings and associations as brands.

In the context of the manifold 'convergence' (Jenkins 2006) of the formerly distinct realms of structure and culture, social and individual, public and private, producer and consumer, corporate and grass-roots, this chapter will first pursue some of the issues raised in Chapter 3 concerning the empowerment-exploitation paradox of social media. It will then turn to consider selected contemporary aspects of how advertising is dealing with social change, particularly in matters of public health, the environment and nationhood in the global era.

Advertising and social identity

> Advertising was the industry quickest to exploit the extent to which identity is something constructed, something invented and controlled.
>
> (Davidson 1992: 178)

In Chapter 3, some key dimensions of the relationship between social media and their users were specified: the advent of user-generated content and value co-creation; the mobilisation of crowd-sourcing and viral marketing; and the privacy problems posed by behavioural targeting. It was suggested there is a contradiction inherent in social media between the apparent empowerment given to the user, and the possibilities for exploitation opened up in the same process. We return now to look at that issue from a more theoretical perspective.

Working for the brand

As noted in Chapter 1, Marxists have long argued that media consumption by audiences is a form of work, in which 'surplus value' is extracted from them. This would be particularly true of 'paying attention' to advertisements. Advertising seeks to command our attention, and even if we don't experience this as work, we are at least aware that it costs us time. This cost is perhaps more evident when corporations seek to engage us in their market research, such as online evaluations of their products and services, and even of their business systems: for example, when Amazon asks you to rate the performance of a third-party supplier. In the 'attention economy' (Davenport and Beck 2001) we now have on the internet, advertisers do not just compete for the attention of consumers as TVCs, magazine ads and billboards have always done, but must offer incentives to attract and retain users. Rather than the eye-catching images of traditional mass media advertising, the popular social media internet sites in particular capture attention through the offer of inter-active personal involvement. Social networking is 'a highly developed technol-ogy of the self' which demands emotional investment in 'the construction, maintenance and performance of cultural identities' (Turner 2010: 146). While such involvement can be seen in the conventional Marxist view as a new form of albeit pleasant 'audience work' (Zwick *et al.* 2008: 180), it also fits a broader theoretical recognition of how important the investment of time and emotion are in economic behaviour (Amin and Thrift 2004: xviii–xix), and how they maintain social discipline (Hearn 2008).

Arvidsson argues that collective personal involvement is the basis of how brands acquire value, as was explained in Chapter 1. In this view, the 'trust, affect and shared meanings' we generate in social interaction becomes a form of 'immaterial labour' exploited by corporate brand managers in their efforts to shape the 'context of consumption' of brands in how they are advertised (2005: 236–37, 244). Furthermore, although social interaction by definition takes place through communities and networks, in the case of the internet, these are virtual rather than geographic. As Graeme Turner observes, the pleasure of watching a video on YouTube brings not just an intrinsic indivi-dual satisfaction, but can have an 'exciting … sense of co-presence' which comes from knowing that the experience is shared with others of similar tastes, perhaps even 'an imagined transnational community' (2010: 144). In this way, YouTube should provide a congenial context of consumption for advertising both global and niche brands.

However, in the postmodern world of social media and reflexive consumers, brands which are either prescriptive or manipulative in how they are adver-tised risk rejection in favour of those that seem to offer a form of personal expression. Holt maintains that contemporary consumers are not just amen-able to brand advertising, but quite well-disposed to communicating with each other through brands. Whereas once social distinction was achieved by 'market-consecrated brands', now it is through how consumers 'individuate market offerings and avoid market influence', choosing to produce themselves through their selection of 'authentic' brands (2002: 83). Thus, he argues that advertisers who directly seek to establish emotional associations with their brand will be less successful than those who take the indirect path of culti-vating 'potent identity myths' (2004: 28). As will be considered further below, national identity myths have this kind of potency. Holt's example in the case of the US is the soft drink Mountain Dew, although it is Coca-Cola which represents the mythic 'America' internationally. Perhaps one of the most suc-cessful US brands ever in this respect is Harley-Davidson, which not only is another American icon, but carries a myth of outlaw masculinity that attracts active 'brand communities' of owners and fans in several countries. In the case of the UK, we can contrast the subcultural cachet of Fred Perry with the cheeky but more marketing-inspired fcuk, while in Australia, national identity might be affirmed with a jar of Vegemite.

Brands that are seen as authentic tend to have their origins in subcultures or popular culture in general, and the mythic qualities of these origins are carried over into how they are marketed. This includes conventional media advertising in which a product becomes rendered as a brand through the mythic associations it is given, much like the 'referent systems', or embedded cultural meanings so definitively analysed by Judith Williamson in magazine advertisements in the 1970s (1978). But in postmodern marketing, branding as a 'context of consumption' also involves various below-the-line strategies such as 'ambient marketing' (Hearn 2008: 210) in which brands are associated with actual social activities and experiences. Holt gives the example of Corona, a rather ordinary Mexican beer which acquired mythic status through first being favoured by US college students going to beach parties in Mexico in the 1980s. This myth of origin and its hedonistic associations were used subsequently to build Corona into a leading brand in the US and elsewhere (2004: 16–20).

In the 'experience economy' (Pine and Gilmore 1999), at one level consumers are enticed into branded spaces like Starbucks and Niketown, but also are offered more tactile and sensory experiences built into the design of branded products themselves (Arvidsson 2005; Moor 2007). There is also sponsorship, where corporations seek to become identified with subcultural communities by associating their brand with activities like extreme sports events, for example Red Bull Crashed Ice (Higgins 2007); and the more subtle 'life world emplacement': that is, the organisation of special events or clubs for brand users (Holt 2002). An online example would be the social networking and games offered by Lego, a versatile experience marketer (Zwick et al. 2008).

The various forms of stealth, viral and buzz marketing mentioned in previous chapters can be classified under the heading of 'social marketing'. Cultural critic Douglas Rushkoff coined the term 'viral marketing' as an early warning about how ideas can spread through the internet, only to find it soon after taken up by brand agencies as a digital-age version of traditional word-of-mouth marketing. Just as some companies, with the help of their agencies, were sending out undercover scouts to 'coolhunt' new subcultural trends on the streets, others began paying 'trolls' to pose as fans of their brands and spread favourable comment over the chat rooms and bulletin boards popular on the internet at that time (2009: 131–32). With the advent of social media, advertisers began to place offbeat TVCs and other branded content strategically so that friends would want to send them on to each other. More recently, the 'Like' and '+1' buttons on Facebook and Google have rationalised and facilitated this practice in accordance with the ever more intense commercialisation of these sites. In all these cases, while it is the advertisers and their agencies who are planting the seeds, it is left up to the consumers to 'discover' them and cultivate their brand value. So, it is not as if only active, content-generating users do 'work' for advertisers: simply giving opinions and relaying them to friends is also a form of participation in 'value co-creation'.

Yet while social marketing strategies have the dual advantage for advertisers of bypassing the scepticism which consumers, especially younger ones, have towards conventional media advertising, and at the same time, of exploiting the interactive, networking capabilities of the internet, advertisers are less in control of the image and hence the value of their brands, than they are with traditional media. The popular culture which advertisers are trying to harness to their purposes is 'generally beyond the direct control of capital' (Arvidsson 2005: 242), as suggested in Chapter 1, while the online consumers are unruly, and even resistant. Their 'tastes and patterns are increasingly fluid, fragmented, heterogeneous, and less amenable to categorization, management, and direction' (Zwick *et al.* 2008: 171).

As just suggested, this may be particularly true of the younger consumers oriented to social media, often characterised as 'generation Y' or the 'millennial' generation, but several influential observers trace the origins of contemporary consumer resistance to the counter-culture generation of the 1960s. As we have now seen parodied on *Mad Men*, the 1950s has become thought of as an age of suburban conformity under the dictates of the men in grey flannel suits on Madison Avenue, against which an emergent critique of advertising and consumerism came to be part of the countercultural quest for individualism and authenticity. According to Thomas Frank, the advertising industry absorbed the creative energy and rebellion in a process of 'co-optation', but this was 'something much more complex than the struggle back and forth between capital and youth revolution'. Rather, business management in fields such as advertising and fashion embarked on its own search for innovation, which drew upon oppositional youth culture and ultimately installed 'hip consumerism' as a constant motive force in capitalist modernity (1997: 235). In similar vein, Dick Pountain and David Robins point to the ethos of 'Cool', an attitude of postmodern irony and detachment that has come to characterise much contemporary advertising directed towards young people in particular. Citing Anthony Giddens' concept of 'reflexive modernization', they argue that it is a form of consumer subjectivity which 'offers a handle by which Cool advertisers can steer the consumer in the desired direction ... Everyone is a rebel now' (2000: 164–66).

The term 'post-Fordism' is often used to contrast the engaging and self-expressive kind of 'work' we willingly do as consumers in the age of 'reflexive modernization' – posting on Facebook, sharing videos on YouTube – with the disciplined work carried out by production workers in the era of industrial capitalism. The Ford factory was a model of the 'scientific management' of labour, and standardised mass production, and hence a metaphor for that era (Allen 1992). Current 'autonomist Marxist' theory argues not only that the work of social networking is a form of 'immaterial labour' which is exploitative in that it involves 'the channelling of age-old human desires into the hollow, promotional terms of post-Fordist capitalist acquisition' (Hearn 2008: 211), but also that contemporary brand-building advertising is to be distinguished from Fordist advertising, which in this view, is the difference between interactivity and discipline (Arvidsson 2006: 93). As we have seen, branding depends on consumers' investment of their personal 'attention, knowledge, and affect' in identifying with brands (Zwick *et al.* 2008: 176). This is post-Fordist. Consumer discipline, on the other hand, can be thought of as the skills which we acquire, and the labour we perform, in learning how to submit to what corporations demand of us as consumers, such as clearing away our own tables at McDonald's 'restaurants', or putting together flat-pack furniture bought at Ikea. Correspondingly, Fordist advertising, which pre-vailed in the US from the 1930s to the 1960s, draws on scientific management to demand that consumers obey the marketers' paternal authority (Holt 2002: 81). Or as Arvidsson has it, the difference is that brands 'work *with* the free-dom of consumers, they say not "You Must!" But "You May!"' (2006: 8, italics in original).

Going beyond this, Marxism shades into Foucauldianism when theorists such as Arvidsson invoke 'bio-political governance: a governance that works from below by shaping the context in which freedom is exercised' (2005: 246). While some theorists in this vein conceptualise a total apparatus of control that ensures 'the smooth functioning of capitalist accumulation' (Hearn 2008: 213), Arvidsson sees a system seeking to manage the social contra-dictions between production and consumption via brand management. This is a balancing act rather than a regime of discipline:

> management must allow for a certain mobility of the brand image ... At the same time this mobility must be controlled and kept within the boundaries of the intended brand identity.... brand management works by enabling or empowering the freedom of consumers *so that it is likely to evolve in particular direction.*
>
> (2005: 244, italics in original)

In this formulation, the theoretical possibility remains open that brand man-agement is not always able to shape consumer choices to its will. Since popular culture, especially in its more subversive manifestations, is 'beyond the control of capital', there is always an opening for critique and resistance. We return to this theme later in the chapter.

Now it's personal

The diffusion of the concept of 'lifestyle' in the 1980s as the foundation of postmodern brand marketing was alluded to in Chapter 1. In that context, influential social theorist Mike Featherstone (1987) cites the thesis of 'cultural intermediaries' that Pierre Bourdieu put forward in his classic work, *Distinction* (1984). This term refers to a new class, a petite bourgeoisie 'who provide symbolic goods and services' in an emergent economy of consumption (1984: 310). For Bourdieu, they are leaders of taste and style, who, on one hand, maintain affinities with the intellectuals and act as a vanguard of the traditional, production-based bourgeoisie; while on the other, perform the role of cultural entrepreneurs, propagating their 'expressive and liberated lifestyles' amongst the popular classes (Featherstone 1987: 90–91). Bourdieu specifically names, as members of this class, managers in advertising and the media, key creative industries which bring 'the art of living' into everyday life (1984: 310), not unlike the 'aestheticization' process later conceptualised by Lash and Urry (1994).

Looking beyond its managers alone to advertising as an occupation and as an institution, Sean Nixon criticises Featherstone's interpretation of the cultural intermediaries concept for its lack of an empirical basis, and its neglect of the actual differences to be found within the whole category of advertising workers (2003). Other observers point out that advertising workers, like creative workers in general, are still workers, by no means an 'aristocracy of labour', and have to survive in an environment of uncertainty. Younger workers in particular who have grown up in the era of neoliberalism have been characterised as 'the precarious generation', obliged to constantly prove themselves in highly competitive and insecure circumstances of employment (Ross 2009: 6).

However much the metaphor of 'immaterial labour' might highlight the input which consumers make to their own subjection in a postmodern economy of brands, in a quite literal way we can rather think of producers in the creative industries as immaterial labour, and a commonsense view suggests that the same cultural pressures will be even more acute for creative workers in contemporary 'enterprise culture' (du Gay 1996). Rushkoff despairs that 'turning into a recognizable brand icon oneself' has become an adaptive strategy in a world of production and consumption defined by brands and corporations, and cites the advice of a self-styled personal branding consultant, Tom Peters,

> ... for anyone who's interested in what it takes to stand out and prosper in the new world of work ... We are CEOs of our own companies: Me Inc. To be in business today, our most important job is to be head marketer for the brand called You.
>
> (quoted in Rushkoff 2009: 142)

Thus, 'the branded self sits at the nexus of discourses of neoliberalism, flexible accumulation, radical individualism, and spectacular promotionalism' (Hearn 2008: 201). As Andrew Wernick has argued comprehensively in his *Promotional Culture* (1991), 'promotional discourse' has become a 'cultural dominant' which can be seen in various situations of competitive individualism, manifested across a whole range of institutional realms beyond media and advertising, not least academia and the university (1991: 183). However, advertising personnel are uniquely positioned as cultural or 'promotional intermediaries' (Aronczyk and Powers 2010: 9), not only because the institution of advertising as such mediates between production and consumption, but because they are themselves consumers as well as producers. This is particularly true of creative personnel.

While advertising 'creatives' distinguish themselves as such professionally, they still are consumers and inhabitants of the world of popular culture from which they derive their inspiration. The convergence of production and consumption thus works both ways. For example, Pountain and Robins argue that advertising 'is not merely a cynical manoeuvre perpetrated by manipulated outsiders whose real interests lie elsewhere', but, harking back to Frank's account referred to above of how counter-cultural opposition became absorbed into 'hip consumerism', they say, 'this mediocracy [of advertising and media personnel] knows how to employ Cool as a selling tool, how to manipulate its icons, precisely because it makes sense to them, it reflects their own values' (2000: 169). Again, Nixon's landmark study of advertising practitioners in London agencies in the 1990s finds that the 'new lad' style of marketing fashionable in the UK at that time was derived from the close identification which the young male creative workers themselves had with 'laddish' forms of consumer behaviour and lifestyle (2003: 165–66).

Since the 1990s, various governments around the world have identified their 'creative industries', including advertising, as national assets: resources to be fostered, cultural activities with economic value (Yúdice 2003). In particular, the creativity of British advertising has been lionised in various ways, notably in the bestowing of knighthoods on figures such as WPP CEO Martin Sorrell. Meanwhile, in the US, advertising agencies have been celebrating their 'creative revolution' since the 1960s (Frank 1998). However, as explained in Chapter 2, there has developed a structural separation between the traditional creative and the specialist media-buying functions of advertising agencies. This division amplifies a longstanding and ubiquitous distinction amongst advertising personnel, even from the days of full-service agencies, between the 'creatives' and the 'suits', those responsible for the business side of the industry. This can be seen in turn as a manifestation of the peculiar fusion of culture and economy which is advertising. Yet even if agency executives see their creatives as a problem to be managed, they also value creativity as the asset which attracts and holds clients. The agencies have their own very considerable investment in the valorisation of creativity and in their mediating role between advertiser clients and their consumer targets. Anne Cronin's interviews with UK agency practitioners make it evident that they see their business as 'a very unstable and competitive field' in which their agencies themselves are brands (as they are often referred to in the trade press), so part of their job becomes 'continually pitching their agency's creative and commercial talents to existing clients and potential clients in a reflexive self-promotional strategy' (2004b: 342).

The creatives, for their part, have a vested interest in maintaining the perception of creativity as an agency's greatest asset, and this is turn motivates self-branding and an 'obsession' with creativity as 'a strategy of distinction' in 'an intensely competitive world of work' (Nixon 2003: 162). Indeed, for all the current discourse on user-generated content and co-creation, the blurring of the line between amateur and professional, and the metaphorical critique of consumption as work, advertising creative personnel evidently retain a clear understanding of the value of having a paid job, and of the branding of their identity as creatives as an essential means to that. Similarly, it is because there are so many young people who are outside the industry but who aspire to securing paid creative employment that their self-branding activities make them vulnerable to exploitation, a reserve army of creative labour (Carah 2011). For those who are on the inside, their career advancement usually involves moving from one agency to another, rather than advancing within the same one, and this will depend on self-branding performances such as their capacity to garner awards, and to make themselves known on 'the industry circuit of award ceremonies, launches and the wider social networks of the industry' (Nixon 2003: 72). These aspects of advertising work are abundantly evident in the trade journals, which, apart from bearing news about the latest changes in client–agency pairings, provide details of the movement of personnel from one agency to another, and reports from a complex world of creative awards which extends from the local to the global.

Rushkoff's judgement is that 'today's system of control depends on a society fastidiously cultivated to see the corporation and its logic as central to its welfare, value, and very identity' (2009: xxiv). In that perspective, advertising personnel, at least creatives in particular, can indeed be seen as cultural intermediaries, both in the sense that they pick up and popularise new styles of consumption, and that they themselves are committed performers of the self-branding practices which global corporations seek to foster in all of our subjective identities, as workers and consumers alike.

Regulating advertising in the public interest

Online behavioural advertising

To return from the actual to the virtual labour market, the issue of online behavioural targeting advertising was raised in Chapter 3: this is when social media send you advertising based on the information which has been gathered from your computer, silently tracking your interests, whether you were aware of that or not. Critical theorists argue that because our freely-chosen online behaviours are being monitored so as to collect information that can then be used to sell us goods and services that this, too, is immaterial labour, in which we produce ourselves as economically valuable resources for advertisers. This informational environment positions each of us, once again, as an 'entrepreneurial self' (Arvidsson 2006: 132–33). Social networking requires that we behave as individuals: ethicist Christine Rosen has called this structured mode of individual expression 'egocasting'. This is 'the thoroughly personalized and extremely narrow pursuit of one's personal taste' in 'a world where we exercise an unparalleled degree of control over what we watch and what we hear' (2005: 52, 67). Yet at the same time as consumers in 'a sea of information' are given 'a chance to differentiate themselves by navigating a wealth of choices', they are permitting others 'to capture and exploit the information they generate in so doing' (Andrejevic 2009: 32). This is what we have referred to already as the empowerment-exploitation paradox of social media.

While many internet users may be naïve or indifferent about having their online behaviour monitored and tracked, such as with 'cookies' routinely being placed as they visit particular sites, there are users' advocacy groups that have taken up the issues posed, and have lobbied governments to assert some control. As indicated in Chapter 3, privacy is the paramount concern, but there are also questions about, for example, the ownership and security of data generated by users, dramatically demonstrated in the 2011 case of the extensive hacking of Sony's Playstation Network (Wakabayashi 2011).

By the end of the 2000s, governments had begun to accept the need for regulation. Over 2006 and 2007 in the UK, a behavioural targeting company, Phorm, conducted trials in conjunction with British Telecom, in which individuals' page views were scanned without their knowledge, and they were sent targeted ads accordingly. In spite of the public outcry which resulted when this became known, there were no laws at that time under which the obvious breach of privacy could be prosecuted. The European Union rebuked the UK for its lack of an independent authority, the looseness of its concept of consent, and the weakness of its sanctions (Hall 2009; 'BT avoids online privacy case' 2011). The Internet Advertising Bureau (IAB), the industry's professional association, did go on to develop a voluntary 'good practice' code, but when the EU's e-Privacy Directive became law in the UK in May 2011, it went further than the IAB's code's opt-out provisions, requiring businesses to obtain 'explicit consent' from internet users before any cookie could be placed on their computer ('New net rules set to make cookies crumble' 2011). Meanwhile, in the US, a bipartisan bill was introduced to Congress that also went beyond rationalising pre-existing self-regulatory arrangements, to require companies to give clear notice to users about what information was being collected from them and why ('Proposed privacy law serves notice to online ad companies' 2011). In response to a growing call for a 'Do Not Track' register in Australia at that stage, the industry formed an association, the Australian Digital Advertising Alliance, to establish a voluntary good practice code and an inquiry website as the IAB had done in the UK, but the government was considering compulsory opt-out provisions (Frith 2011).

Thus, with these moves towards regulation, the irony is that, in the era of reflexive modernisation, privacy has become a matter of public interest. As we have seen above, the internet is a vehicle for expressive individualism and personal branding, particularly via the wildly popular social media. The interest of government in this is not just a response to the user pressure groups that are alert to the vulnerabilities, but is consistent with broader principles of what government sees itself to be for, albeit attenuated by the neoliberal mood of the times. That is, although many, perhaps most, individuals may not care about the information about themselves which they are constantly surrendering (nor even less about the 'work' involved), government sees a need to intervene on their behalf. This is not so much the 'nanny state' seeking to save individuals from themselves, as some critics see restrictions on alcohol and tobacco advertising, but more like statutory forms of regulation aimed specifically at 'unfair and deceptive acts or practices in commerce', to borrow a phrase from the relevant code of the US Federal Trade Commission (FTC). Traditional areas subject to such regulation, that is, not necessarily by advertising regulatory authorities, are the marketing of pharmaceuticals, therapeutic goods and financial services. The recent government initiatives noted above in fostering privacy regulation suggests that the internet has come to be seen as a 'public good', the commercial and civil benefits of which can be undermined by deceptive practice. As Cronin shows, there is a long history of advertising regulation, but that has tended to focus on what is assumed to be 'the powerfully persuasive effect of advertising's textual address': that is, on advertisements (2004a: 45). The issues raised by regulating to protect the 'new media consumer citizen', as against the 'vulnerable mass media subject' of the past 'extend well beyond the effects of advertising texts, to how consumers come to be targeted by certain types of advertising in the first place', notably behavioural targeting (Spurgeon 2008: 87).

While there is some statutory regulation governing advertising on the books in the US (as in the case of the FTC just cited), the UK (notably the Independent Television Commission Codes) and Australia (mainly in the Competition and Consumer Act), the advertisers and agencies in these and many other countries, in the face of pressure from consumer, community and environment groups, have sought strenuously to keep statutory regulation to a minimum, and to set up their own self-regulation arrangements instead. All within the last 50 years or so, the Advertising Standards Authority was set up in the UK; the US industry established its National Advertising Division and National Advertising Review Council; and in Australia the Advertising Standards Bureau and Board were implemented (Cronin 2004a; Mattelart 1991). These are bodies which are funded by the advertising industry in each case, but operate with formal independence and greater or lesser degrees of cooperation with government.

As Mattelart has argued, the trend to minimise regulation is similar, but distinct from, the drive to privatisation which has characterised the neoliberal economic policies which have become the orthodoxy of the West. It shifts authority from public to private institutions, and pits the free speech of the citizen against notions such as 'commercial free speech' (1991: 87). Yet while cynics might deride self-regulation as putting the fox in charge of the hen-house, in practice 'co-regulation' has been the price paid by the manufacturing/marketing/media complex to stay free of statutory control, at least in the UK and Australia. This is where government agencies require advertisers, agencies and media to devise and uphold their own codes in areas such as television advertising. So, it is not as if 'self-regulation' means the total relinquishment of government authority. Rather, the industry has sought and been granted an institutional structure which keeps statutory regulation at bay in return for ostensibly responsible conduct. Yet, as we shall see, such arrangements have proven to be much more satisfactory to the industry than to consumers and their organisations.

The case of childhood obesity

Advertising has been for some time the object of much public debate about eating disorders, such as concerns about its role in fostering unrealistic body images. More recently, attention has turned towards the extent to which advertising is implicated in what has become a bona fide public health issue throughout the world, namely obesity, especially amongst children. This is both a local issue, in that it has mobilised concerned parents' groups at community level, and a global one, in that it raises questions about the commercialisation of food in general within global culture. Importantly, although this public debate has focused specifically upon television advertising, this is often more a metonym not just for advertising in general, but the whole host of marketing practices pursued by FMCG corporations in fast food franchises and soft-drink, cereal and snack food manufacturing. These include giveaways, contests and events, all 'below the line' promotional methods which do not involve the purchase of media time or space, even for example, driveway signage and point-of-sale material in fast food outlets. A good part of this public disquiet about television advertising and childhood obesity has arisen in a wider context of apprehension about a quite evident trend for commercial interests to cultivate children as a market (Frith and Mueller 2003; Schor 2004). One commentator in the US, where this tendency began, refers to 'the consumer group formerly known as children. ... Children are the darlings of corporate America' (Linn 2004: 1). Whether the focus on children's television advertising is because of its high visibility, or because it is a certain kind of advertising over which regulation is politically possible, that is where the blame for obesity has been directed by community groups. At the same time, medical authorities have been urging governments to act against television advertising of food to children, in the UK, the US, Australia and elsewhere. That is, there is a 'discourse' taking place in the everyday sense of a public debate, one in which medical bodies and advocacy groups are lined up against the corporate interests of food advertisers, their agencies and the media.

Looking over the extensive research, obesity is said to be 'multi-factorial' (Young 2003): that is, the primary factors of physical activity and diet are mediated in a highly complex manner by sociocultural, genetic and environmental variables, and television watching itself seems to be a factor. Thus, children's ethnic inheritance; how close they live to a public park, as against a McDonald's outlet; and how much they watch television (as distinct from how many ads they see), are all part of their whole 'obesogenic' environment. There is no 'smoking gun' apparent, so it becomes a matter of faith rather than science, in which the interested parties can choose the research which legitimises their own position, and repudiate or ignore all the rest. This ambiguity is a source of comfort to all the interest groups with a stake in food advertising to children on television, that is, the manufacturing/marketing/media complex, while for the critics, it means that the necessary hard evidence of a demonstrable causal link between advertising as such and childhood obesity eludes them. In this situation, the food advertising interests always can evade the charges against them, while the critics have to make their stand on the basis of circumstantial rather than scientific evidence, fortified by their own visceral convictions.

Nevertheless, governments have responded by putting regulatory regimes in place, but these differ greatly in their form and effectiveness. The UK system is one of the strictest in the world, with a ban, introduced in 2006, on the advertising of HFSS – products that are high in salt, fat or sugar – during children's airtime. A review in 2010 concluded that it had been successful in reducing children's exposure (Ofcom 2010). In the US, the federal government has been seeking to establish standards to which the industry would voluntarily submit, but is facing industry resistance in favour of its own self-regulatory regime under looser standards (Neuman 2010). In Australia, there is a 'co-regulation' regime: a complex mix of statutory regulation supported by voluntary codes formulated by the relevant industry associations, but which falls far short of the extensive bans that the lobby groups are demanding (Parents Jury 2010; Sandev 2011).

Given the strengthening will of government, pressure from the constellation of professional organisations and community-based groups looking more and more like an emergent social consensus, and advertisers' fear of possible litigation from consumers, corporations have had to respond concretely to public concerns. In the US, Kraft is amongst several major advertisers that have cut back on the advertising of foods high in fat and sugar. In Australia, McDonald's claims to have reduced its advertising in children's viewing time by 60 per cent since 2001 (Lee 2005). While it is difficult to gauge the international influence of public criticism, it seems more than a coincidence that McDonald's committed itself to promoting 'healthy menu options' within a year of the global screening of *Super Size Me*, Morgan Spurlock's 2004 film about McDonald's (Smith 2006).

Thus, even if it is only in defence of their own interests, global corporations have been obliged to respond to local community concerns, particularly as in this case, when they are amplified with professional support on a public health issue.

The greening of advertising

Another major area in which the manufacturing-marketing/media/complex has shown itself responsive to public concerns, albeit on its own terms and only to the extent necessary, is the issue of advertising and the environment. While significant pockets of diehard climate change sceptics remain, since the 1960s and 1970s there has been a growing public consciousness of the impact which human behaviour has been having upon the environment, particularly as regards consumption and waste. At first, works such as *The Limits to Growth* (Meadows 1972) met with a controversial public reception, and environmental concerns were regarded as problems only for the counter-culture cranks and hippies in activist organisations such as Friends of the Earth. However, subsequent decades have seen environmental problems become mainstream political issues, thanks to international advocacy by the United Nations, national government initiatives, and the channelling of green activism into parliamentary parties.

In the critical literature, advertising is deeply implicated as a prime force behind the 'culture of consumption' embedded in modern subjectivities (Gabriel and Lang 2006: 17). It is believed to have 'an exceptionally powerful impact on consumers' outlooks, desires and shopping patterns' on a global scale (Myers and Kent 2004: 124). In addition to its general influence in fostering demand by investing products with attractive cultural meanings, advertising is seen specifically to encourage consumer desires for eternal novelty. Thus, in performing its traditional function of closing the gap between production and consumption, advertising also accelerates the turnover rate at which consumers discard their old goods for new ones, and so contributes to global waste (Schor 2010: 40–41).

Yet while consumers still continue to buy advertised products like cars and white goods periodically, and elaborately-packaged FMCG on a daily basis, a vague cultural awareness has arisen that something needs to be done, as evidenced by the dutiful take-up of domestic rubbish recycling in several countries over recent years (Hawkins 2006). Corporations tapped into this feeling early on with an approach to advertising that quickly became dubbed by environmentalists as 'greenwashing'. Investigative activist group Corpwatch defines this as 'The phenomenon of socially and environmentally destructive corporations attempting to preserve and expand their markets by posing as friends of the environment', and gives as example that, as of Earth Day 1990, a quarter of new household products in the US were advertised as 'recyclable' or similar (Corpwatch 2001). More than the labelling and advertising of products, greenwashing extends into corporate public relations and rebranding, perhaps the most egregious example being British Petroleum's attempt to make BP stand for 'Beyond Petroleum'. This kind of cynical exploitation of public sentiment has been counterproductive, however, causing consumers to lose even more confidence in advertising (Smart 2010: 205).

So, recognising that such a 'brand risk' is involved in failing to respond credibly to environmental concerns, some leading global manufacturers of FMCG, including the world's biggest advertiser, Procter & Gamble, are seeking to develop environmentally responsible products and packaging. Coca-Cola and PepsiCo are working on bottles made from renewable materials, for example. Their motivation is 'at once altruistic and mercenary', says the 'director of sustainability' at Nestlé, while counterparts in other corporations concede that these efforts are being made in order to head off any threat of statutory regulation ('Brand giants get green' 2011). Similarly, the US and global retailer Walmart has taken a leading role in laying down sustainability criteria for their suppliers and their products to meet, but claim that this is in response to customer demand ('Move over government' 2011). Meanwhile in the UK, a 2011 study of 300 firms on the London Stock Exchange found that nearly all had environmental policies, a measurable increase over two years before, but very few were 'adequately managing' their environmental footprint ('Gillette leads eco charts' 2011).

So far, consumers are not impressed. A US industry study in 2011 found that 75 per cent of respondents wanted more transparency and meaningful information in packaging and advertising, while more than half said they had little confidence in corporate claims to green credentials ('"Green gap" persists in US' 2011). This compares to a previous study in the UK that had found that although environmental concerns played a major part in purchase decisions for two-thirds of the sample, 70 per cent said that advertising does not help them to establish which companies have credible claims ('Green issues still matter to UK shoppers' 2009). In any case, environmentalist critics argue that consumers' access to reliable information, and being able to understand it, is not enough: 'it is questionable whether "buying green" constitutes a sufficiently effective response to the scale and gravity of environmental concerns' (Smart 2010: 202).

In other words, this is about much more than advertising. Even if corporations and their products all truly met valid sustainability standards and could convey that credibly in their advertising to consumers, that would only be dealing with a minor and superficial part of the global environmental problem. What is at stake is the challenge of the environmental crisis to the 'consumer society' model itself, from the 'overconsumption' of the developed countries (Humphery 2010) to its embrace by the 'new consumers' of the developing world (Myers and Kent 2004).

'Resistance is futile'

> At this point, mainstream environmentalism stalls out, for it has not yet
> focused on developing a politically practical language for analyzing and con-
> fronting the explosion of wants ... What instead emerges is simplistic mor-
> alizing about consumption that little advances the intellectual analysis or
> collective action necessary for taking on the consumption question. This mor-
> alizing takes three forms: rhetorical lambasting of advertising, condemnation
> of the immorality of overconsumption, and a rosy-eyed, apolitical romantici-
> zation of the joys of simple living.
>
> (Maniates 2002: 206)

It is thus consumption, rather than advertising as such, which is now the issue.
However, advertising is seen as having a unique role in generating not only consumption, but the whole complex of problems which has been addressed in the
barrage of anti-globalisation books that have appeared at least since the turn of the
century – not only the environment, broadly understood, but related issues such as
the use of public space, identity politics, outsourced labour, human rights and
global inequality. One of the most influential of such works, Naomi Klein's *No
Logo* (2000), drew attention to the growth of organised resistance to advertising in
the form of 'culture jamming'. This began as the creative defacement of billboards
in the 1980s, such as by the Australian group BUGA UP (Billboard Utilising
Graffitists Against Unhealthy Promotions), and became institutionalised with the
Adbusters Media Foundation in Vancouver. Adbusters publishes a magazine, and
in more recent years, maintains a website, in the cause of 'mental envir-
onmentalism', and the 'uncooling' of brands. With their 'noncommercials', 'sub-
vertisements' and other media parodies, Adbusters wages 'meme warfare' against
corporate advertising with a missionary zeal (Adbusters 2011; Bordwell 2002).

As Pountain and Robins observe, the predominant ethos of Cool in youth-
oriented marketing favours apolitical and ultimately acquiescent consumption,
since 'ironic detachment is ... extremely difficult to harness to any sort of
collective endeavour' (2000: 174). Hence, Adbusters' project of uncooling is

Figure 4.1 Culture jamming: BUGA UP's creative defacement of a billboard makes a
protest against plastic bottles

intended as a form of seeding and spreading active resistance to advertising. However, Adbusters also has its critics. Notably, Joseph Heath and Andrew Potter (also Canadian, like Klein and Adbusters) take a position in line with Frank's argument cited earlier in this chapter about 'the conquest of cool', namely that even this form of explicit resistance can be co-opted by the manufacturing/marketing/media complex (2004). Klein agrees, and goes further, casting the issue in the context of coolhunting: 'There will always be new spaces to colonize – whether physical or mental – and there will always be an ad that will be able to penetrate the latest strain of consumer cynicism'. Typical of her examples is Coca-Cola's 'Image is nothing ... Obey your thirst' campaign for Sprite (2000: 298–300). From such a viewpoint, Adbusters' and other forms of subcultural resistance are doing 'work' for capitalism, by showing where the bounds of opposition lie, and articulating its forms. It can even be argued that the dialectic between subcultural resistance and the continuous drive to co-opt it is the leading edge of commercial cultural innovation, or as Holt puts it: 'What has been termed "consumer resistance" is actually a form of market-sanctioned cultural experimentation through which the market rejuvenates itself' (2002: 89).

So, if the 'rhetorical lambasting of advertising' turns out to be so counter-productive, what about the other forms of moral suasion listed by Maniates – condemnation and lifestyle responses? The very concepts of 'consumerism' and 'overconsumption' are themselves heavily laden with 'a high moralism' (Humphery 2010: 7). This gives a tone of exasperated denunciation of the consuming masses to a number of recent books, including three – one in the UK, one in the US, and one in Australia – all with the same title, *Affluenza*. Using the metaphor of consumerism as social disease, blame is laid on consumers for allowing themselves to be lulled into a state of false consciousness by emulation of each other, and of course, by advertising (Humphery 2010: 35–36). As for lifestyle responses, those consumers who pursue a greater or lesser degree of 'voluntary simplicity' may find themselves co-opted by the advertisements in 'new age' magazines with titles like *Simplicity* (Maniates 2002: 230), and caught up in 'green consumerism'(Smart 2010: 206), which could range from eating 'ethical eggs' to buying a Prius. At the extreme end of this trend are the 'bourgeois bohemians', or 'Bobos'. These new cultural intermediaries 'express their conscience in their consumerism', such as riding in their luxury four-wheel drive 'to the nearest haute-design shops and local purveyors of Third World treasures' (Wittstock 2000). Yet if the critics continue to only ever seek the higher moral ground, it is difficult to see where real change is to come from.

Advertising and the nation

Brands and national belonging

For all the contemporary rhetoric about globalisation, the fact remains that it is the nation-state which is the dominant and effective unit of political, economic, and cultural organisation in the world. However porous their borders have become to transnational influences, sovereign national governments still are ultimately responsible for the running of national economies and for holding together a national culture. The historian Benedict Anderson famously referred to the nation in the latter sense as an 'imagined community' (1983), but whereas he saw 'print capitalism' as first bringing about such a modern consciousness, it has been argued in Chapter 1 that commercial television has more recently led so many contemporary nations to become 'imagined communities of consumption' (Foster 1991: 250). Thus, in addition to the various traditional popular cultural forms, narratives of national belonging, and the 'shared meanings' of nationhood which are expressed in televisual and media culture in general, it is also the case that branded goods and services, 'as advertised on television', and elsewhere, now become mediators of membership of the nation (Sinclair 2008a).

When we talk about national identity, we not only mean the identity of the nation in relation to other nations, but also the identity of those persons who see themselves as belonging to the nation, and for whom that is a dimension of their personal identity. The images and narratives in advertising can be powerful vehicles of myth, in the sense used by Roland Barthes in his classic analysis of how nationhood in France was expressed in images of goods (1973). Holt argues that the most important of such myths, as in this case, 'concern how citizens are linked to the nation-building project', insofar as these myths motivate and are performed in acts of everyday consumption of advertised goods that encourage the consumer to identify with the 'populist world' of the nation (2004: 57–58). In this sense, national identity can be taken to refer to things as well as persons. To the extent that governments have progressively given over their authority to commercial interests and 'market forces' as the guardians of national culture and identity, the 'official nationalism' of the nation-state is now infused with what has been called the 'commercial nationalism' of the market (James 1983: 79). Thus, in advertising, people are addressed in their capacity as members of the nation, but as consumers, not as citizens, nevertheless calling upon the same 'trust, affect and shared meanings' involved in national belonging (Arvidsson 2005: 236).

In the golden age of mass media, advertising was seen by both its critics and advocates not only as an expression of the times, but also of the place: that is, the nation. To speak of 'advertising' meant advertisements for the nationally-marketed brands which a given people came to know from the TVCs, radio jingles, newspaper and magazine pages, and billboards that formed the commercial environment of the nation. As already suggested in previous chapters, the global brands of today had local origins: for example, Coca-Cola had to build its market from its origins in the city of Atlanta to the state of Georgia, then to other southern states and eventually the US as a nation before it could become a multinational, transnational or global corporation (Pendergrast 2000). Similarly, the capacity of companies to grow to national scale depended on parallel growth in the media which could carry their advertising. The particular role of nationally-networked broadcast television in the golden age of mass media has already been remarked upon in Chapter 2.

As for the advertising agencies, they are crucial 'not only in mediating the economic strategies of clients, but also in culturally defining the geographic boundaries of markets and consumer identities' (Leslie 1995: 411). In the context of nation-building and consolidation, advertising thus addresses consumer-citizens in terms of their national belonging: in the context of globalisation, the formation of transnational markets calls for different consumer identities, based on factors such as mobility, ethnicity and regional belonging.

Advertising and minorities in the era of transnational markets

One of the principal features of the global era is the large-scale transnational movement of peoples, yielding a complex 'ethnoscape' of immigrant minorities in most countries of the world (Appadurai 1990). Given the advertising and brand-saturated cultural environment of contemporary capitalism, in conjunction with the trend to ever more fragmented and hence targetable audiences, we might expect the resultant culturally diverse minorities to attract intensive commercial exploitation as consumer markets via 'ethnic' media. For example, one might think that with the settlement needs which burgeoning populations of new immigrants have in setting up a household, they would form a target market for a wide range of goods and services, from electrical appliances to health insurance, or that advertising in selected minority languages would be an effective way to reach longer-established, even second-generation migrants who are still most comfortable with their language of origin, and can not be easily reached through mainstream media. Yet, on the contrary, one of the anomalous aspects of the increased movements of peoples across borders in recent decades is that they are for the most part ignored by the large corporate advertisers in their countries of destination. Even in mass media advertising such as TVCs, members of minorities are represented far less frequently than their actual incidence in the population, and then often only as walk-on stereotypes that can be recognised by majority audiences (Institute of Practitioners of Advertising 2011).

Most advertiser avoidance of minority marketing has to do with uncertainty about the target. Often there is a perception that minorities, particularly recently-arrived immigrants and refugees, do not have enough spending power to be worth the effort, while with long-established groups, the perception is that they will have assimilated and do not require any special targeting. The sheer diversity of the range of minorities now present in countries of immigrant destination is another reason why advertisers might not want to engage in minority marketing. This is a problem of 'critical mass', in the sense that each prospective minority audience is too small and perhaps also too widely distributed to be reached on a cost-effective basis (Sinclair and Cunningham 2001: 22). Sometimes marketers have sought to deal with this by the 'aggregation' of minorities who seem to have some factor in common, but this runs the risk that the category so created will be too abstracted to have any sense of identification for the target groups. Furthermore, when it fails to attract them, this becomes a self-justifying reason why advertisers feel that 'minority marketing' doesn't work (Pires and Stanton 2005). Even such a successful marketing category as that of 'Hispanics' in the US is really an aggregation, and it is not necessarily accepted by people who see themselves primarily as Mexican Americans, Cuban Americans and so on (Dávila 2001). Another reason may be where advertisers fear that their brand will become associated with an ethnic underclass, or more defensibly, where they reject the use of minority media because these media can not provide audited circulation or audience figures. The media of minority communities suffer as a result of the fact that large advertisers favour the mainstream media attended to by the dominant majority, and in the same process, the minorities themselves are disenfranchised from the national culture.

On the other hand, the resistance or mere indifference which large advertisers show towards minority marketing should not be exaggerated, since there are several major corporations that do take it seriously, and both the advertising industry and government advocate it in certain markets. The British Institute of Practitioners of Advertising, for example, has encouraged advertisers to pursue 'the brown pound', but at the same time, regulators warn against the traps of tokenism and stereotypes in doing so, advertisements directed to ethnic minorities being subject to the same tendencies to stereotype them as when ethnic minorities are represented in mainstream advertisements ('Advertisers miss out on ethnic pound' 2003). In Australia, government subsidises minority media and offers awards for 'multicultural marketing' (Sinclair 2009b). The mode and degree to which minority marketing is institutionalised varies considerably from one country to another, and indeed, from one minority to another: 'some ethnic groups are more different than others' (Pires and Stanton 2005: 79).

For example, we can contrast the case of Spanish-speakers in the US with that of Chinese-speakers in Australia. The Spanish-speaking minorities in the US, aggregated for purposes of governmentality and marketing as 'Hispanics', amount to more than 15 per cent of the population, and are in a unique position in that they are served not only by two national television networks, but also abundant local press and radio media. The scale of this audience is great enough to merit the production of both programming and advertising specifically for and by them, but although the networks attract many mainstream corporate advertisers, this is partly because the cost of advertising is cheaper, so there is some sense of a discount for difference. The Australian Chinese, at around 2 per cent of the population, form a minority group with enough critical mass to exist as a market and sustain local media, though when it comes to television, they have no locally available, only global narrowcast, services (Sinclair 2009b).

In both cases, these minorities are aristocrats relative to the very many other minorities in their respective countries, most of whom struggle to maintain their local media, and are marginalised from the mainstream. It might be thought that to remain aloof from the pervasive commercialisation of capitalist modernity is a desirable condition, but if we recall Martin Davidson's argument that 'it is in consumerism that we most express our sense of social belonging' (1992: 123), then to be excluded from consumer culture can be seen as yet another form of alienation from the nation experienced by minorities. National networked free-to-air commercial television, in its dual historical role of nation-building and the forming of national markets for advertisers, has created contemporary developed nations as 'imagined communities of consumption', to cite Robert Foster once again (1991: 250). To be at the margins of the world of goods so created, is to live a restricted form of the citizen-consumership which now links all of us to our contemporary nations, and thus enforces a diminished cultural citizenship.

The nation as brand

Nation-states have their own interests to pursue in promoting images of national unity and belonging, and in cultivating support for their policies both at home and abroad. They do so increasingly as a form of branding – the US has been called 'The mother of all brands' (Anholt and Hildreth 2004), while Cool Britannia (McLaughlin 2002), Australian Made/True Blue (Australian Made 2003) and India Shining (Bijoor 2004) are examples of nation-branding exercises from recent decades, implemented in conjunction with extensive advertising campaigns. That is, the nation itself now presents itself as a brand, both internally and externally. Internally, in the interests of governance and as the custodian of the national culture with which it legitimises its authority, the nation-state addresses its citizens as members of the 'imagined community' of the nation, and hence as participants in its supposed 'deep horizontal comradeship' (Anderson 1983: 6). Externally, many nations now cultivate a brand identity, each seeking to position itself vis-à-vis other nations in the global marketplace, competing in cultural terms for economic objectives such as trade, tourism and investment, or to protect the unique 'nation of origin' status of their exports (Anholt 2000; Moor 2007). In that light, nation branding can be seen as a particular level of place branding in general, since not just nations but states, cities and districts within a given nation now also compete globally for these purposes.

Nation branding has a political dimension, in which a nation may seek to extend its influence via 'public diplomacy' in the form of 'soft power'. In the current literature on globalisation-as-cultural imperialism, this strategy is seen to involve media, marketing and consumption (Fraser 2005). However, of more interest in the present context, is when the nation presents itself as a brand for commercial purposes. An instructive and recent case in point, one which brings together global media, celebrity culture, corporate sponsorship and branded content in a high-profile nation branding exercise, was the 2010 visit to Australia by the *Oprah Winfrey Show*. This was a major step in the Australian federal government's Brand Australia campaign launched that year. The principal sponsor of the event was the national tourism authority, Tourism Australia, buttressed with substantial contributions from state governments and the privatised national air carrier, Qantas. There were also 'partners', mainly the Ten Network, the national broadcast television network which screens the *Oprah Winfrey Show* in Australia, but as well, global corporations such as McDonald's and Motorola, who paid for product placements in the shows that were produced, and in their promotion.

The visit was first announced on a regular *Oprah Winfrey Show* in the US in mid-September, when Oprah invited 300 of her studio audience to join her. Subsequent promotion included a trailer programme watched by ten million Americans, *Oprah's Aussie Countdown*. Early in December, Oprah arrived in Australia with her 300 guests and a crew of 150 (from her own production company, not an advertising agency), travelling widely and very publicly, and shooting what was to become a four-part 'television event', *Oprah's Ultimate Australian Adventure*. This was subsequently shown not only in Australia and in the US, the main target audience, but in all the 145 countries to which the US network CBS distributes the regular show (Meade and Sinclair 2010).

What is remarkable about this spectacular campaign is that it brought together and serves to illustrate several of the key elements in marketing today: the global scale involved in both creating and showing such an event; the mobilisation of national identities, both those of Australia and the US; the exploitation of the contemporary fascination with celebrity, or the person as a brand; the fact that corporate investment took the form of sponsorship rather than advertising; and perhaps most tellingly, the fact that the means of distribution was the 'old' medium of television (albeit with social media tie-ins), for which the campaign supplied high-quality branded content, but without any 'advertising' as such. *Oprah's Ultimate Australian Adventure* can be seen as a preview of a post-advertising future.

This chapter has reviewed a diverse range of social issues in which advertising is implicated, and more often than not, assumed to be guilty by association. Even as new forms of communication displace and disperse the forms of advertising which were ubiquitous and seemingly carried cultural authority in the past, advertising does not go away. On the contrary, as was seen in the previous chapter, it assumes new forms consistent with the rise of social media, while at the same time shoring up traditional media, notably free-to-air television. Social media and marketing have made advertising more of an individual than a collective phenomenon. Thus, instead of the mass manipulation feared by critics of advertising in the past, the concern now is with the willingness of the 'new media consumer citizens' to give up their personal information, to make brands out of themselves, and to 'work' for social media in exchange for opportunities for personal expression and social networking. To the extent that advertising still has a highly visible and public role in social communication, it is the usual suspect in contemporary issues in which there are millions of witnesses, but insufficient evidence for a conviction, namely obesity, and the environment. Finally, even in the global era, advertising has a role not only in defining the nation as a community of consumption, but a say in who belongs to it.

Chapter 5

Advertising, globalisation and world regions

Globalisation is not a total and uniform process, equally affecting every part of the globe, as the word might imply. When it comes to taking a close look at what is actually happening with advertising, the media and globalisation at ground level, it becomes apparent that in fact there are not many truly global advertisers, agencies or media. Although the concept of 'globalisation' flags the territorial ambitions of the manufacturing/marketing/media complex and reflects the fact of their presence in ever more parts of the world, it remains very much a figure of speech, a strategic exaggeration in the ideological rhetoric of globalism. At the beginning of the 2000s, one baseline study showed that the major 'global' corporations at that time made most of their sales within their own world-regional domicile, or within what Kenichi Ohmae called the 'triad' of North America, the European Union and Asia. Even then, of all the companies in the *Fortune 500*, only Coca-Cola had more than 20 per cent of its sales in Asia, while McDonald's had less than 14 per cent (Rugman and Verbeke 2004, 8–9). One might think, then, so much for fears of 'Coca-Colonization' (Kuisel 1991) or 'McDonaldization' (Ritzer 1993). To take another measure, Procter & Gamble, the world's biggest advertiser by far, with over 300 brands (such as Hugo Boss, Max Factor, Olay, Vicks, Braun and Gillette), was spending only 20 per cent of its global advertising expenditure in Asia at that time, even though it appeared amongst the top ten advertisers of most major markets of the region (Endicott 2005). On such evidence, and as Table 5.1 shows, with the singular exception of Japan, the present century began with North America and Europe still the regions with the largest national markets, even if there was already much corporate interest and activity in cultivating fast-growing markets elsewhere in Asia, and in the developing world, notably Brazil, Russia, India and China, as we shall see.

Similarly with the agency holding groups: even in 2008, for example, UK-based WPP produced most of its income in Europe; the US groups Omnicom and Interpublic generated more than half of theirs in North America; and Publicis derived over 80 per cent of theirs more or less equally from both those regions. From the rest of the world – the Asia-Pacific, Middle East, Latin America and Africa, where by far the majority of the world's population

Table 5.1 Global advertising expenditure, 2010 estimates by country

National Market	Adspend 2010	Rank 2010	Rank 2000
United States	$151.5	1	1
Japan	43.3	2	2
Germany	24.6	3	3
China	22.6	4	10
United Kingdom	18.0	5	4
Brazil	14.2	6	12
France	12.9	7	5
Italy	10.8	8	6
Australia	9.4	9	8
Canada	8.9	10	9
Spain	7.9	11	7
Russia	7.8	12	42
South Korea	6.7	13	13
Netherlands	5.2	14	11
India	5.1	15	33

Figures are in billions of US dollars.
Copyrighted 2011 Crain Communications. 75587-nlpf.
('Global Marketers 2010' 2010).

lives – WPP obtained 24 per cent, Omnicom 16, Interpublic 20 and Publicis 18 per cent ('Agency Report 2009'). Yet, as will be seen in this chapter, agencies either wholly or partly-owned by the global groups dominate the advertising markets in most countries of the world. In other words, even if the activities of the manufacturing/marketing/media corporations in the countries outside of their North Atlantic home markets have been a comparatively minor part of their total operations, their presence in those countries may loom large.

Notwithstanding these caveats, this chapter will show how significant shifts are under way which are likely to result in a considerable rebalancing of the territorial investments and income of the global corporations, and at the same time, a substantial extension of their impact in the world outside the North Atlantic, as ever more people are brought into the global consumer culture which they exist to foster. Yet, by looking at selected nations within their regions, it will become evident that the impact of globalisation is mediated by national and regional factors, so that global corporate influence is neither homogeneous nor uncontested.

Regional roundup – trends in major world regions

Given the inherent interconnectedness of nations in the present era, to consider globalisation in any one country is a contradiction in terms. However, if we are truly to understand globalisation, we must take into account its impact within each nation, and in most cases, of each nation in a given region. While it is not feasible to examine the situation in each and every country, this chapter will provide an overview of the major ones in each world region, having regard to the largest advertisers, the most significant agencies, and the state of play between advertising and the media. The annual rankings of the 'top ten' advertisers in each national market, as published by the authoritative US-based but internationally-oriented trade journal, *Advertising Age*, is used here as a comparative measure and source for identifying the largest advertisers, using data for 2009, which became available in 2010. Using top ten lists may be an arbitrary and partial measure, but it does provide a concise way of seeing where most of the money is coming from.

For advertising agencies, however, there are no such rankings. Since the Sarbannes-Oxley Act was passed by US Congress in 2002, annual rankings of agencies based on their declared billings are no longer permitted to be published as they once were routinely by trade, professional and research organisations in various countries of the world. The Act was intended to tighten up rules governing financial disclosure in the US, but precisely because of the globalised nature of the advertising industry, with US-based agencies in every market, it has had the effect internationally of stopping the publication of league tables of agency billings, such as had been available to a previous generation of advertising researchers (Sinclair 2005). Accordingly, while various estimates are available in some instances and cited in the chapter, there is no common and authoritative source for identifying the leading agencies in each national market. As for the distribution of advertising expenditure across the various media, fortunately there are data available from appropriate national bodies in most countries, though it is not always comparative, as the categories used may differ. This is certainly true also, incidentally, of how advertised products and services are categorised from one country to the next. On that score, in what follows here, 'FMCG', fast-moving consumer goods, is used in a broad sense to include fast food as well as packaged food and drink; and health and beauty products along with personal care and household cleaning products.

North America

Although this is a region which geographically includes Canada and Mexico, it is massively dominated by the US, which remains by far the world's largest advertising market. Although it has just 5 per cent of the world's population, the US accounted for 20 per cent of global gross domestic product, and nearly 34 per cent of worldwide advertising expenditure in 2009. Expenditure in Canada, by contrast, although one of the world's top ten advertising markets, amounted to an estimated 2 per cent. Of the largest 100 global advertisers measured by *Advertising Age* that year, 46 of them were US-based, by far the largest number of any other nation. First amongst them, its customary position, was FMCG conglomerate Procter & Gamble, which by then was

Table 5.2 Top ten national advertisers, United States, 2009

Measured media spending	2009	2008	% chg
Procter & Gamble	$4,188.9	$4,838.1	−13.4
Verizon Communications	3,020.0	3,282.6	−8.0
AT&T	2,797.0	3,073.0	−9.0
General Motors	2,214.9	2,825.0	−21.6
Pfizer	2,097.0	1,906.4	10.00
Johnson & Johnson	2,060.9	2,529.2	−18.5
Walt Disney	2,003.8	2,217.6	−9.6
Time–Warner	1,848.1	2,070.6	−10.7
L'Oréal	1,833.6	1,841.8	−0.4
Kraft	1,748.4	1,687.0	3.6

Figures are in millions of US dollars.
Copyrighted 2011 Crain Communications. 75587–nlpf.
('100 Leading National Advertisers 2010' 2010).

investing two-thirds of its measured expenditure and generating 62 per cent of its revenue outside of the US: such a distribution was fairly typical of the top 100 (Johnson 2010). In the other countries of the region, half of Canada's top ten advertisers were US-based corporations, although there were only two in Mexico ('Global Marketers 2010' 2010).

Table 5.2 shows the top ten advertisers within the US national market itself in 2008–9. It would be apparent that media expenditure was well down for most of these advertisers, reflecting the effects of the global financial crisis (GFC) over the period, but the corporations listed are mostly the same as over previous years. By a large margin, Procter & Gamble leads a field of huge telecommunications, automotive, drug, media and assorted FMCG corporations, mostly also global in their operations, though only one of them, L'Oréal, is foreign-based. If this list of US national advertisers is compared with the *Advertising Age* top 100 global advertiser rankings of the same year ('Global Marketers 2010' 2010), only Procter & Gamble is ahead of L'Oréal amongst those advertisers that appear on both lists, followed closely in the global top ten by General Motors, Johnson & Johnson, and Kraft; and with Pfizer, Disney and Time-Warner in the top 25. In other words, of the US top ten, only the two US telecommunications companies are not also global advertisers.

As to agencies, *Advertising Age* has published a ranking of 'Top US Advertising Agencies' for the same period, based on the journal's own estimates of their revenue. To take the top ten of these, all of them are well-known for their operations on a global scale as well as in the US, and are affiliated to one or the other of the global holding companies – six of them with the non-US global groups WPP, Publicis and Havas, while the US groups Interpublic and Omnicom have two each ('Agency Report 2010' 2010). As outlined in Chapter 2, since the 1980s certain iconic US agencies have been taken over by the British and French groups: J Walter Thompson (now JWT) and Leo Burnett, for example, so to that extent, the US advertising agency business itself has been the object as well as an agent of globalisation.

As noted above, advertising expenditure was down in 2008–9 in response to the GFC, the sharpest fall ever recorded in these rankings, but the distribution of this expenditure across the various advertising media was consistent with previous trends: that is, newspapers and magazines had the biggest falls, along with television and radio 'spot' advertising. Although the internet's share increased, it was still attracting only a relatively small proportion of the whole, less than 8 per cent, compared to over 48 per cent for all television advertising, 35 per cent for all print, 6 per cent for radio and less than 3 per cent for outdoor ('Total US Advertising Spending by Medium, 2010 Edition' 2010).

Europe

As shown in Table 5.1, Europe embraces six of the world's top 15 advertising markets, as based on estimates of 2010 expenditure by Publicis media agency ZenithOptimedia. In order of size, these are Germany, the UK, France, Italy, Spain and the Netherlands. The table also shows their ranking at the beginning of the decade, from which we can see some downward movement, slight in most cases: much more striking has been the degree of upward movement by China, Brazil, Russia and India, to be examined later in the chapter. Note, incidentally, that these 15 markets account for nearly 78 per cent of total world advertising expenditure ('Global Marketers 2010' 2010).

We will examine the UK situation in some detail below, but without making an exhaustive identification and analysis of the top ten advertisers for each of the other European markets, let the following summary suffice:

- In Germany, large supermarket chains such as Metro Group and Aldi are prominent, along with Volkswagen, German media groups, and global advertisers based elsewhere in Europe, namely L'Oréal, Ferrero and Unilever. The only US-based global advertiser is the ubiquitous Procter & Gamble. Note that Aldi and Volkswagen are also global advertisers.
- In France, L'Oréal heads a list of predominantly French and other corporations in media, automotive, telecommunications and retail fields, once again with Procter & Gamble being the only US presence. There are six French global advertisers on this list: L'Oréal, Vivendi, PSA Peugeot-Citroën, Renault, France Telecom and Carrefour.
- Italian telecommunications, FMCG (products such as Barilla pasta and Ferrero's Nutella for example), media and automotive companies form the majority of that country's top ten, two of which are global advertisers, with three other European-based global advertisers and, needless to add, Procter & Gamble rounding out the list.
- In Spain, global corporations based elsewhere in Europe predominate, in automotive, finance and FMCG fields, with the Corte Inglés retail chain

and the global telecommunications company, Telefónica, the only Spanish companies listed. From the US, Johnson & Johnson are there – in addition to Procter & Gamble.

- The top advertiser in the Netherlands is the Anglo-Dutch FMCG conglomerate Unilever, which is second only to its great rival Procter & Gamble as a global advertiser. Reflecting Dutch culture, there is also a dairy and a coffee corporation, along with a telecommunications and a retail company, while the global advertisers are L'Oréal and the British household FMCG company Reckitt-Benckiser from Europe, and Coca-Cola, Kraft, and Procter & Gamble from the US ('Global Marketers 2010' 2010).

Looking now at the UK, the most notable feature on Table 5.3 is that the largest advertiser is the British Government. The Central Office of Information (COI) exists to rationalise and control marketing and advertising across the whole spectrum of government responsibilities – such as disseminating information on benefits, rights and welfare, and running campaigns for public safety and health: 'Coughs and sneezes spread diseases' is a classic from the COI's post-Second World War beginnings. As just seen in continental Europe, the world's three largest FMCG advertisers have a major presence in the UK too, in this case together with one of the UK's own global advertisers, Reckitt-Benckiser (owner of brands such as Nurofen, Durex and Mr Sheen).

It should be added that the joint Anglo-Dutch Unilever was the largest advertiser in nearly 20 per cent of the national markets surveyed by *Advertising Age* in 2009 (Johnson 2010). Its hundreds of brands include Flora and Lipton in foodstuffs; Dove and Lux in soaps; and Omo or Surf in household products. Unilever is also responsible for the fact that, as with their Impulse

Table 5.3 Ten largest advertisers, United Kingdom, 2009

Measured media spending	2009	2008	% chg
Central Office of Information	333.2	345.1	−3.4
Procter & Gamble Co.	283.2	401.4	−29.4
Unilever	201.4	276.9	−27.2
L'Oréal	195.5	233.7	−16.4
British Sky Broadcasting	170.6	169.4	0.7
Tesco	168.2	190.1	−11.5
Walmart Stores	153.0	141.2	8.3
DFS Furniture Co.	146.9	153.7	−4.4
Reckitt-Benckiser	134.3	177.7	−24.4
Kellogg Co.	126.8	144.8	−12.5

Figures are in millions of US dollars. Data from Nielsen Co.
Copyrighted 2011 Crain Communications. 75587–nlpf.
('Global Marketers 2010' 2010).

brand for women in past decades, so many men around the world now seem to smell the same, whether their deodorant is called Axe or Lynx, the same product having different names in different markets for trademark reasons (Hamm 2007). The largest of the British corporate advertisers on the list is BSkyB, with the retailers Tesco and DFS not far behind. Interestingly, of the US-based global advertisers here, Walmart ranks more highly than in its home market, whilst Kellogg's, although a global advertiser, is by no means one of the largest – 34 in the top 100 that year – which tempts the suggestion that Britain may be a more fertile market for their products than many other nations. Whatever the reasons for that, FMCG and retail are clearly the most advertised categories in the UK.

Turning to advertising agencies, the British marketing and advertising trade journal *Brand Republic* publishes an annual ranking of both creative and media agencies ranked by billings estimates provided by the professional measurement company Neilsen. For 2010, reporting 2009 data, of the top ten creative (and some full-service agencies), there were only two not affiliated with one of the global holding groups, and one of those was subsequently acquired by such a group during 2010 ('Interpublic Group to acquire Delany Lund Knox Warren from Creston' 2010). For the whole top 100, agencies tied to WPP had the lion's share of billings, followed by Publicis, Omnicom, Interpublic and Havas ('Top 100 Creative Agencies 2010' 2010). By these measures, we would have to say that British advertising is highly globalised, but with the British WPP group dominating its domestic market just as much as it does globally.

Finally, as to the distribution of advertising expenditure, the UK Advertising Association breakdown for 2009 shows that, notwithstanding the discourse about the decline of 'old' media, print continued to attract the greatest proportion of expenditure, 29.6 per cent, leading television with 26.2 per cent and the internet with 24.2 per cent. Direct mail garnered 10.7 per cent, while outdoor, radio and cinema together totalled 9.3 per cent (Advertising Industry Statistics 2010). As noted in Chapter 3, other sources have declared that internet expenditure actually overtook that of television in 2009. Certainly, given the restricted amount of time available on British television for advertising, whatever is the exact proportion of expenditure attracted to the internet, Britain must lead the world ('Online adspend overtakes TV in UK' 2009).

Asia-Pacific

Only a few decades ago, Asia as a communication region was mainly a mass of state-controlled national media systems dutifully distributing government propaganda, maintaining socially conservative values, and showing little interest in cultural innovation or exchange with regional neighbours. Advertising opportunities were limited, though even so, US- and European-based advertisers were making their presence felt, represented by the same agencies as served them in their home markets. Based on research carried out the 1970s, Michael H Anderson's *Madison Avenue in Asia* was the first attempt to comprehensively document and analyse the advent and impact of the international advertising industry across the region. Anderson criticised what he saw as the 'advertising imperialism' of that era, namely its part in the subjection of the 'Third World' countries of Asia to the West, particularly the US (Anderson 1984).

However, by the early 1990s, processes of market 'liberalisation' were under way in the major countries of the region, and the rapid economic growth achieved by the 'Asian Dragon' nations at that time was taken to be a refutation of Asia's alleged dependence, even if that growth did falter in the crisis of 1997–8. Much as Europe had experienced it in the 1980s, liberalisation meant an influx of foreign investment, including advertisers and their agencies, as well as the opening up of new media outlets, especially television channels, by both national and foreign corporations. This was the beginning of a total transformation in the mediascape of the region.

From the point of view of the critical study of the advertising industry, Asia has some very interesting characteristics. But what do we really mean by 'Asia'? Taken as a whole, broadly-defined world region, Asia encompasses two of the world's biggest national markets outside of the US (namely Japan and China), and two others in the top 15, South Korea and India. Asia also is home to the world's very biggest single advertising agency (Dentsu, of Japan). China and India in particular are both undergoing exceptionally rapid economic growth, and seeing the emergence of new categories of consumers, not only the much-vaunted 'middle class' of those societies. This growth continues to attract global advertisers and agencies, and at the same time, Chinese and Indian brands have begun to venture on to the world market. Not only have Chinese brands like Haier and Lenovo become marketed into the Asian region, but they have been launched into the West: meanwhile, India's Tata Motors has bought the prestige Jaguar and Land Rover marques from Ford.

Yet Asia is defined more by its geographical unity than anything else, for in most relevant aspects, the diversity of Asia is arguably greater than any other world region, presenting advertisers and their agencies, and media, with complex barriers, not only between nations, but within them. As will be explained below, the economic logic of globalisation might motivate the huge global marketers active in the region to seek the economies of scale and other theoretical advantages of standardising their marketing efforts, but the experience that they and their agencies have had with the realities of linguistic, cultural, regulatory and other differences have obliged them to go some distance towards tailoring advertising campaigns at different levels: regional, sub-regional, national, and sub-national. Significantly, it was Asia where the concept and practice of 'glocalisation' was invented.

Figure 5.1 McDonald's glocalises their 'I'm lovin' it' global campaign in Singapore

For all the exceptional rates of growth in advertising expenditure recorded in the first half of the 2000s, and the breathless rhetoric of the trade press, the level of involvement which the global advertisers and their agencies have with Asia needs to be put into perspective. In relative terms, the global advertising industry is still a late developer there. According to the latest available annual report on 'Global Marketers' from the leading trade journal *Advertising Age* in 2010, the world's biggest 100 advertisers were spending just less than 24 per cent of their total volume of expenditure on media advertising in the Asia-Pacific region (that includes the world's second and soon-to-be third biggest national markets, Japan and China respectively, as well as Australia and New Zealand). This compares to 56 per cent in North America, although not far behind 29 per cent in Europe. Interestingly, while that proportion of expenditure far outstrips that of other former developing regions, some of those others are seeing much higher rates of growth. Notably, Latin America increased by 14 per cent over the year, while Asia was just a touch over 6 per cent (Johnson 2010).

The global advertisers with the greatest presence in Asia are the familiar conglomerates behind the FMCG brands. Looking at the ten advertisers with the biggest expenditure on media in each of 14 major national markets of the region in 2009, stretching from South to East Asia, we find Procter & Gamble in six of them and Unilever in ten. The Swiss-based Nestlé is found in five of these markets, with brands Maggi, Nescafé, and several milk and water branded products, while the French-based L'Oréal is marketing brands such as Maybelline, Helena Rubenstein and Giorgio Armani in four. The US-based Yum Brands, owner and franchiser of KFC (formerly Kentucky Fried Chicken) and Pizza Hut, appears in three markets. Interestingly, while the automotive category on a global basis is the second-largest in spending after 'personal care', it is represented in this albeit cursory survey by five companies only. Honda, Toyota and Mitsubishi are in the top ten in their home market of Japan, with Honda appearing on a mere two other lists and Toyota on one, while Hyundai and Kia do not figure on any list outside their home market of South Korea ('Global Marketers 2010' 2010).

The relevance of all this for the media is that, as already noted, FMCG advertisers have strongly favoured television as their preferred advertising medium, which suggests that the immense growth of television in Asia in recent decades has been powerfully propelled by their advertising revenue. A regional measure in the mid-2000s puts television as accounting for 66 per cent of main media expenditure in the region ('Asia-Pacific Ad Enjoys Double Digit Growth' 2006). Although the use of the internet and other new media is rapidly gaining ground in terms of rates of increase, television still dominates in absolute terms, and unlike the trend in some more developed societies, is also still experiencing strong growth. Particularly in China and India, this situation reflects the fact that the majority of the population in the most populous countries of the region, and the world, do not have access to the internet. This is changing: while penetration in India is 6.9 per cent of the population, in China it is 31.6 per cent. However, these figures should be compared to 78 per cent for Japan and 81 per cent for South Korea (Internet World Stats 2010). Furthermore, while the major FMCG advertisers are found in the top ten in most countries of the world, categories like automotive and retail which figure prominently in the top ten of European and North American markets, as seen above, are relatively absent in the developing countries of Asia, and indeed, this can be taken as indicative of their status as emergent markets.

Historically, certain US- and European-based advertising agencies had been active in a few Asian markets, such as Thailand, prior to the era of globalisation proper, but they were largely excluded from the largest markets, China and India, until the 1980s and 1990s respectively. By this time, the agencies had been gathered into the global holding groups, and some of these groups have now become particularly intent upon gaining influence in the region. The favoured mode of market entry, even when it was not mandated by national governments wishing to maintain control over the industry, has been the joint venture: that is, the globally-linked agency forms a partnership with a 'local' agency. This is mutually advantageous, as it gives the outsiders access to inside knowledge about how to do business in the foreign environment, as well as to local familiarity with the culture, and perhaps business and government contacts. For their part, the local agency gets access to the accounts of the global clients that the global agency brings with it, an opportunity which would otherwise be unlikely, given the trend to global alignment discussed in Chapter 2.

For example, we have seen that the huge British-based WPP Group has the formerly US-owned full-service agencies J Walter Thompson (JWT), Ogilvy & Mather, Young & Rubicam, and Grey Advertising all under its umbrella globally, as well as a number of media-buying agencies, all co-ordinated as Group M. To take the notable example of China, they operate through 19 joint venture companies, and maintain offices not only in the first-tier cities of Beijing and Shanghai, but many provincial cities as well. This is typical of the Western-based agencies: to be concentrated into holding groups at the global level, and integrated into decentralised joint ventures at the local (Sinclair 2008b). However, at this stage, it is pertinent to note that the first foreign agency to be admitted to China, and whose joint venture there, Beijing Dentsu, is the top-ranking agency by revenue (Adbrands 2010a), is neither part of a holding group, nor Western: this is Dentsu, Japan's leading agency, and a considerable power not only in China, but throughout the whole region.

For all the rapid growth and involvement of the global manufacturing/marketing/media complex in China and India, it is Japan which, at least until the disasters of 2011, remained Asia's largest, and the world's second-largest, national advertising market. Being largely self-contained and resistant to the Western world, it is unique in Asia, and it makes Asia unique as a world region. Just as US-based transnational corporations of the 1960s and 1970s led their advertising agencies to follow them overseas, so have Japanese advertising agencies followed the international expansion of their major clients, notably manufacturers in the automotive and consumer electronics categories. And just as the US-based global corporations dominate their domestic advertising market, so is the list of the top ten advertisers in Japan dominated by Japan-based globalised companies: Panasonic, Toyota, Honda and Mitsubishi, for example, plus Kao Corp, one of Japan's own FMCG global corporations ('Global Marketers 2010' 2010).

Much more than their US-based counterparts, Japanese advertising agencies derive most of their income from their domestic market, but for a number of reasons, it is difficult to compare them. First, as mentioned in Chapter 2, the Japanese agencies do have some affiliations with the Western-based global holding groups, but for the most part they operate as agencies in their own right. When compared to the leading individual Western international agencies, as distinct from the global groups into which those agencies are combined, Dentsu has been the world's biggest advertising agency for decades. Hakuhodo, the next largest agency in Japan, is also in that particular top ten ('Agency Report 2010' 2010). Second, there are significant differences in the business conventions under which the advertising industry developed in Japan. Notably, client conflicts are not seen as a problem, at least not in the domestic market. For example, Dentsu can handle accounts for competitors in the same industry, such as Toyota and Honda, Ford and BMW, and those clients will also have accounts with Hakuhodo (Kawashima 2006, 2009). However, outside of Japan, the Japanese agencies are seeking to become more international, so they have been developing links with the global groups, and have to be more respectful of global clients' concerns with conflicts.

One more important difference in how the advertising business is conducted in Japan compared to the West is that close relations between agencies and media are the norm in Japan. Historically, as we have seen, such relations have been anathema in the West, since advertisers have been suspicious of the conflict of interest entailed by any corporate link between an agency and the media: they fear that agencies would be able to corral clients into their own media. However, in Japan, the agencies operate on a full-service basis: that is, they retain a media-buying function, and their market power is based on their capacity to earn commissions on the massive purchases of media time and space they buy and resell to their clients (Kawashima 2009).

We shall return to examine China and India as advertising markets later in the chapter, but before leaving the Asian region, mention must be made of the world's thirteenth largest market, South Korea. Apart from its size, South Korea is worthy of note because, like Japan, it has shown itself resistant to penetration by the global manufacturing/marketing/media complex. This is evident in two ways: first, the top ten advertisers' list is comprised exclusively of South Korean corporations, most of which are global brands, ranging over consumer electronics (such as Samsung and LG); automotive (Hyundai and Kia); telecommunications; retail; and FMCG ('Global Marketers 2010' 2010). Second, with regard to the advertising agency business, several of South Korea's manufacturing conglomerates, the *chaebols*, have their own in-house advertising agencies – this is true of Samsung, LG and Hyundai specifically. Some of these *chaebol* agencies form partnerships with the globally-linked agencies to pursue marketing campaigns outside of South Korea, but within the domestic market, roughly half of the top ten in recent years have been *chaebol* agencies, with the other half being the usual globally-affiliated international agencies based in the West (Kim and Cha 2009).

To summarise: until recent decades Asia has attracted little interest from the global manufacturing/marketing/media corporations, relative to their activities in other regions. However, rapid growth in both China and India in particular has now attracted a great deal of corporate attention, so we find that the largest advertisers in the major markets of the region are the North Atlantic-based FMCG marketers. However, we shall see that national FMCG companies also figure in both China and India, along with telecommunication providers, ahead of regional automakers and other manufacturers, notably those which feature in Japan. As to advertising, global agencies have been setting up in Asia for some time, mainly through joint ventures with local partners, and this combination of global FMCG marketers and agencies has stimulated the growth and proliferation of the different national systems of commercial television. Beyond this, it is difficult to generalise about Asia as a region, as each national market has its own distinctive characteristics. We will consider China and India in more detail below in the section on 'BRICs'.

Latin America

Outside of North America and Europe, Latin America is the world region with the longest history and closest engagement with the globalisation of the advertising industry. US-based advertising agencies were opening up offices in certain Latin American capitals as early as the 1920s, and Mexicans and Brazilians had their own thriving agencies before the Second World War. The establishment and growth of radio on a commercial basis in the major countries of the region was decisive in laying the basis for the subsequent commercialisation of television, not only as the premium advertising medium, but also as a political and cultural institution which remains uniquely 'Latin'. In the present era, the advertising industry in Latin America largely has been incorporated into the same global holding companies as dominate the industry elsewhere in the world, but not without independent traditions of creative work having established themselves and winning international peer recognition.

The major national markets of the region are Brazil, Mexico, Argentina, Colombia, Venezuela and Chile, in that order, although 80 per cent of the total advertising expenditure of the whole region is in the first three of these (AAAP 2009). It should be acknowledged that as a world region, Latin America attracts a comparatively small share of global advertising expenditure. In 2010, this was 6.5 per cent, ahead of the Middle East and Africa at 5.0 per cent, but well behind the Asia-Pacific's 23.6 per cent. Nevertheless, Latin America has shown very strong growth in relative terms, and it was the only world region not to have experienced a downturn during the GFC. In the period of recovery which has followed, Latin American advertising is expected to continue to grow at a rate more than twice that of any other region (Johnson 2010). Most of this expected expansion is in Brazil, the world's fifth biggest country in both size and population (Wentz 2010) and sixth biggest market as seen on Table 5.1. Thus, just as growth rates in China and India account for most growth in Asia, so too does Brazil in Latin America. Brazil will be examined in detail along with these Asian counterparts, and also the case of Russia, under the 'BRICs' heading below. Suffice it to say here that Brazil's profile as a major advertising market is quite diverse and sophisticated by regional standards. Brazilian agencies continue to own a stake in the advertising business, albeit with global partners, and Brazilian creative work is highly regarded internationally. Amongst the leading advertisers, major Brazilian-owned retail and banking interests are well-represented.

In turning to Mexico, Latin America's other major market, two common features with Brazil become evident, in that television is the medium most favoured by the major advertisers, and that the national television industry in each case is dominated by one major player which faces only relatively weak competition in the capture of advertising revenues. In Brazil, this is TV Globo, while in Mexico, it is Grupo Televisa, which not only derives the most advertising revenue, but also heads the list of biggest advertisers. Televisa is one of the six Mexican advertisers on that list, which also includes its only real competitor, Televisión Azteca, along with the Mexican Government and Mexican-based international companies such as Bimbo and América Movil, the holding company of Mexican telecommunications mogul Carlos Slim. Global FMCG corporations occupy the other four slots, namely Procter & Gamble, Unilever, Nestlé and Colgate-Palmolive. In Argentina, US and also European-based global FMCG advertisers such as these dominate, with only one slot being filled by an Argentine company ('Global Marketers 2010' 2010). As for the advertising business, agencies linked to the global holding groups preponderate, whether wholly-owned or via local partnerships, in both Mexico and Argentina (Sinclair 2009a).

Latin American television seems to be in a strong position to withstand competition from the internet as a new advertising medium, particularly in Brazil and Mexico, where free-to-air television attracts at least 60 per cent of advertising expenditure. The average for the region is 52.7 per cent (ACHAP 2007). The commercialisation of popular culture via television is deeply entrenched and longstanding: the *telenovelas* which form the backbone of television programming in Latin America today have descended from the *radionovelas* which were expressly developed as cultural vehicles for advertising in the region by FMCG sponsors such as Procter & Gamble in the decades between the World Wars (Luis López 1998). Furthermore, most Latin American countries were quite unlike the rest of the developing world, in that they opted for a commercial, advertising-supported model of broadcasting during that era. Given that long history, it is not surprising that entrepreneurial media dynasties have emerged and become entrenched in the major Latin American countries, based on their market dominance of television in particular.

In the absence of comparative figures for the ratio of free-to-air to pay-TV, suffice it to say that access to television in Latin America corresponds to the sharp social stratification which still typifies the region: that is, free-to-air continues to be a truly mass medium, while pay-TV is an elite one. In Mexico, pay-TV is in a third of TV homes, while it is little over a quarter in Brazil ('Web reach rises in Latin America' 2010). Although internet penetration is highly variable – from 64.4 per cent in Argentina, to 37.8 per cent in Brazil and 27.2 per cent in Mexico (Internet World Stats 2010), industry data suggest that the share of advertising expenditure going to the internet is small, and indeed, inversely related to degree of penetration, around 3, 4 and 5 per cent respectively. This situation can be expected to change as more and more people access the internet via mobile phones rather than computers. Marketing industry sources in fact predict strong growth in internet ad spending, but off a low base, and hampered by frugal user behaviour and inadequate infra-structure ('Research: eMarketer predicts ad spending growth in Latam of 6–9% annually through 2014' 2010).

In summary, the form assumed by the manufacturing/marketing/media complex in Latin America is one of thoroughly embedded nationally-owned media oligopolies continuing to thrive on advertising revenue from the large global (though also major national and regional) corporations that are being given access to mass audiences through free-to-air television, which is not only the most widely-distributed but also the most culturally embedded of the media. As to the advertising industry itself, the global groups have con-solidated their presence through their affiliations with global clients outside of the national markets, and access to local cultural knowledge and creative talent via partnerships within them.

Standardisation, localisation and 'glocalisation'

In the process of becoming ever more globalised, the practices of marketing in general and advertising in particular have had to learn how to come to terms with the realities of cultural and other differences. While past decades saw campaigns for products such as Marlboro run on a uniform, 'standardised' basis in every country where they were sold – 'one sight, one sound, one sell' – (Mattelart 1991: 55), cultural adaptation has become a fundamental strategic principle for marketers in the age of globalisation.

Nevertheless, standardisation had considerable influence amongst global marketers in the 1980s. In particular, a Harvard management guru, Theodore Levitt, proclaimed 'the emergence of global markets for standardised consumer products on a previously unimagined scale' which had overcome 'accustomed differences in national or regional preference' and now required 'the standar-dization of products, manufacturing, and the institutions of trade and com-merce' (1983: 92–93). It was noted in Chapter 2 how the leading British advertising agency of the 1980s, Saatchi & Saatchi, built itself into a global corporation: this was partly because it took up Levitt's doctrine. Not only did standardisation fit neatly with the rhetoric and organisational transformations of the emerging global era, but it was and is seen to have economic advan-tages: 'the creation of a stronger global international identity through con-sistent positioning and image across markets over time ... cost reduction through economies of scale in advertising production, sharing of experience and effective use of advertising budget' (Tai 1997: 56–57). In other words, corporations have a strong economic disincentive against cultural adaptation, so, what needs to be explained is why advertisers would want to engage in cultural adaptation at all.

One major reason was the manifest failures of certain celebrated global campaigns during the 1980s and early 1990s. Many of these were hilarious or bizarre and have passed into urban legend: for example, that one of Levitt's favourite global marketers, Coca-Cola, once had its name mistranslated into Chinese as 'bite the wax tadpole' (Mooney 2008). There have been entire books dedicated to such marketing blunders (Ricks 1999). But as well as obvious linguistic and cultural differences, including religious strictures and variations in tastes, marketers were also encountering practical differences in national regulatory regimes and distribution systems. Such experience turned attention to alternative ways of approaching global marketing, the clearest being defined by Nestlé which has pursued a more localised, or 'multidomestic' strategy of differentially formulating products like their instant coffee in accordance with the taste preferences of various national markets. So, although standardisation has continued to be attractive to global marketers for economic reasons, the realities of cultural and other differences have forced them to develop adaptive strategies to cope with market-by-market variations.

The result of all this has been a kind of a continuum in marketing theory and practice between standardisation and localisation, but some middle ground was being cleared by the beginning of the 1990s with the concept of 'glocalisation'. This had its origins in the strategies of Japanese marketers in Asia, notably Sony, who pursued 'global localisation', rather than 'global standardisation' (Iwabuchi 2002). Glocalisation subsequently came to be embraced in global marketing as the practical wisdom of creating the right balance between minding the bottom line of standardisation while meeting the demands of localisation. It was noted early in Chapter 1 that marketing wisdom conventionally distinguishes between the four 'Ps' in the 'marketing mix': product, place, promotion and price. In the case of glocalisation, certain elements in the mix can be held constant, while others can be varied. For instance, in her study of regional advertising strategies in Asia, Tai distinguished between strategic factors, such as main campaign theme, market segmentation and product positioning; as against tactical ones like creative execution and media placement. The former tend to be standardised, but the latter localised: she calls this an 'adaptation strategy' (1997: 58). In such ways, the marketer hopes to maximise the organisational and economic advantages of standardisation, while responding to the necessities of cultural and other differences between markets. This is what glocalisation means in practice.

On the issue of segmentation strategies, Saatchi & Saatchi enthused about how global advertising could target 'segments', or similar socioeconomic groups, not just in the one country but as a transnational market in different countries or regions: 'there are probably more social differences between midtown Manhattan and the Bronx, ... than between midtown Manhattan and the 7th Arrondissement of Paris' (Quoted in Mattelart 1991: 52–53). This does seem to be true for certain kinds of products, such as services that are intrinsically international, like credit cards, and goods which carry international prestige, such as designer brands (Herbig 1998). Yet as more and more companies, usually based in the US or Europe, enter the rapidly developing regions of the erstwhile 'Third World', they are needing to find strategies to cope with the cultural and other barriers that confront not elite but mass market goods and services, such as the various FMCG categories.

If segments are to be targeted in such a way, this suggests that adaptation might be deployed at a number of levels: the sub-national as well as the national, and perhaps even the world-regional. Furthermore, to the extent that adaptation is being made on cultural-linguistic grounds, rather than, for example, to meet national regulations, then geocultural or geolinguistic regions come into consideration, that is, nations or even groups within nations which are not geographically connected (Sinclair 2004). To return to the case of Asia as a region, Tai observes, 'Asia is really a series of localized markets with their own characteristics, rather than a region' (1997: 49). However, she argues that China, Taiwan, Hong Kong and Singapore might form a Chinese market, that is, as a geocultural or geolinguistic region. Shu-mei Shih conceives of such a virtual region as 'the Sinophone Pacific' (2007), although Michael Curtin is more sceptical: he sees 'global China' as a media market, and hence an advertising medium, as being more potential than actual (2007).

An example of a global corporation pursuing a regional, in this case, a pan-Asian, marketing strategy would be Coca-Cola and its non-carbonated juice-based drink called Qoo (pronounced 'coo'). Qoo was first launched as a successful brand in Japan in 1999, and subsequently 'rolled out' in South Korea, Singapore, China, Thailand and Taiwan, albeit with some national variations being required in its market positioning (Osborne 2001; Wang 2008). On the other hand, it is well-documented that McDonald's regularly tailors menus to meet various cultural and religious laws and customs, as well as taste preferences in particular countries, such as vegetarian hamburgers in India (Watson 1997). This is true of its advertising also: for instance, in adapting North American TVCs based around the 'I'm Lovin' It' theme for China, the American singer Justin Timberlake was replaced by Wang Leehom, a popular local singer performing a Mandarin version of the campaign jingle. This strategy was repeated with other minor variations in each of McDonald's Asian markets (Madden 2003). Coca-Cola's approach could be called 'strategic regionalism', or marketing a product to multiple countries on a regional basis with minimum variation (Sinclair and Wilken 2009), while McDonald's is a clear example of a more multidomestic strategy.

Respectively, these cases illustrate region-wide and market-by-market forms of adaptation. Far from the standardisation advocated by Leavitt, and its flip side, the homogenisation seen by critics of globalisation, these examples suggest how product-market strategy and advertising in fact can be globally aligned or locally adapted to differing degrees depending on corporate organisation, the product, the market and several other relevant circumstances. Global marketing corporations seek to manage the conflict between the advantages of standardisation and the realities of cultural and other differences in a kind of practical compromise, though also try to ensure that campaigns are not glocalised any more than is strictly necessary. More generally, actual marketing practices point up the degree to which globalisation is in practice mediated not only by national factors, but also by regional ones, which suggests that critics of globalisation should be more wary of corporate influence in its adapted forms, rather than when it makes no concession to regional and national differences and openly declares its alien origins.

'BRICS' and 'CHINDIA' in comparative perspective

The once fundamental distinction between the 'developed' and the 'developing' nations of the world has been thrown into disarray by the rapid economic growth and social change exhibited over the last decade by Brazil, Russia, India and China. In spite of their obvious and very considerable differences in geographical attributes, economic base, historical and political formation, and not to mention sociocultural composition, these countries have been united in contemporary business discourse under the acronym BRICs (Kowitt 2009). One of the major features of this apparent unity is the growth of their national markets for consumer goods and services, usually seen in conjunction with the rise of an ostensible 'middle class' in each country. Such a development implies a key role being played by marketing in general and advertising in particular in the making of BRICs. Indeed, as seen in Table 5.1, all of the BRICs countries were included in the world's biggest 15 advertising markets in 2010, having dramatically increased their rankings over the previous decade – Russia in particular came from 42nd to 12th place, while India came into 15th place from 33rd ten years before. At that time, China and Brazil were already in the top dozen('Global Marketers 2010' 2010).

In the period since the GFC, it has been the BRICs nations taken together which have been 'the main drivers of growth' in the global recovery of advertising expenditure: 2011 percentage estimates of growth put Brazil at 19.8, Russia at 16.5, India at 16, and China at 13 ('Global adspend to rise 4.8%' 2011). This makes these markets much more crucial to the interests of the manufacturing/marketing/media complex than in decades past. Sir Martin Sorrell, the head of WPP, the world's biggest global group, sees a 'shift in power' and a 'transfer of influence' from the mature developed economies to the more dynamic ones of the BRICs nations, and beyond them to the 'Next 11', a grouping led by countries such as South Korea, Mexico and Turkey (Quoted in Whiteside 2009).

Brazil

As mentioned above, the foundations of advertising in Brazil were laid by US-based agencies early in the imperial phase, and the first Brazilian agencies developed very much under their tutelage (Woodard 2002). However, after the Second World War Brazilian advertising assumed its own character, and began to enjoy the international reputation for creativity which it enjoys today (O'Barr

Table 5.4 Ten largest advertisers, Brazil, 2009

Measured media spending	2009	2008	% chg
Casas Bahia	566.8	605.0	−6.3
Unilever	363.8	363.8	0.0
Anheuser–Busch InBev	167.5	136.2	22.9
Caixa	157.4	127.0	23.9
Hyundai Motor Co.	141.8	91.2	55.5
Bradesco	138.3	131.4	5.3
Fiat	135.1	133.0	1.6
Hypermarcas	129.3	95.6	35.3
Telecom Italia	107.8	58.1	85.5
Petrobras	104.7	90.6	15.6

Figures are in millions of US dollars, discounted by *Advertising Age*.
Data from Ibope Brazil.
Copyrighted 2011 Crain Communications. 75587–nlpf.
('Global Marketers 2010' 2010).

2008). This occurred in association with the emergence of TV Globo as the pre-eminent national television network (Sinclair 1999).

Table 5.4 shows Brazil's ten largest advertisers ranked by their 2009 expenditure. There are five Brazilian and five foreign-owned advertisers: four of them are based in Europe, and one in Asia. The Brazilian advertisers are Casas Bahía, a chain of furniture and electrical goods stores; Caixa Econômico Federal, the national savings bank; Bradesco, a major private bank; Hypermarcas, a manufacturer of a wide range of FMCG; and rounding out the ten, the largest company in Latin America, Petrobras, a predominantly public-owned petroleum corporation. Of the foreign-based advertisers, Unilever has been either the second, or more often, the largest advertiser in Brazil at least since 1996. Fiat has been in the top ten since 2001, although more predictably, Ford and General Motors also have usually featured in this list. Anheuser-Busch InBev is a truly global merger formed in 2008, bringing together the former Brazilian Ambev and the US brewer of Budweiser under the former Interbrew of Belgium, creating one of the world's two biggest brewers. Hyundai and Telecom Italia are interesting newcomers: Telecom Italia trades as TIM, a major mobile telephone provider in Brazil, mobile telephony being a rapidly-expanding and competitive market, both in Latin America and across all the BRICs nations.

With regard to the advertising agencies, data from an industry source which has ranked them according to their 2008 billings indicate that each of the four biggest global groups has at least one agency amongst the top-ranked ten, either wholly-owned or in Brazilian partnership. There are five such partnerships, but not one of the top ten is completely Brazilian. The groups are predominantly US-based (namely Omnicom and Interpublic), but the British WPP is well-represented with three of its agency networks. The mix illustrates the distinct phases of the internationalisation of the industry in Latin America, from the 'imperial' phase, up until the present global era, when we find that some of the most acclaimed Brazilian creative agencies of recent decades – Almap, DM9 and Africa – have been incorporated into the one global group, Omnicom (Adbrands 2010b). Indeed, in the recovery period following the GFC, Brazil continues to experience something of a boom, given its high growth rate and its expanding 'middle class', even if that social category is implausibly estimated as being half the population. Accordingly, foreign advertising agencies are continuing to arrive, mostly looking for Brazilian partners (Wentz 2010).

Brazilian researchers calculate that the top ten agencies bill around half the total media expenditure in the country (Ferriera Simões *et al.* 2007). How is expenditure distributed across the various media? Data cited by Brazil's Internet Advertising Bureau put free-to-air television at over 63 per cent. The major beneficiary of this large proportion of revenue going to television is TV Globo, which garners an estimated 70 per cent. However, internet advertising has not taken off in Brazil as it has in other large world markets, measuring only 4.2 per cent in 2010 (IAB Brazil 2010).

In light of the world-wide trend noted in Chapter 2, that of unbundling formerly full-service agencies into creative and media-buying specialisms, the Brazilian case is worth noting. It appears that unbundling has been prevented from happening in Brazil by national regulations designed to protect the television industry from global groups gaining a monopoly over media buying. The principal beneficiary of this is TV Globo (Ferriera Simões *et al.* 2007), although it is also argued that revenue from media-buying enables full-service agencies to pay high salaries to their creative staff: hence the celebrated reputation for creative work and the high status accorded to creative professionals in Brazil (Wentz 2010).

Russia

Although Russia has only become a significant advertising market since the dissolution of the former Soviet Union at the beginning of the 1990s, there is a little previous history which should be sketched in. Just as in the UK and the US, there had been advertising agencies setting themselves up since towards the end of the nineteenth century, but with the Russian Revolution of 1917, advertising became a state monopoly. Of course, Western-style advertising was totally unacceptable on ideological grounds, but interestingly, the Soviet regime came to recognise that advertising had a key function to serve in the distribution of goods, even in a command economy (Hanson 1974). From the mid-1960s, foreign advertising was organised under Vneshtorgreklama, a special authority within the Ministry of Foreign Trade, while domestic advertising was handled through a network of regional organisations (O'Keefe and Sheinkopf 1976).

The end of Soviet influence in Eastern Europe and the breakup of the USSR opened up several national markets in an entire region that had previously been inaccessible to the Western manufacturing/marketing/media complex. Russia is by no means the only, but certainly the largest, of these markets formerly behind the 'Iron Curtain' that have proved so attractive to US- and European-based corporations. By the end of the first decade of Russia's post-Soviet existence, the leading advertising agencies were all, either then or now, members of the global groups: Young & Rubicam and Grey (WPP); BBDO, DDB and TBWA (Omnicom); D'Arcy, Leo Burnett and Saatchi & Saatchi (Publicis); and McCann Erickson (Interpublic) (Adbrands 2011a). The only leading Russian agency at that time was Video International, which by 2005 had formed a joint venture arrangement with WPP (Pfanner 2005). The Japanese marketing conglomerate Dentsu made a notable entrance in 2008 when it acquired Smart Communications and became Dentsu-Smart ('Dentsu-Smart, advertising subsidiary, set up in Russia' 2008). That same year, in digital advertising, Google purchased advertising agency and search engine ZAO Begun (Ellis 2008).

Although there are thousands of businesses called 'advertising agencies' in Russia, these are mainly print and promotion boutiques. Given the recent Soviet background, the absence of experienced, large-scale agencies is no surprise, and this has left the market wide open to the usual suspects such as those just mentioned, who arrive already holding the accounts of the global advertisers who have opened up business in Russia (Repieve 2008). Table 5.5 lists Russia's top ten advertisers, all but one of which are major global marketers, predominantly European-based. The only Russian advertiser is Sistema, a diverse conglomerate active in various fields, including mobile tele-communications, and controlled by one of the several entrepreneurs in the oligarchy which quickly emerged after the collapse of the USSR. Wimm-Bill-Dann

Table 5.5 Ten largest advertisers, Russia, 2009

Measured media spending	2009	2008	% chg
Procter & Gamble Co.	98.8	128.1	−22.9
L'Oréal	78.2	73.2	6.7
Henkel	50.7	53.0	−4.3
Mars Inc.	49.7	50.4	−1.3
Unilever	49.1	59.6	−17.7
Wimm–Bill–Dann	40.9	36.3	12.5
Nestlé	40.6	37.0	9.9
Reckitt-Benckiser	36.5	39.0	−6.4
Danone Groupe	35.6	40.9	−12.9
Sistema	32.4	41.0	−20.8

Figures are in millions of US dollars, discounted by *Advertising Age*.
Data from TNS Russia/Part of Kantar Media Network.
Copyrighted 2011 Crain Communications. 75587–nlpf.
('Global Marketers 2010' 2010).

is a juice and dairyfood company which was Russian until December 2010 when it was taken over by PepsiCo, thus making Russia its biggest market outside of the US ('Pepsi's Russian Challenge' 2010).

It is evident that all of these global advertisers are in one branch or other of FMCG. As already noted, FMCG advertisers in general tend to prefer television as their advertising medium, and this is certainly true for this group of advertisers. In the same year of 2009, television was attracting 55 per cent of all advertising expenditure in Russia, with the top ten advertisers being responsible for a quarter of all expenditure on television. Online advertising expenditure in Russia, by contrast, not only lags well behind television, but is below the average of 15–20 per cent in most developed markets ('Russian Advertising Market Set for Growth' 2010). Interestingly, outdoor advertising is a significant medium in Russia, a field in which News Corporation has been expanding its presence (Pfanner 2005).

India

India is a nation where advertising can mean anything from viral videos to branded messages painted on a cow's horn or a brick in the village well, reflecting the huge gap between the 'middle class' glorified in pro-globalisation discourse, and the rural masses. India's history of contact with the Western manufacturing/marketing/media complex dates from an initial involvement beginning between the World Wars, followed by a period of disengagement. This was initiated by the Foreign Exchange Restriction Act of 1974, which affected advertisers and agencies alike. Notably, Coca-Cola left the country entirely, while J Walter Thompson, which had arrived in 1929, survived by forming a joint venture, Hindustan Thompson. It was not until the large-scale economic liberalisation of the 1990s that the international agency networks were encouraged to enter India (Mazzarella 2003). Even after liberalisation, the joint venture model continued to be favoured in advertising, not because it was mandated, but because it was strategic for the foreign agencies seeking local market knowledge, and reciprocally, for the local agencies to gain access to the global clients that the agencies brought with them. We shall see shortly that this is also characteristic of the advertising industry in China.

Liberalisation across various economic sectors allowed global consumer corporations access to the Indian market (including the return of Coca-Cola), so that after nearly two decades of liberalisation, they figure prominently in the tally of largest advertisers, particularly in FMCG, as seen in Table 5.6. Yet in addition to three of the biggest US-based and two European corporations of this kind, plus two Asian-based global corporations, there is a firm presence of Indian corporations. These are first, the Tata Group, already mentioned as an example of an Indian-based conglomerate in the process of becoming global; Bharti Group, a major provider of telecommunications in India and internationally, including of mobile services

Table 5.6 Ten largest advertisers, India, 2009

Measured media spending	2009	2008	% chg
Unilever	98.1	62.7	56.5
Reckitt-Benckiser	30.6	19.7	55.5
Tata Group	27.1	29.9	−9.5
Procter & Gamble Co.	20.1	17.8	12.9
Coca-Cola Co.	16.8	9.1	83.9
Bharti Group	16.2	16.7	−3.1
PepsiCo	15.3	13.0	17.5
ITC	15.0	13.7	9.5
Honda Motor Co.	14.0	10.4	34.6
LG Group	13.9	13.3	4.4

Figures are in millions of US dollars, discounted by *Advertising Age*.
Data from TAM India.
Copyrighted 2011 Crain Communications. 75587–nlpf.
('Global Marketers 2010' 2010).

under the Airtel brand; and ITC, a conglomerate whose diverse fields of business includes FMCG. Thus, global, regional and national advertisers are all represented on this list, although it is apparent that the Indian corporations drastically curtailed their advertising expenditure during the GFC, unlike most of the global advertisers here.

Although Indian agencies have their own creative traditions, the advertising industry exhibits the typical pattern of domination by the global holding groups, either with their own fully-owned offices or via joint ventures with Indian agencies, dating from the 1970s and 1980s. Amongst the 'most admired' agencies in India, WPP is strongly represented with its Ogilvy & Mather, JWT and Grey networks, as well as through the Indian-based agency Contract Advertising, and an international joint venture, Rediffusion DY&R (Adbrands 2011b). WPP has claimed it has half the market, in fact (Sanders and Madden 2005). Omnicom has two joint venture agencies, one with Mudra (DDB) and the other with RK Swamy (BBDO). Interpublic is represented by McCann-Erickson and a joint venture known as DRAFTFCBplusUlka, while Publicis has Leo Burnett. On the media buying side of the business in particular, the global groups between them have over 80 per cent of the market (Srivastava 2005).

As far as media are concerned, India's experience of liberalisation has taken television from a restrictive government monopoly to a cornucopia of channels, posing a challenge to print's traditional dominance as an advertising medium. The most profitable channels are entertainment channels in Hindi, which attract about 35 per cent of all ad spending. Notable amongst these are Star Plus, one of News Corporation's greatest international successes, and Zee TV, owned by the Indian entrepreneur Subhash Chandra (Hiscock 2009). As an indicator of the nexus between television and the biggest advertisers, a 2009 industry study found that 73 per cent of TVCs on Indian television in 2008 were for brands owned by the top 50 advertisers, notably in FMCG and telecommunications ('Indian TV advertising continues to grow' 2009).

Conversely, there is relatively little FMCG advertising on the internet: rather, the BFSI sector dominates (banking, financial services and insurance), along with travel (Internet & Mobile Association of India 2010). This is because, as noted, internet penetration in India is a low 6.9 per cent of the population. However, its growth in the decade 2000–2010 was more than 1500 per cent (Internet World Stats 2010), indicating rapid take-up amongst the 'middle class', who form the market for BFSI. Defining this category as those having a household income between $US7,495 and 37,495, one authoritative study put the middle class at 13 per cent of the population, or 160 million individuals, with the prediction they would reach 267 million by 2016. Significantly, this numerous but minor proportion of the population accounted for over half computer ownership in India in 2010 ('India's middle class population to touch 267 million in 5 yrs' 2011). However, mobile phone use extends astonishingly far into the mass population beyond the middle class, so, as telecommunications infrastructure expands and smartphones become cheaper, mobile internet access can be expected to increase in India, thus making computer ownership much less of a crucial factor, and greatly enlarging the market for internet advertising in the near future ('India will become world's No. 1 mobile market by 2013' 2010).

China

Of all the markets outside of the English-speaking world, China is by far the most spectacular in its size and growth. There are various estimates of this: suffice it to refer to its rapid rise in the decade 2000–2010 from tenth to fourth place as a world market, as seen in Table 5.1, and predictions common in the trade press that it is soon destined to overtake both Germany and Japan to become the largest national market outside of the US.

Table 5.7 shows that, as in Brazil, there is a balance between global and national advertisers on the top ten list. Three of the former are from the US and two from Europe, all of which are by now familiar from their persistent presence in other such lists. Of the Chinese companies, two are different branded divisions of the same publicly-listed pharmaceutical conglomerate, Harbin Sixth Factory and Hayou Sanchine, which produce a very wide range of hospital as well as over-the-counter drugs, both Western and traditional Chinese. Hangzhou Wahaha Group is a private company which has several brands of packaged drinks based on water, milk and juice, along with similar products; while Ting Hsin has instant noodle, packaged drinks, fast food and convenience store divisions: in other words, both companies are in the field of FMCG, broadly understood. China Mobile's presence stands as a strong

Table 5.7 Ten largest advertisers, China, 2009

Measured media spending	2009	2008	% chg
Procter & Gamble Co.	990.3	1,117.3	−11.4
Unilever	575.5	503.0	14.4
L'Oréal	537.5	341.8	57.3
Harbin Pharma Group Pharmaceutical Sixth Factory	446.8	446.0	0.2
Yum Brands	361.3	302.3	19.5
Hayao Group Sanchine Pharmacy	268.8	209.5	28.3
Hangzhou Wahaha Group	259.5	170.5	52.2
Coca-Cola Co.	252.0	185.5	35.8
Ting Hsin International Group	241.5	136.8	76.6
China	237.3	226.5	4.7
Mobile			

Figures are in millions of US dollars, discounted by *Advertising Age*. Nielsen Co. also monitors advertising spending in China. Data from CTR (part of Kantar Media). Copyrighted 2011 Crain Communications. 75587–nlpf. ('Global Marketers 2010' 2010).

reminder of the rapid rise of telecommunication devices in China, and also represents one of the few Chinese consumer durable brand names which could be considered truly 'national'. Others, further down the list, would include Lenovo computers, Haier whitegoods, TCL televisions and Bird mobile phones (Spurgeon 2008).

As to the agencies, it was already mentioned that Dentsu was the first foreign agency to be admitted to China, in 1979, with the first phase of market liberalisation. It was closely followed by McCann Erickson, then other Western agencies, such as J Walter Thompson, arrived in the 1980s, with a further influx in the early 1990s. These set up offices not only in Beijing, but also Shanghai and Guangzhou, representing the three major markets in which their clients were then active, largely global advertisers like Procter & Gamble and General Motors. In accordance with government regulation of foreign ownership at the time, the agencies' offices were either outposts of their base in Hong Kong, or joint ventures with Chinese partners (Wang 2000). This restriction was lifted in January 2006, yet as has been noted above, although the way is now clear for foreign agencies to buy out their joint venture partners, this has not been happening. The foreign managers argue that apart from the fact that their joint venture partners are in a comfortable position with no incentive to sell, the partners are valuable in providing 'local connections' to clients they would not attract otherwise, and furthermore, are 'a huge help in getting things done in China', presumably a reference to the partners' role as intermediaries in an alien culture and political system (Trombly 2006). Thus, for the present, apart from several Chinese agencies, the list of leading agencies in China is characterised by joint ventures, notable amongst which are Beijing Dentsu, Shanghai Leo Burnett, Saatchi & Saatchi Great Wall, McCann Erickson

Guangming and Shanghai Advertising (partner to both Ogilvy & Mather and Hakuhodo) (Adbrands 2010a).

China presents formidable natural barriers against building a national market, even for Chinese brands. For one thing, the sheer physical size of its territory and population are a challenge just for the logistics of distribution of goods and services, let alone for advertising them. Then, from a demographic and sociological point of view, there is extreme internal differentiation within China as a consumer market: there is no 'Chinese market' as such. For all the hype about the emergent 'middle class', there are in fact vast socioeconomic and regional gaps between, say, the urban elites and the peasants of the remote provinces, so marketing has to seek to differentiate itself accordingly. One study puts the 'upper middle class', one of the world's largest markets for luxury goods, at around 1 per cent of the population ('China takes luxury lead' 2011). This is manifestly more upper than middle. In her *Brand New China*, Jing Wang cites research that suggests that if a meaningful definition is applied, the 'middle class' amounts to around 5 per cent of the population (2008: 189–92).

The mass of Chinese consumers outside of Beijing and the coastal metropolises have not been acculturated into seeing products as brands (Doctoroff 2005), and have a stubbornly pre-modern inclination to buy goods on the basis of their price and reliability, or other pragmatic values such as safety (Wang 2008), rather than the kind of brand image imparted by Western-style advertising. Yet this is not just a question of the relative susceptibility of rural and urban dwellers to advertising images and appeals, but of income distribution and purchasing power, which in turn limits their actual consumption and experience of brands. In response, global marketers such as Procter & Gamble have been developing 'brand extensions', cheaper versions of their advertised brands, so as to give consumers an affordable product with which they may experience and come to recognise the brand ('P&G adapts in emerging markets' 2011). Urban youth, on the other hand, the most media-aware and brand-conscious segment of the population, might know and want advertised global brands, but in line with their income, instead purchase cheaper local substitutes, or the counterfeit versions of global brands for which China is notorious (Saywell 2000). Given the size, distribution and demographics of the population, marketers have had to extend their operations from the metropolises where they began into the industrial and provincial cities, and the global advertising agencies have been obliged to follow in their support (Hargrave-Silk 2004; Sinclair 2008b).

An exceptionally high percentage of total advertising expenditure goes on television, almost 80 per cent in 2010 ('CTR reports China advertising expenditure grew 13.5 per cent in 2009' 2010). However, television is highly decentralised, with thousands of channels ranged over local to national levels, so advertising campaigns on a national basis do not necessarily reach a national audience. Nevertheless, the state-owned China Central Television (CCTV) still attracts the bulk of revenue, in spite of the rise of regionally-based competitors, notably Hunan Satellite TV (Wang 2008). As well, it must be appreciated just how massive the internet is in China. Almost a third of the population is on line, making it the largest national internet market in the world (Internet World Stats 2010), albeit a carefully controlled one. The Chinese are provided with equivalent versions of all the popular internet services known in the West – Tudou and Youku instead of YouTube, for instance, though there are some Western services – and most users have mobile access (Klassen 2010). Accordingly, as in India, the internet has become an attractive medium for advertising, and is growing at a rate three times faster than television or print (Chang 2010). This trend can be expected to continue to expand, with over half of the citizens in the main cities having smartphones ('Smartphones surge in Asia' 2011).

The huge and rapid take-up of mobile phones is just one of several points of comparison that can be made about China and India. The term 'Chindia' became current in the mid-2000s to bracket off these two Asian members of BRICs, itself a term which dates from 2001, coined to identify the incorporation of all four of those nations into the global economy (Kowitt 2009). Indeed, at the most obvious level, China and India have in common their billion-plus populations, and thriving economies which have been opened up in recent decades to foreign investment, and otherwise liberalised to produce growing consumer markets after decades of heavy-handed state control. In the present context, if we return to Tables 5.6 and 5.7, at least three points of comparison can be made between the Indian and the Chinese top advertiser lists: namely, the massive dominance of the world's very biggest global advertisers; the presence nonetheless of national corporations; and the incidence of both global and local companies in the FMCG categories. These points can be taken as an indication of the incipient stage of development of consumer capitalism in both countries; the adaptation of large national companies to the modes of marketing introduced by the global advertisers and their agencies; and the instrumental role played by those modes in the process.

However, it is not only less mature consumer capitalist advertising markets that are dominated by the FMCG giants, as all the BRICs countries share this characteristic with both the US and Europe, as we have seen. Furthermore, there is at least one telecommunications corporation amongst the top ten in each of the BRICs nations, indicative of the globalisation of communication infrastructure which is giving support to their economic transformation. Less commonly represented are fields such as retail and automotive, as found characteristically amongst the largest advertisers in the more developed countries.

Looking beyond 'Chindia' to all members of BRICs, Russia is the most subject to the domination of global FMCG corporations, an ironic realisation of the worst fears of the 1970s critics of 'cultural imperialism', while Brazil is the least, with a strong presence of national companies across various fields. Arguably, Brazil's profile is more like that of a developed country than any other in this group. Yet when one looks across all the top advertiser lists, the most striking feature is how each one of these nations manifests both its experience of globalisation, and at the same time, its own specific national realities in political economy and culture. In Brazil, the national institutions Petrobras and Caixa feature along with large Brazilian-owned retailers. In Russia's case, we find a representative of the capitalist oligarchy which has arisen in the post-Soviet era. In India, two of its largest private conglomerates appear on its list, while the biggest Chinese advertisers include pharmaceutical companies which, amongst other things, make and market traditional medicines.

Such an observation, that a nation's largest advertisers reflect its particular economic and cultural character, would not be surprising nor even worth remarking upon, but that the discourse of globalisation (both pro and anti), like that of cultural imperialism before it, has created the impression that the influence of global corporations is a total and direct rather than a partial and complexly-mediated phenomenon. Certainly, as we have seen time and again, the advertising industry itself is predominantly globalised, though often via mutually-beneficial joint ventures between the global networks and nationally-based agencies, and there are certain advertisers, notably the free-spending FMCG marketers Procter & Gamble and Unilever, that appear on most top ten lists, but none of the lists considered is totally global. On the contrary, what those lists bring to light is the identification of the national and regional corporations which are the participants in, and beneficiaries of, the drive towards capitalist modernity. Thus, the manufacturing/marketing/media complex operates across global, regional and national, and arguably also, sub-national levels.

Decades ago, Latin American critics of 'dependency' coined the concept of 'the internationalization of the internal market', and this still today provides insight upon advertising's key role in creating markets on a national basis, and opening them up to the global marketers, yet at the same time, enabling national companies to benefit as they become drawn in to the process. Similarly, in the case of the media's role, 'The sector of the national bourgeoisie that owns the media is closely tied to the industrial bourgeoisie and constitutes a central link to metropolitan interests' (Salinas and Paldán 1979: 90). We have seen how this applies to television in particular. The commercialisation of television has triumphed in all of the BRICs nations. It was noted how in Brazil, television was commercial from the beginning, and came to be dominated by one major network. In Russia, television was a state monopoly and carried no advertising in the Soviet era, but subsequently was partly privatised and commercialised, albeit with its oligarchic owners still subject to arbitrary state control. Prior to the liberalisation of the 1990s, both India and China had state-controlled systems also, but they did accept advertising. Since then, there has been a proliferation of commercial channels in both nations, with some prominent entrepreneurs emerging in India, while China has some public–private companies which successfully compete with CCTV. As we have seen, television is the dominant advertising medium in all these nations, attracting from 55 per cent of total advertising expenditure in Russia, up to 80 per cent in China. These figures compare to the global average of over 41 per cent estimated for 2012 (Bush 2010).

Finally, as to the audience for television and its advertising, there may indeed be an emergent 'middle class' in the BRICs countries, understood in the broadest sense, but the rhetoric of neoliberal modernity conceals the huge gap which still prevails between the privileged classes' access to new consumption possibilities, and that of the vast mass of the people. While the former might be ready and willing to value and to consume the same branded goods as in the West, the latter have much less spending power, and like the Chinese consumers mentioned earlier, value price and reliability, but have no predisposition to admire and desire brands for their own sake. In this context, advertising, and all the other dimensions of marketing which underlie it, assumes the task of 'teaching' prospective consumers to acquire the modern orientation towards branded goods: advertising agencies thus cast themselves as the pedagogues of consumer citizenship in the global era. This is a role in which the global advertising agency networks have decades of experience. As one early advocate earnestly enthused:

> In what is called its pioneering phase, advertising's function is not to rob sales from competitors, or gull the unsophisticated, but to teach new consumption behaviour. Western European/North American-style advertising has demonstrated itself as an enormously effective teacher of new ways of living.
>
> (Stridsberg 1974: 77)

Sometimes this aim is still quite explicit: a L'Oréal brand manager in Russia declares: ' ... we try to educate the consumer on the necessity of following the basic rules of hygiene' ('Adaptation key in Russia' 2011). While it is an open empirical question as to what advertising actually does teach, and how effectively, it is at the very least arguable that audiences for advertising in these settings are shown how to place themselves as subjects addressed by advertisements, how to make the associations amongst the meanings which advertising seeks to bestow upon goods, and even how to interpret the unfamiliar visual language of TVCs (Wang 2003), all part of the repertoire of cultural competencies required for consumer citizenship. In this respect, advertising and marketing in general have a key role to play in the making of a middle class in these developing societies, thus bringing these societies into the ambit of the global manufacturing/marketing/media complex, the prime agents of capitalist modernity.

Coda

This book has outlined and examined the contemporary transformations in the advertising industry and its assemblage of relations with its clients and the media, referred to throughout as the manufacturing/marketing/media complex. This fluid situation has been approached from a number of perspectives, each chapter offering its own take.

First, theoretical positions on advertising which were influential during the golden age of mass media are critically reviewed, particularly in terms of their adequacy or otherwise in accounting for the challenges presented by the advent of the internet, with its unprecedented interactive and individualising capacities. It is argued that the very meaning of 'advertising', at least as it has been understood in the humanities and social sciences, has been largely overtaken by recent developments, both in media and in theory. The Marxist political economy of value, the 'cultural turn' offered by semiological analysis of advertisements, and even the more recent ethnographic forays into advertising agencies have all been superseded to a greater or lesser extent by the reorientation of advertising within a broader conceptual landscape of 'consumer culture', and by contemporary work on branding. Branding has been theorised as simultaneously an economic and a cultural phenomenon, and this is shown to be manifested in brand value being both a form of intellectual property, and a commercial appropriation of popular culture.

Second, the globalisation of the manufacturing/marketing/media complex is approached here via an historical overview. While some of the corporations behind today's global brands have had an international presence since before the First World War, it was the 1960s and 1970s that saw the ground being laid for the globalisation era. Advertising agencies facilitated the process, and in the 1980s, radically reorganised themselves as global corporations in their own right. The former supremacy of US-based advertising agency networks became eclipsed by 'mega-groups', overarching financial and management structures fuelled by international capital. Advertising functions were first divided into separate 'creative' and 'media-buying' agencies, and then gathered together with other marketing 'disciplines' under the umbrella of 'integrated marketing communications'. The global mega-groups, because they have the benefit of access to the largest global clients, have been able to put pressure on nationally-owned agencies to sell out or enter into joint venture with them in a process of 'global alignment'. None of this could have happened without the globalisation of the media also taking place over this time, first with the spread of television from one nation to another, and then with the exceptional medium of the internet.

The third perspective is found at the heart of the book, where direct attention is given to the current destabilisation of the global manufacturing/marketing/media complex, and how this has been provoked by the internet. It is made clear that this is not about 'new' media replacing 'old', but rather, the incapacity of the traditional business models to cope with a form of communication which, although most certainly a new advertising medium, is so much more than that in its commercial applications. Google's command over search advertising is taken as the paradigm case of how strategic exploitation of the properties of the internet by an entrepreneurial company can be consolidated into a new corporate form of business. While advertising agencies have in the process become threatened with 'disintermediation', traditional media corporations have had to cast around for new ways of maintaining ownership and control over their content, in the face of a new medium, and its users, that favour content being free. Consequently, print, mobile telephony and television have all entered upon an era of intense technological and commercial innovation. As for media consumers, they are to some extent 'empowered' by the new media, in ways impossible for mass media audiences, such as the capacity to generate their own content. However, this empowerment is counteracted by forms of commercial exploitation which were also previously unavailable, notably 'value co-creation'.

The fourth perspective is from the point of view of this empowerment-exploitation paradox, and the broader social issues raised by the current upheaval in the manufacturing/marketing/media world. The quest for individualisation and authenticity in consumption is now seen to be harnessed into forms of 'work' which consumers carry out for advertisers, particularly via marketing on social media. The primary issue discussed is behavioural targeting, now recognised by governments as a matter in need of regulation. Food advertising aimed at children is another such issue. As to environmental concerns, advertisers have scrambled to establish their green credentials. On these and other issues, the advertising industry is shown to be on the defensive, not only against government, but also against community, advocacy and professional groups who are mobilised along with activists and critics of consumption in general. Meanwhile, there is the question of whether advertising agency personnel, particularly creative workers in their own consumption behaviour, might be acting as 'cultural intermediaries' in fostering consumer lifestyles. More broadly, advertising is examined in the context of the nation, looking at the conditions under which minorities may or may not be targeted by advertising, and the contemporary trend for nations to brand themselves in a global competition for trade and tourism.

The fifth and final perspective from which the book approaches advertising, the media and globalisation, is predominantly empirical and comparative. Recent industry data is presented to give an overview of the major advertisers, the most significant agencies, and the state of play between advertising and the media in the main world regions. That includes Europe and North America, as well as the Asia-Pacific and Latin America. The emerging new markets of the 'BRICs' nations are given special attention. Questions of standardisation, localisation and 'glocalisation' in global marketing strategies are examined. The global predominance of television as the biggest advertisers' preferred medium is made evident, although this may change with the spread of mobile telephony. The accumulated data show how a process of rebalancing the territorial investments and income of the manufacturing/marketing/media complex is under way, and how this trend entails a substantial extension of their impact in the world outside the North Atlantic, as ever more people are brought into the global consumer culture in which they have such a heavy stake. Nevertheless, in looking at selected nations within their regions, it becomes evident that the impact of globalisation is mediated by national and regional factors, so that global corporate influence is neither homogeneous nor uncontested.

The initial premise of this book, that advertising is the economic force behind media development, tends to be taken for granted as a truism in media studies, and similar humanities and social science perspectives on contemporary communication. Although there continues to be interest in advertising as a cultural form, there is relatively much less active analysis of the advertising industry, meaning the advertiser clients and the agencies which serve them, and their relation to each other and the media, referred to throughout here as the manufacturing/marketing/media complex. As a contribution to such an analysis, this book demonstrates that even in an era of intense technocommercial innovation and institutional transformation, the most successful media forms are still those that are capable of assembling the prospective consumers that advertisers will pay to reach. We have seen that it is not a question of new media superseding the old, for television still holds its dominant position in most countries of the world, given its capacity to aggregate mass audiences, and at the same time, search advertising has emerged as the most profitable form of advertising on the internet, yet precisely because of its ability to disaggregate and target consumers' specific interests. Accordingly, we find that, even on a global scale, the largest advertisers prefer television, while the internet has opened up advertising opportunities to a host of small, local businesses.

Audiences, for their part, largely consent to these regimes as if in a Faustian bargain: in much the same way as watching commercials on television is tolerated in return for receiving free information and entertainment, just so do internet users render up information about themselves in the course of their everyday searching and social networking activities. Nevertheless, consumers are reflexive and resistant, and their acquiescence has to be won, so advertisers and their agencies are engaged in a constant process to attract and engage them. At present, the massive takeup of mobile communications in developed and developing societies alike seems to represent the latest front in the pursuit of consumers by large and small advertisers alike. For a book about all this, there can be no conclusion: the dogs bark and the caravan moves on.

Bibliography

'100 Leading National Advertisers 2010' (2010) *Advertising Age*, 20 June.

AAAP (Asociación Argentina de Agencias de Publicidad) (2009) 'Informe Oficial Latinoamericano de Inversión Publicitaria 2009'. Online. Available HTTP: <http://www.aaap.org.ar/inversion-publicitaria/2009/latam/informe_inversion_publicitaria_latinoamerica_2009.pdf> (accessed 16 December 2010).

Aaker, D.A. (1991) *Managing Brand Equity: Capitalizing on the value of a brand name*, New York: The Free Press.

ACHAP (Asociación Chilena de Agencia de Publicidad) (2007) 'Cuadro Comparativo de Inversión Publicitaria Latinoamérica 2006'. Online. Available HTTP: <www.achap.cl/estudios_05.php> (accessed 7 May 2008).

'Adaptation key in Russia' (2011) *WARC News*, 4 August.

Adbrands (2010a) 'China: Leading Agencies in 2006 by Revenues'. Online. Available HTTP: <http://www.adbrands.net/cn/index.html> (accessed 9 March 2011).

Adbrands (2010b) 'Brazil: Advertisers/Agencies'. Online. Available HTTP: <http://www.adbrands.net/br/> (accessed 21 March 2011).

Adbrands (2011b) 'India: Advertisers/Agencies'. Online. Available HTTP: <http://www.adbrands.net/in/index.html> (accessed 21 March 2011).

Adbrands (2011a) 'Russia: Advertisers/Agencies'. Online. Available HTTP: <http://www.adbrands.net/ru/index.html> (accessed 21 March 2011).

Adbusters.org (2011) Adbusters blog. Online. Available HTTP: <www.adbusters.org/blogs> (accessed 18 May 2011).

Adetunji, J. (2009) 'UK to follow US lead by allowing product placement on television'. *The Guardian*, 14 September.

Adorno, T. and Horkheimer, M. (1977) 'The culture industry: enlightenment as mass deception', in J. Curran, M. Gurevitch, and J. Woollacott (eds) *Mass Communication and Society*, London: Edward Arnold.

'Advertisers miss out on ethnic pound' (2003) *BBC News* (Online), 22 September.

Advertising Industry Statistics (2010) *Advertising Association*. Online. Available HTTP: <www.adassoc.org.uk> (accessed 10 February 2010).

'Agency Family Trees 2010' (2010) *Advertising Age*, 26 April. Online. Available HTTP: <http://adage.com/datacenter/agencyfamilytrees2010> (accessed 15 September 2010).

'Agency Report 2009', (2009) *Advertising Age*, 27 April. Online. Available HTTP: <http://adage.com/datacenter/article?article_id=136094> (accessed 15 October 2009).

'Agency Report 2010', (2010) *Advertising Age*, 25 April. Online. Available HTTP: <http://adage.com/article/datacenter-agencies/agency-report-2010-index/142925/> (accessed 30 August 2011).

'Agency Report Card' (2009) *Ad News*, 10 April: 22–33.

Allen, J. (1992) 'From Fordism to Post-Fordism', pp. 184–95, in Hall, S., Held, D. and McGrew, T. (eds.), *Modernity and Its Futures*, Cambridge, UK: Polity Press.

Amin, A. and Thrift, N. (eds.) (2004) *The Blackwell Cultural Economy Reader*, Cornwall, UK: Blackwell.

Amjadali, S. (1999) 'Ads online: A boom waiting to happen', *The Australian*, 4–5 September.

'And then there were three' (2007) *Campaign Brief*, 22 November. Online. Available HTTP: <http://www.campaignbrief.com/2007/11/droga5-australia-announcesnew.html#mouse%20run> (accessed 28 October 2009).

Anderson, B. (1983) *Imagined Communities: Reflections on the origin and spread of nationalism*, London: Verso.

Anderson, C. (2006) *The Long Tail*, New York: Hyperion.

Anderson, C. (2008) 'Free! Why $0.00 is the future of business', *Wired Magazine*, 25 February.

Anderson, C. (2010) *Free: How today's smartest businesses profit by giving something for nothing*, London: Random House Business Books.

Anderson, M.H. (1984) *Madison Avenue in Asia*, Rutherford, NJ and London: Fairleigh Dickinson University Press/Associated University Presses.

Andrejevic, M. (2009) 'The twenty-first-century telescreen', pp. 31–40, in Turner, G. and Tay, J. (eds.), *Television Studies after TV*, London and New York: Routledge.

Angwin, J. and Steel, E. (2009) 'MySpace's play for ex-Facebook chief', *The Australian*, 24 April.

Anholt, S. (2000) *Another One Bites the Grass: Making sense of international advertising*, Chichester, New York: Wiley.

Anholt, S. and Hildreth, J. (2004) *Brand America: The mother of all brands*, London: Cyan Communications.

Appadurai, A. (ed.) (1986) *The Social Life of Things: Commodities in cultural perspective*, Cambridge, UK: Cambridge University Press.

Appadurai, A. (1990) 'Disjuncture and difference in the global cultural economy', *Public Culture*, 2(2): 1.

Aronczyk, M. and Powers, D. (eds) (2010) *Blowing Up the Brand*, New York: Peter Lang.

Arthur, C. (2010) 'Twitter unveils "promoted tweets" ad plan', *The Guardian*, 13 April.

Arvidsson, A. (2003) *Marketing Modernity: Italian advertising from fascism to post-modernity*, London: Routledge.

——(2005) 'Brands: a critical perspective', *Journal of Consumer Culture*, 5: 235–58.

——(2006) *Brands: Meaning and value in media culture*, London: Routledge.

'Asia-Pacific Ad Enjoys Double Digit Growth' (2006) *AMCB: Asian Media and Communication Bulletin* 36(1): 18.

Australian Made (2003) 'Together again – Australian Made and True Blue celebrate 21 years'. 26 August. Online. Available HTTP: <http://www.australianmade.com.au/news/6944.asp> (accessed 18 March 2011).

Baran, P.A. and Sweezy, P.M. (1968) *Monopoly Capital: An essay on the American economic and social order*, Harmondsworth, UK: Penguin.

Barnet, R.J. and Müller, R.E. (1975) *Global Reach: The power of the multinational corporations*, London: Jonathan Cape.

Barnett, E. (2010) 'Sir Martin Sorrell: Pay TV platforms will control the future of the UK broadcasting business', *Telegraph.co.uk*, 1 July.

Barnouw, E. (1979) *The Sponsor*, Oxford: Oxford University Press.

Barthes, R. (1973) *Mythologies*, St Albans, UK: Paladin.

Baudrillard, J. (1981) *For a Critique of the Political Economy of the Sign*, St Louis: Telos Press.

Beal, A. (2007) 'Yahoo fully acquires Right Media', *Marketing Pilgrim*, 30 April. Online. Available HTTP: <www.marketingpilgrim.com/2007/04/yahoo-fully-acquires-right-media.html> (accessed 12 September 2011).

Belch, G.E. (2009) *Advertising and Promotion: An integrated marketing communication perspective*, Sydney: McGraw Hill Australia.

Berman, D.K., Ovide, S. *et al.* (2008) 'Top US newspaper group confronting bankruptcy', *The Australian*, 9 December.

Bijoor, H. (2004). 'Branding the govt of India', *The Hindu Business Line*, 19 February. Online. Available HTTP: <http://www.thehindubusinessline.com/catalyst/2004/02/19/stories/2004021900180400.htm> (accessed 18 March 2011).

Bordwell, M. (2002) 'Jamming culture: Adbusters' hip media campaign against consumerism', pp. 237–53, in Princen, T., Maniates, M. and Conca, K. (eds.) *Confronting Consumption*, Cambridge, MA: MIT Press.

Bourdieu, P. (1984) *Distinction: A social critique of the judgement of taste*, trans. Richard Nice, London: Routledge and Kegan Paul.

'Brand giants get green' (2011) *WARC News*, 9 May.

'Brand giants get social' (2011) *WARC News*, 17 February.

Brand Republic Staff (2009) 'News Corp bids to form online content consortium', *Brand Republic*, 21 August.

Brand, S. (1987) *The Media Lab: Inventing the future at MIT*, New York, Viking, Penguin.

Brat, I. (2009) 'Vegemites happy as Kraft spreads the decision-making', *The Australian*, 1 October.

Bruns, A. (2008) *Blogs, Wikipedia, Second Life, and Beyond: From production to produsage*, New York: Peter Lang.

'BT avoids online privacy case' (2011) *WARC News*, 15 April.

Bulik, B.S. (2006) 'It doesn't fall far from the tree', *Advertising Age*, 31 July.

Bunce, R. (1976) *Television in the Corporate Interest*, New York: Praeger.

Bunnell, D. and Leuke, R.A. (2000) *The Ebay Phenomenon: Business secrets behind the world's hottest internet company*, New York: Wiley.

Burns, J. (2010) 'Murdoch pitches iPad as newspaper saviour', *The Australian*, 8 April.

Bush, M. (2010) 'Slow recovery notwithstanding, global ad outlook improves', *Advertising Age*, 18 October.

Canning, S. (2010) 'MySpace sets itself up as one-stop shop', *The Australian*, 28 October.

Cappo, J. (2003) *The Future of Advertising: New media, new clients, new consumers in the post-television age*, New York: McGraw-Hill.

Carah, N. (2011) 'Breaking into The Bubble: Brand-building labour and "getting in" to the culture industry', *Continuum: Journal of Media & Cultural Studies*, 25(3): 427–38.

Castro, J. (1985) 'Call from Philip Morris', *Time*, 7 October. Online. Available HTTP: <http://www.time.com/time/magazine/article/0,9171,960035,00.html> (accessed 30 September 2009).

Cato, S. (2010) 'Murdoch's army marches on', *Business Spectator*, 12 March.

Chalaby, J.K. (2008) 'Advertising in the global age: Transnational campaigns and pan-European television channels', *Global Media and Communication*, 4: 139–56.

Chang, R. (2009) 'Google acquires AdMob to bolster mobile-display business', *Advertising Age*, 9 November.

Chang, B. (2010) 'Limit on TV ad time give web firms the edge', *ChinaDaily.com.cn*, 21 April.

Cheng, R. (2011) 'Google unveils Wallet and Offers', *The Weekend Australian*, 28–30 May.

'China, India Set for Adspend Growth' (2009) *WARC News*, 7 September, available HTTP: <http://www.warc.com/News/TopNews.asp?ID=25636&Origin=WARCNews Email2009> (accessed 11 September 2009).

'China takes luxury lead' (2011) *WARC News*, 10 March.

Clifford, S. (2008) 'YouTube feature tells video creators when and where a clip is being watched', *New York Times*, 27 March.

Cochoy, F. (2004) 'Is the modern consumer a Buridan's donkey? Product packaging and consumer choice', in K. M. Ekström and H. Brembeck (eds.) *Elusive Consumption*, Oxford and New York: Berg.

Comanor, W.S. and Wilson, T.A. (1974) *Advertising and Market Power*, Cambridge, MA: Harvard University Press.

Corlette, P. (2010) 'The rise of branded content', *Ad News*, 10 September.

Corpwatch (2001) 'Greenwash fact sheet', 22 March. Online. Available HTTP: <www.corpwatch.org> (accessed 12 November 2010).

Creamer, M. (2009) 'In a first, web advertising outpaces TV in U.K.', *Advertising Age*, 29 September.

Cronin, A.M. (2004a) *Advertising Myths: The strange half-lives of images and commodities*, London and New York: Routledge.

Cronin, A.M. (2004b) 'Currencies of commercial exchange', *Journal of Consumer Culture*, 4(3): 339–60.

'CTR reports China advertising expenditure grew 13.5% in 2009', (2010) CTR Market Research, *www.ctrchina.cn*, 28 January.

Curtin, M. (2007) *Playing to the World's Biggest Audience: The globalization of Chinese film and TV*, Berkeley: University of California Press.

Davenport, T.H. and Beck, J.C. (2001) *The Attention Economy: Understanding the new currency of business*, Boston: Harvard Business School Press.

Davidson, M.P. (1992) *The Consumerist Manifesto: Advertising in postmodern times*, London: Routledge.

Dávila, A. (2001) *Latinos Inc.: The marketing and making of a people*, Berkeley, CA: University of California Press.

Dawber, A. (2009) 'Murdoch blasts search engine "kleptomaniacs"', *The Independent*, 10 October.

'Dentsu-Smart, advertising subsidiary, set up in Russia' (2008) *Goliath Business News*, 19 December. Online. Available HTTP: <http://goliath.ecnext.com> (accessed 30 September 2009).

Deuze, M. (2010) 'Convergence culture in the creative industries', pp. 452–67, in Thussu, D.K. (ed.) *International Communication: A Reader*, London and New York: Routledge.

Doctoroff, T. (2005) *Billions: Selling to the new Chinese consumer*, New York, NY: Palgrave Macmillan.

Douglas, M. and Isherwood, B. (1979) *The World of Goods: Towards an anthropology of consumption*, London: Allen Lane.

Du Gay, P. (1996) *Consumption and Identity at Work*, London and Thousand Oaks, CA: Sage.

Dyer, D., Dalzell, F. and Olegario, R. (2004) *Rising Tide: Lessons from 165 Years of Brand Building at Procter & Gamble*, Boston: Harvard Business School Press.

'Editorial' (2007) Indian Institute of Planning and Management. Online. Available HTTP: <http://www.iipm.edu/> (accessed 12 November 2012).

Efrati, A. (2010a) 'Google goes social in fight with Facebook', *The Australian*, 16 September.

Efrati, A. (2010b) 'Twitter revamps site as it searches for ads' *The Australian*, 16 September.

Efrati, A. (2010c) 'Google wants to make online display ads "sexy"', *The Wall Street Journal* (online), 26 September.

Efrati, A. (2010d) 'Google TV in deal with NBC, Amazon', *The Australian*, 6 October.

Elkin, N. (2010) 'The real battle between Facebook and Google is for your phone', *Advertising Age*, 16 November.

Elliott, G. (2010) 'The online charge is well advanced', *The Australian*, 4 February.

Ellis, L.R. (2008) 'Google buys begun ad agency from Russia's third largest search engine firm rambler', *SearchEngineWorld*, 18 July. Online. Available HTTP: <www.searchengineworld.com> (accessed 12 November 2010).

Ellis, S. (2002) 'AOL magic goes AWOL', *The Australian*, 18 April.

Endicott, R. (2005) *Advertising Age*'s 19th Annual Global Marketing Report. *Advertising Age*, 14 November.

Ewen, S. (1976) *Captains of Consciousness*, New York: McGraw Hill.

Farber, D.R. (2002) *Sloan Rules: Alfred P. Sloan and the triumph of General Motors*, Chicago: University of Chicago Press.

Featherstone, M. (1987) 'Lifestyle and consumer culture', *Theory, Culture & Society*, 4: 55–70.

Fernandez, M.E. (2006) 'ABC's "Lost" is easy to find, and not just on a TV screen', *Los Angeles Times*, 3 January.

Ferriera Simões, C., Demartini Gomes, N. and Fernando Jambeiro, O. (2007) personal communication.

Fildes, N. and Frean, A. (2011) 'Google maps out its master plan', *The Australian*, 17 August.

Flew, T. (2007) *Understanding Global Media*, Basingstoke, Hampshire and New York: Palgrave Macmillan.

Foster, R.J. (1991) 'Making national cultures in the global ecumene', *Annual Review of Anthropology*, 20: 235–60.

Fowler, G. and Schechner, S. (2010) 'TV shows emerge as the new digital battlefield', *The Weekend Australian*, 4–5 September.

Frank, T. (1997) *The Conquest of Cool*, Chicago: University of Chicago Press.

——(1998) *The Conquest of Cool: Business culture, counterculture and the rise of hip consumerism*, Chicago and London: University of Chicago Press.

Fraser, M. (2005) *Weapons of Mass Distraction: Soft power and American empire*, New York: Thomas Dunne Books.

Frith, D. (2010) 'Big battle looms for internet TV gadgets', *The Australian*, 21 September.

Frith, D. (2011) 'Beware the cookie monster: how to avoid those online ad pushers', *The Australian*, 12 April.

Frith, K.T. (1997) *Undressing the Ad: Reading culture in advertising*, New York: Peter Lang.

Frith, K.T. and Mueller, B. (2003) *Advertising and Societies: Global issues*, New York: Peter Lang.

Gabriel, Y. and Lang, T. (2006) *The Unmanageable Consumer: Contemporary consumption and its fragmentation*, London: Sage.

Garfinkel, H. (1967) *Studies in Ethnomethodology*, Englewood Cliffs, NJ: Prentice-Hall.

Garnham, N. (1979) 'Contribution to a political economy of mass-communication', *Media, Culture and Society*, 1: 123.

'Gillette leads eco charts' (2011) *WARC News*, 9 May.

'Global adspend to rise 4.8%' (2011) *WARC News*, 8 November.

'Global marketers: multinational agency network assignments' (2008) *Advertising Age*, 8 December. Online. Available HTTP: <http://adage.com/images/random/datacenter/2008/globalaccounts2008.pdf> (accessed 23 October 2009).

'Global Marketers 2010' (2010) *Advertising Age*, 6 December.

Goldman, R. (1992) *Reading Ads Socially*, London and New York: Routledge.

Goldman, R. and Papson, S. (1998) *Nike Culture: The sign of the swoosh*, London: Sage.

Goldman, R. and Papson, S. (2011) *Landscapes of Capital*, Wiley.

'Google gets "creative"' (2009) *WARC News*, 8 October.

'Google launches targeted ad scheme' (2009) *WARC News*, 12 March.

Google Trends (2010) 'Facebook.com, MySpace.com trends in the US', *Google Trends*. Online. Available HTTP: <http://www.google.com/trends> (accessed 18 October 2010).

Graham, J. (2005) 'Video websites pop up, invite postings', *USAToday.com*, 21 November.

'"Green gap" persists in US' (2011) *WARC News*, 9 May.

'Green issues still matter to UK shoppers' (2011) *WARC News*, 9 May.

Haig, M. (2002) *Mobile Marketing: The message revolution*, London: Kogan Page.

Hall, E. (2009) 'U.K. falls behind on online privacy', *Advertising Age*, 5 November.

Hall, E. (2010) 'U.K tightens rules on newly approved TV product placement', *Advertising Age*, 15 February.

Halliday, J. and Graser, M. (2005) 'BMW pulls out of branded entertainment', *Advertising Age*, 3 October.

Hamm, S. (2007) 'Children of the web', *Business Week*, 2 July.

Hansell, S. (2009) 'Advertisers are watching your every tweet', *The New York Times*, 16 July.

Hanson, P. (1974) *Advertising and Socialism*, London: Macmillan.

Hargrave-Silk, A. (2004). 'Third-tier city consumers spark a rethink', *Media*, 22 October.

Hau, L. (2006) 'Newspaper killer', *Forbes.com*, 12 November.

Hawkins, G. (2006) *The Ethics of Waste: How we relate to rubbish*, Lanham, MD: Rowman & Littlefield.

Hay, J.G. (2006) 'The new game plan', *Marketing Media Survival Guide, www.inshot.com.au*, October.

Hearn, A. (2008) "Meat, mask, burden: Probing the contours of the branded 'self'", *Journal of Consumer Culture*, 8(2): 197–217.

Heath, J. and Potter, A. (2004) *The Rebel Sell: Why the culture can't be jammed*, Toronto: HarperCollins.

Helft, M. (2007) 'Google aims to make YouTube profitable with ads', *New York Times*, 22 August.

Helmore, E. (2006) 'Murdoch goes all out for cyberspace domination', *Observer*, 26 March.

Herbig, P.A. (1998) *Handbook of Cross-cultural Marketing*. New York: Haworth Press.

Herman, E.S. and McChesney, R.W. (1997) *The Global Media: The new missionaries of corporate capitalism*, London and Washington: Cassell.

Higgins, M. (2007) 'Red Bull's headlong frozen dash is a crash course in marketing', *The New York Times* (online), 3 March.

Himelstein, L., Neuborne, E., *et al.* (1997) 'Web ads start to click', *Business Week*, 6 October.

Hirsch, F. (1977) *Social Limits to Growth*, London: Routledge and Kegan Paul.

Hiscock, G. (2009) 'Creative side is key to India's huge TV ad market', *The Australian* (online), 13 April.

Holt, D.B. (2002) 'Why do brands cause trouble? A dialectical theory of consumer culture and branding', *Journal of Consumer Research*, 29: 70–90.

Holt, D.B. (2004) *How Brands Become Icons: The principles of cultural branding*, Boston, MA: Harvard Business School Publishing.

Howard, T. (2004) 'Burger King promotes tongue-in-beak chicken fight', *USA Today*, 11 May.

Hulu (2010) 'Hulu Help'. Online. Available HTTP: <http://www.hulu.com/help> (accessed 12 November 2010).

Humphery, K. (2010) *Excess: Anti-consumerism in the West*, Cambridge: Polity Press.

IAB Brazil (2010) 'Participação dos Meios em Abr/2010', Internet Advertising Bureau Brazil. Online. Available HTTP: <http://www.iabbrasil.org.br/arquivos/doc/Indicadores/Indicadores-de-Mercado-IAB-Brasil.pdf> (accessed 27 August 2010).

IAB UK (2010) 'Full Year 2009: Internet advertising worth £3.54 billion', Internet Advertising Bureau UK.

IAB US (2010) 'IAB Internet advertising revenue report 2009 full year results', Internet Advertising Bureau US.

'Indian TV advertising continues to grow' (2009) *WARC News*, 9 April.

'India's middle class population to touch 267 million in 5 yrs' (2011) *The Economic Times*, 9 February.

'India will become world's No. 1 mobile market by 2013' (2010) *The Hindu Business Line*, 21 May. Online. Available HTTP: <http://www.thehindubusinessline.in/2010/05/22/stories/2010052252590700.htm> (accessed 8 March 2011).

Institute of Practitioners of Advertising (2011) 'New data on BAME representation in commercials'. Online. Available HTTP: <http://www.ipa.co.uk/Content/New-data-on-BAME-representation-in-commercials> (accessed 25 August 2011).

Internet & Mobile Association of India (2010) 'Online Display Advertising Market in India to Grow by 28%'. Online. Available HTTP: <http://www.iamai.in/PRelease_Detail.aspx?nid=2204&NMonth=12&NYear=2010> (accessed 8 March 2011).

Internet World Stats (2010) 'Usage and Population Statistics'. Online. Available HTTP: <http://www.internetworldstats.com> (accessed 8 March 2011).

'Interpublic Group to acquire Delany Lund Knox Warren from Creston' (2010) *Trading Markets*. Online. Available HTTP: <http://www.tradingmarkets.com> (accessed 10 February 2011).

'Interview with Richard Rosenblatt, Intermix and MySpace' (2006) *socaltech.com*, 30 January.

Iwabuchi, K. (2002) *Recentering Globalization*, Durham, NC: Duke University Press.

James, P. (1983) 'Australia in the corporate image: A new nationalism', *Arena Journal*, 63: 65–106.

Jenkins, H. (2006) *Convergence Culture: Where old and new media collide*, New York: New York University Press.

Jhally, S. (1987) *The Codes of Advertising: Fetishism and the political economy of meaning in the consumer society*, New York: St. Martin's Press.

Johnson, B. (2010) 'Top 100 Global Advertisers see world of opportunity' *Advertising Age*, 6 December.

Jones, G. (2005) *Renewing Unilever: Transformation and tradition*, Oxford and New York: Oxford University Press.

Kane, Y.I. and Steel, E. (2010) 'Apple control behind slow launch of iAds', *The Australian*, 17 August.

Kawashima, N. (2006) Advertising agencies, media and consumer market: The changing quality of TV advertising in Japan. *Media, Culture & Society* 28(3): 393–410.

Kawashima, N. (2009) 'The structure of the advertising industry in Japan: The future of the mega-agencies', *Media International Australia*, 133 (November): 75–84.

Kelty, C.M. (2008) *Two Bits: The cultural significance of free software*, Durham and London: Duke University Press.

Kemper, S. (2001) *Buying and Believing: Sri Lankan advertising and consumers in a transnational world*, Chicago and London: The University of Chicago Press.

Kim, K.K. and Cha, H. (2009) 'The globalisation of the Korean advertising industry: Dependency or hybridity?' *Media International Australia*, 133 (November): 97–109.

Klaassen, A. (2009) 'Google uses twitter to sell ads', *Advertising Age*, 6 April.

Klassen, A. (2010) 'Behind China's great firewall: A booming internet', *Advertising Age*, 28 October.

Klein, N. (2000) *No Logo*, London: Flamingo.

Kowitt, B. (2009) 'For Mr. BRIC, nations meeting a milestone', *CNNMoney.com*, June 17.

Kraft Foods Inc. (2002) 'Company history', International Directory of Company Histories, 45, St James Press. Online. Available HTTP: <https://www.fundinguniverse.com/company-histories/Kraft-Foods-Inc-Company-History> (accessed 30 September 2009).

Kuisel, R.F (1991) 'Coca-Cola and the Cold War: The French face Americanization, 1948–53', *French Historical Studies* 17(1): 96–116.

La Monica, P.R. (2006) 'Google to buy YouTube for $1.65 billion', *CNNMoney.com*, 9 October.

Lash, S. and Urry, J. (1994) *Economies of Signs and Space*, London and Thousand Oaks, CA: Sage.

Lawson, A. (2002) 'Big Brother, big business', *The Age Green Guide*, 28 June, pp. 8–9

Learmonth, M. (2009) 'Why free-ride YouTube is finally winning ad dollars', *Advertising Age*, 13 April.

Learmonth, M. (2010) 'What big brands are spending on Google', *Advertising Age*, 6 September.

Learmonth, M. (2011b) 'Rupert Murdoch shows off his new baby', *Advertising Age*, 2 February.

Learmonth, M. (2011a) 'Eric Schmidt: the post-PC "platform" war', *Advertising Age*, 1 June.

Lears, J. (1994) *Fables of Abundance: A cultural history of advertising in America*, New York: Basic Books.

Lee, E. (2010a) 'Google will make $2.5 billion in display advertising', *Advertising Age*, 14 October.

Lee, E. (2010b) 'Twitter begins publishing ads in users' streams', *Advertising Age*, 1 November.

Lee, E. (2011) 'Facebook books $1.86B in advertising', *Advertising Age*, 17 January.

Lee, J. (2005) 'Marketing chiefs put junk-food ads on the scales', *smh.com.au*, 17 February.

Leslie, D.A. (1995) 'Global scan: The globalization of advertising agencies, concepts, and campaigns', *Economic Geography*, October 71(4): 402–26.

Levitt, T. (1983) 'The globalization of markets', *Harvard Business Review*, May–June: 92–102.

Linn, S. (2004) *Consuming Kids: The hostile takeover of childhood*, New York and London: The New Press.

Luis López, O. (1998) *La Radio en Cuba*, 2nd corrected edn. La Habana, Cuba: Editorial Letras Cubanas.

Lury, C. (2004) *Brands: The logos of the global economy*, London: Routledge.

M&C Saatchi (2009) Corporate website. Online. Available HTTP: <http://www. mcsaatchi.com/index.php> (accessed 29 October 2009).

M&C Saatchi (2011) 'Brutal Simplicity of Thought'. Online. Available HTTP: <http://www.mcsaatchi.com> (accessed 17 August 2011).

McChesney, R.W. (1999) *Rich Media, Poor Democracy: Communication politics in dubious times*, Urbana: University of Illinois Press.

McFall, L. (2004) *Advertising: A cultural economy*, London: Sage.

McKendrick, N., Brewer, J. and Plumb, J.H. (1982) *The Birth of a Consumer Society: The commercialization of eighteenth-century England*, London: Europa Publications.

McLaughlin, E. (2002) 'Re-branding Britain', Open2.net. Online. Available HTTP: <http://www.open2.net/society/socialchange/new_brit_coolbritainnia.html> (accessed 18 March 2011).

MacLennan, N. (2008) 'Photon gets Naked', *Ad News*, 5 February.

McLeod, A. (2007) *Abundance: Buying and selling in post-war Australia*, Melbourne: Australian Scholarly Publishing.

McQueen, H. (2001) *The Essence of Capitalism: The origins of our future*, Sydney: Sceptre.

Madden, N. (2003) Spotlight. *Advertising Age*, 6 October.

'Madison Avenue goes multinational' (1970) *Business Week*, 12 September.

Magnet, M. (1986) 'Saatchi and Saatchi will keep gobbling', *Fortune*, 23 June.

Mandese, J. (2007) 'Why the internet does not need Madison Avenue', *Admap*, February.

Maniates, M. (2002) 'In search of consumptive resistance: The voluntary simplicity movement', pp. 199–235, in Princen, T., Maniates, M. and Conca, K. (eds.) *Confronting Consumption*, Cambridge, MA: MIT Press.

Marx, K. (1967) *Capital*, Vol. 1, New York: International Publishers.

Mattelart, A. (1979) *Multinational Corporations and the Control of Culture: The ideological apparatuses of imperialism*, trans. Chanan, M., Brighton, Sussex: Harvester Press and Atlantic Highlands, NJ: Humanities Press.

Mattelart, A. (1991) *Advertising International: The privatisation of public space*, London: Routledge.

Mazzarella, W. (2003) *Shovelling Smoke: Advertising and globalization in contemporary India*, Durham: Duke University Press.

Meade, A. and Sinclair, L. (2010) 'When Oprah educates Yanks on our "hip" McCafes, it's the dollar talking', *The Australian*, 6 December.

Meadows, D.H. (1972) *The Limits to Growth: A report for the Club of Rome's project on the predicament of mankind*, New York: Universe Books.

Miller, D. (1997) *Capitalism: An ethnographic approach*, Oxford and New York: Berg.

Miller, D. (2002) 'The unintended political economy', in Du Gay, P. and Pryke, M. (eds.) *Cultural Economy: Cultural analysis and commercial life*, London: Sage.

Millward Brown (2010) 'Brand Z Top 100 – Tech triumphs with Google, Microsoft, Apple and IBM scoring top marks in Millward Brown's Ranking of the World's most Valuable Brands' (Press release), Millward Brown.

Moeran, B. (1996) *A Japanese Advertising Agency: An anthropology of media and markets*, Surrey, UK: Curzon.

Mooney, P. (2008) 'Bite the wax tadpole?', *Coca-Cola Conversations*. Online. Available HTTP: <http://www.coca-colaconversations.com/my_weblog/2008/03/bite-the-wax-ta.html> (accessed 18 February 2011)

Moor, L. (2007) *The Rise of Brands*, Oxford and New York: Berg.

Mort, F. (2000) 'The politics of consumption', in Lee, M.J. (ed.) *The Consumer Society Reader*, Malden, MA and Oxford: Blackwell.

Mosco, V. (1996) *The Political Economy of Communication*, London: Sage.

'Move over government, Walmart's the new regulator in town' (2011) *Advertising Age*, 7 March.

Myers, C. (2009) 'From sponsorship to spots: Advertising and the development of electronic media' pp. 69–80 in Holt, J. and Perren, A. (eds), Media Industries: History, Theory, and Method, Oxford: Wiley-Blackwell.

Myers, N. and Kent, J. (2004) *The New Consumers: The influence of affluence on the environment*, Washington, DC: Island Press.

Needleman, S. E. (2009) 'Firms learning to befriend social media sites', *The Australian*, 4 August.

Neuman, W. (2010) 'Ad rules stall, keeping cereal a cartoon staple', *The New York Times* (online), 23 July.

'New Dell-WPP shop: Synarchy is dead, long live Enfatico!' (2008) *WARC News*, 11 June.

Newman, E. (2008) 'Study: marketers think TV less effective', *Brandweek*, 20 February.

'New net rules set to make cookies crumble' (2011) *BBC News* (online), 8 March.

Nielsen Wire, (2010) 'Bing overtakes Yahoo! as the #2 U.S. search engine', *Nielsen Wire*, Nielsen, 14 September.

Nixon, S. (2003) *Advertising Cultures: Gender, commerce, creativity*, London: Sage.

O'Barr, W.M. (1994) *Culture and the Ad: Exploring otherness in the world of advertising*, Boulder, CO: Westview Press.

O'Barr, W. (2008) 'Advertising in Brazil', *Advertising & Society Review* 9(2).

O'Keefe, M. and Sheinkopf, K. (1976) 'Advertising in the Soviet Union: Growth of a new media industry', *Journalism Quarterly* 53(1): 80–87.

Ofcom (2010) Office of Communication (UK) HFFS Advertising Restrictions Final Review. Online. Available HTTP: <http://stakeholders.ofcom.org.uk/binaries/research/tv-research/hfss-review-final.pdf> (accessed 25 March 2011).

'Online adspend overtakes TV in UK' (2009) *WARC News*, 1 October.

'Online adspend set for further growth in UK' (2010) *WARC News*, 29 September.

Osborne, M. (2001) 'Qoo is coup for Coke in Asia', *Advertising Age*, 8 October.

Ovide, S. and Vranica, S. (2010) 'Publishers, admen queue up for iPad's launch', *The Australian*, 26 March.

'P&G adapts in emerging markets' (2009) *WARC News*, 16 December.

Parekh, R. and Bush, M. (2009) 'WPP folds ill-fated Dell agency Enfatico into Y&R Brands', *Advertising Age*, 9 April.

Parents Jury (2010) 'Regulation of food and drink advertising to children'. Online. Available HTTP: <http://www.parentsjury.org.au/tpj_browse.asp?ContainerID=tpj_the_regulators> (accessed 25 March 2011).

Patel, K. (2010a) 'FTC greenlights Google's AdMob purchase', *Advertising Age*, 21 May.

Patel, K. (2010b) 'Mobile to become a $1 billion business in the U.S next year', *Advertising Age*, 18 October.

Patel, K. (2011) 'Google buys Zagat: It's all about local', *Advertising Age*, 8 September.

Pavlik, J.V. (2008) *Media in the Digital Age*, New York: Columbia University Press.

Pendergrast, M. (2000) *For God, Country, and Coca-Cola: The definitive history of the great American soft drink and the company that makes it*, 2nd ed. London and New York: Basic Books.

'Pepsi's Russian Challenge' (2010) *The Economist* (online), 9 December.

Pfanner, E. (2005) 'On Advertising: Russia rises to the top in ad world', *The New York Times*, 23 May.

Pfanner, E. (2006) 'Publicis buys digitas, an online marketer, for $1.3 billion', *International Herald Tribune*, 20 December.

Photon Group (2009) 'Our divisions'. Online. Available HTTP: <http://www.photongroup.com/companies/> (accessed 28 October 2009).

——(2011) 'Company List'. Online. Available <HTTP://www.photongroup.com/company-list> (accessed 10 February 2012).

Pincas, S. and Loiseau, M. (2006) *A History of Advertising*, Cologne: Taschen.

Pine, B.J. and Gilmore, J.H. (1999) *The Experience Economy: Work is theatre and every business a stage*, Boston: Harvard Business School Press.

Pires, G.D. and Stanton, P.J. (2005) *Ethnic marketing: Accepting the challenge of cultural diversity*, London: Thomson.

Pountain, D. and Robins, D. (2000) *Cool Rules: Anatomy of an attitude*, Reaction Books.

Procter & Gamble (2009) 'Global products A to Z'. Online. Available HTTP: <http://www.pg.com/company/who_we_are/global_products.shtml> (accessed 7 September 2009).

'Proposed privacy law serves notice to online ad companies', (2011) *Advertising Age*, 12 April.

Repiev, A. (2008) 'A glimpse of Russia's advertising and marketing'. Online. Available HTTP: <http://www.repiev.ru/articles/glimps_en.htm> (accessed 12 January 2010).

'Research: eMarketer predicts ad spending growth in Latam of 6–9% annually through 2014' (2010) *Portada*. Online. Available HTTP: <http://www.portada-online.com/article.aspx?aid=7097> (accessed 30 August 2011).

Ricks, D.A. (1999) *Blunders in International Business*, Malden, MA: Blackwell Publishers.

Ritzer, G. (1993) *The McDonaldization of Society: An investigation into the changing character of contemporary social life*, Newbury Park, CA: Pine Forge Press.

Rivlin, G. (2005) 'A retail revolution turns 10', *The New York Times*, 10 July.

Rosen, C. (2005) 'The age of egocasting', *The New Atlantis*, Fall 2004 – Winter 2005: 51–72. Online. Available HTTP: <http://www.thenewatlantis.com/publications/the-age-of-egocasting> (accessed 29 April 2011).

Ross, A. (2009) *Nice Work if You Can Get It: Life and labor in precarious times*, New York: New York University Press.

Rugman, A.M. and Verbeke, A. (2004) 'Regional and global strategies of multinational enterprises', *Journal of International Business Studies*, 35(1): 3–18.

Rushkoff, D. (2009) *Life Inc.: How the world became a corporation and how to take it back*, New York: Random House.

'Russian advertising market set for growth' (2010) *WARC News*, 17 March.

Saba, J. (2011) 'News Corp sells Myspace, ending six-year saga', *Reuters.com*, 29 June.

Salinas, R., and Paldán, L. (1979) 'Culture in the process of dependent development: Theoretical perspectives' pp. 82–98 in Nordenstreng, K. and Schiller, H.I (eds), *National Sovereignty and International Communication*, Norwood, NJ: Ablex Publishing Corporation.

Sanders, L., and Madden, N. (2005) 'Agency holding companies rush to stake claims in China and India', *Advertising Age*, 19 September.

Sandev, M. (2011) 'Junk food advertising ban gathers steam', *B&T*, 9 May.

Sauvant, K. (1976) 'The potential of multinational enterprises as vehicles for the transmission of business culture', in Sauvant, K. and Lavipour, F. (eds.) *Controlling Multinational Enterprises: Problems, strategies, counter-strategies*, London: Wilton House.

Saywell, T. (2000) 'Fakes cost real cash', *Far Eastern Economic Review*, 5 October.

Schechner, S. and Efrati, A. (2010) 'US broadcasters block Google web TV', *The Weekend Australian*, 23–24 October.

Schechner, S. and Fowler, G.A. (2010) 'Amazon eyes net movies on subscription', *The Australian*, 2 September.

Schiller, H. (1979) 'Transnational media and national development', in Nordenstreng, K. and Schiller, H. (eds.) *National Sovereignty and International Communication*, Norwood, NJ: Ablex.

Schor, J. (2004) *Born to Buy: The commercialized child and the new consumer culture*, New York: Scriber.

Schor, J. (2010) *Plenitude: The new economics of true wealth*, Melbourne: Scribe.

Schultz, D.E., Tannenbaum, S. and Lauterborn, R.F. (1994) *The New Marketing Paradigm: Integrated marketing communications*, Lincolnwood, IL: NTC Business Books.

Schulze, J. (2005) 'News clicks on to next big thing', *The Australian*, 20 July.

Schulze, J. (2006). 'Google ads cash to news', *The Australian*, 9 August.

Shoebridge, N. (1984) 'One sight, one sound, one sell', *B&T*, 12 October.

Shu-mei, S. (2007) *Visuality and Identity: Sinophone articulations across the Pacific*, Berkeley, CA: University of California Press.

Sinclair, J. (1987) *Images Incorporated: Advertising as industry and ideology*, London and New York: Croom Helm.

Sinclair, J. (1997) 'The business of international broadcasting: Cultural bridges and barriers', *Asian Journal of Communication*, 7(1): 137–55.

Sinclair, J. (1999) *Latin American Television: A global view*, Oxford and New York: Oxford University Press.

Sinclair, J. (2004) 'Globalization, supranational institutions, and media', pp. 65–82 in Downing, J.D.H., (ed.), *The Sage Handbook of Media Studies*, London and Thousand Oaks, CA: Sage.

Sinclair, J. (2005) 'Global advertising data SOX-ed up', *Flow*, 1(8).

Sinclair, J. (2006) 'Globalisation trends in Australia's advertising industry', *Media International Australia incorporating Culture and Policy*, 119: 112–23.

Sinclair, J. (2008a) 'Branding and belonging: Globalised goods and national identity', *Journal of Cultural Economy*, 1(2): 217–31.

Sinclair, J. (2008b) 'Globalization and the advertising industry in China', *Chinese Journal of Communication*, 1(1): 77–90.

Sinclair, J. (2009a) 'The advertising industry in Latin America: A comparative study', *International Communication Gazette*, 71(8): 713–33.

Sinclair, J. (2009b) 'Minorities, media, marketing and marginalization', *Global Media and Communication*, 5(2): 177–96.

Sinclair, J. and Cunningham, S. (2001) 'Diasporas and the media', pp. 1–34, in Cunningham, S. and Sinclair, J. (eds) *Floating Lives: The media and Asian diasporas*, Lanham, MD: Rowman & Littlefield.

Sinclair, J. and Wilken, R. (2009) 'Strategic regionalization in marketing campaigns: Beyond the standardization/glocalization debate', *Continuum: Journal of Media and Cultural Studies*, 23(2): 147–56.

Sinclair, L. (2008) 'Consumers switch off traditional channels', *The Australian*, 28 April.

Sinclair, L. (2010) 'Advertisers turn on to television again', *The Australian*, 29 March.

Smart, B. (2010) 2010 *Consumer Society: Critical issues and environmental consequences*, London: Sage

'Smartphones surge in Asia' (2011) *WARC News*, 14 March.

Smith, B. (2006) 'McDonald's dishes up PR entrée to fast food film', *The Age* (online), 27 September.

Smith, E. and Vascellaro, J.E. (2009) 'Warner, YouTube near licensing pact', *The Australian*, 30 September.

Smith, S. and Atkin, C. (2003) 'Television advertising and children', in Palmer, E.L. and Young, B. (eds.) *The Faces of Televisual Media*, Mahwah, NJ: Lawrence Erlbaum.

Smythe, D. (1977) 'Communications: Blindspot of Western Marxism', *Canadian Journal of Political and Social Theory* 1(3): 1–27.

Sophocleous, A. (2006) 'Droga opens up', *Ad News*, 18 May.

Spurgeon, C. (2006) 'Advertising and the new search media', *Media International Australia incorporating Culture and Policy* 119: 51–61.

Spurgeon, C. (2008) *Advertising and New Media*, London: Routledge.

Srivastava, A. (2005) 'Passage to India', *Campaign*, 11 November.

Stearns, P.N. (2006) *Consumerism in World History*, New York: Routledge.

Steel, E. (2008) 'WSJ.com to retain subscription component', *The Wall Street Journal*, 25 January.

Steinberg, B. (2009) 'The future of TV', *Advertising Age*, 30 November.

Story, M. (2007) 'WPP Group to buy 24/7 Real Media, an online ad company', *New York Times*, 18 May.

Stridsberg, A. (1974) 'Can advertising benefit developing countries?', *Business and Society Review*, 11: 76–77.

Sullivan, D. (2004) 'Google releases Orkut social networking service', *www.search-enginewatch.com*, 22 January.

Tabakoff, N. (2007) 'Dow Jones one of News Corp's most important acquisitions: Rupert Murdoch', *The Australian*, 18 September.

Tabakoff, N. (2008) 'News plunges as profit tumbles', *The Australian*, 7 November.

Tabakoff, N. (2009) 'Adland awaits Harvey's will', *The Weekend Australian*, 10–11 January.

Tai, S.H.C. (1997) 'Advertising in Asia: Localize or regionalize?' *International Journal of Advertising*, 16: 48–61.

Taraborrelli, J.R. (2004) *Michael Jackson: The magic and the madness*, Pan Macmillan.

Teinowitz, I. and Klaassen, A. (2008) 'Google completes merger of DoubleClick', *Advertising Age*, 11 March.

Terranova, T. (2000) 'Free labor: Producing culture for the digital economy'. Online. Available HTTP: <http://www.electronicbookreview.com/thread/technocapitalism/voluntary> (accessed 15 October 2009).

Thomas, A.O. (2005) *Imagi-Nations and Borderless Television*, New Delhi: Sage.

Thomas, A.O. (2006) *Transnational Media and Contoured Markets: Redefining Asian television and advertising*, New Delhi, Thousand Oaks, CA and London: Sage.

Thussu, D.K. (ed.) (2007) *Media on the Move: Global flow and contra-flow*, London and New York: Routledge.

Toffler, A. (1980) *The Third Wave*, New York: Morrow.

'Top 100 Creative Agencies 2010' (2010) *Brand Republic*. Online. Available HTTP: <http://www.brandrepublic.com/league_tables/1023067/top-100-creative-agencies-2010> (accessed 10 February 2011).

'Total US Advertising Spending by Medium, 2010 Edition' (2010) *Advertising Age*, December.

Trombly, M. (2006) 'China meets WTO demands', *AdAgeChina*, 25 January.

Truman, R. (2006) 'On the radar', *B&T*, 6 October.

Tungate, M. (2007) *Adland: A Global history of advertising*, Philadelphia: Kogan Page.

Tunstall, J. (1977) *The Media are American: Anglo-American media in the world*, London: Constable.

Turner, G. (2009) *Television and the Nation: Does this matter any more?* London and New York: Routledge.

Turner, G. (2010) *Ordinary People and the Media: The demotic turn*, London: Sage.

Turner, G. and Tay, J. (eds.) (2009) *Television Studies after TV*, London and New York: Routledge.

Varley, M. (2010) 'Newspapers show no sign of decline', *B&T*, 5 October.

Vascellaro, J.E. (2009) 'Follow the money: Twitter watches as firms look for ways to cash in on growing chatter', *The Australian*, 26 March.

Vascellaro, J.E. (2010) 'Facebook right in the ad picture as it closes in on net rivals', *The Australian*, 13 May.

Veblen, T. (1965) *The Theory of the Leisure Class*, New York: A.M. Kelley.

Verna, P. (2010) 'Why Netflix has already won the digital TV/video war', *Advertising Age*, 23 September.

Vernon, R. (1971) *Sovereignty at Bay*, New York: Basic Books.

Volkswagen Group (2009) 'Automotive and financial'. Online. Available HTTP: <http://www.volkswagenag.com/vwag/vwcorp/content/en/brands_and_companies/automotive_and_financial.html> (accessed 29 September 2009).

Vranica, S. and Byron, E. (2010) 'Wal-Mart, Procter & Gamble in "family" film', *The Australian*, 12 February.

Wakabayashi, D. (2011) 'Sony's online network dream lies in tatters', *The Australian*, 29 April.

Walker, R.R. (1967) *Communicators: People, practices, philosophies in Australian advertising, media, marketing*, Melbourne: Lansdowne.

Walker, R.R. (1973) *The Magic Spark*, Melbourne: Hawthorn Press.

Wang, J. (2000) *Foreign Advertising in China: Becoming global, becoming local*. Ames, IA: Iowa State University Press.

Wang, J. (2003) 'Framing Chinese advertising: Some industry perspectives on the production of culture', *Continuum: Journal of Media and Cultural Studies*, 17(3): 247–60.

Wang, J. (2008) *Brand New China*, Cambridge, MA: Harvard University Press.

Wang, J. (2009) 'New media technology and new business models: Speculations on "post-advertising" paradigms', *Media International Australia* 133: 110–19.

Warhol, A. (1975) *The Philosophy of Andy Warhol*, New York: Harcourt Brace Jovanovich.

Watson, J.L. (1997) *Golden Arches East: McDonald's in East Asia*, Stanford, CA: Stanford University Press.

'Web reach rises in Latin America' (2010) *WARC News*, 10 December.

Wentz, L. (2010) 'Why so many agencies are storming road to Sao Paulo', *Advertising Age*, 6 December.

Wernick, A. (1991) *Promotional Culture: Advertising, ideology and symbolic expression*, London: Sage.

Whitehead, J. (2010) 'U.K.'s YouView internet TV determined to launch in 2011', *Advertising Age*, 30 September.

Whiteside, S. (2009) 'The view from the top', *WARC News Exclusive*, November.

Wilken, R. and Sinclair, J. (2009) 'Waiting for the kiss of life: Mobile media and advertising', *Convergence* 15(4): 425–27.

Williams, D. (2011) 'How Google+ will transform search and search marketing', *Advertising Age*, 21 July.

Williamson, J. (1978) *Decoding Advertisements*, London: Marion Boyars.

Wittstock, Melinda (2000) 'Are you a BOurgeois BOhemian?', *The Observer*, 28 May.

Woodard, J. (2002) 'Marketing modernity: The J. Walter Thompson Company and North American advertising in Brazil, 1929–39', *Hispanic American Historical Review*, 82(2): 257–90.

Worden, N. (2010) 'News Corp drops plan for multi-publisher digital news hub', *The Australian*, 22 October.

'World press trends: Digital revenues won't replace print' (2009) *World Association of Newspapers*, 1 December.

'World's Top 50 Agency Companies' (2009) *Advertising Age, Ad Age DataCenter*. Online subscription. Available HTTP: <http://adage.com/agencyfamilytrees09/> (accessed 15 October 2009).

'World's 50 Largest Agency Companies 2011' (2011) *Advertising Age, Ad Age DataCenter*. Online subscription. Available HTTP: <https://adage.com/datacenter/datapopup.php?article_id=227071> (accessed 15 September 2011)

'WPP takes Dell's $4.5bn global biz' (2007) *WARC News*, 3 December.

Wright, G. (2008) 'Planet Google', *The Weekend Australian Magazine*, 6–7 September.

Yiannis, G. and Lang, T. (2006) *The Unmanageable Consumer*, London and Thousand Oaks, CA: Sage.

York, E.B. (2009) 'Domino's reacts cautiously, quietly to YouTube gross-out video', *Advertising Age*, 14 April.

York, E.B. and Mullman, J. (2009) 'DDB, Crispin, Goodby can't compete with Doritos crotch joke', *Advertising Age*, 2 February.

Young, Brian (2003) 'Does food advertising make children obese?', *International Journal of Advertising and Marketing to Children*, April–June: 19–26.

YouView, (2010) 'youview.com'. Online. Available HTTP: <http://www.youview.com/> (accessed 15 October 2010).

Yúdice, G. (2003) *The Expediency of Culture: Uses of culture in the global era*, Durham: Duke University Press.

Zenith Optimedia (2007) 'Press release: Time Warner heads new ranking of the world's top media owners', 21 February.

Zwick, D., Bonsu, S.K. and Darmody, A. (2008) 'Putting consumers to work: "Co-creation" and new marketing govern-mentality', *Journal of Consumer Culture*, 8(2): 163–96.

Zyman, S. (2002) *The End of Advertising As We Know It*, Hoboken, NJ: John Wiley and Sons.

Index

Lightning Source UK Ltd.
Milton Keynes UK
UKOW05f2119280314

229051UK00006B/68/P